My Teaching Life

Inspirations and Experiences of an Overachiever

David A. Cicci, Ph.D.

First edition

Dynamic Solutions Publishing

Auburn, Alabama

ISBN: 979-8-9866183-4-0

Cover photo: David A. Cicci, 2018

Back photo: Christine M. Cicci, 2021

Book design: Darby Cicci

Printed in the United States of America

To all my former students…
Thanks for making it fun!

CONTENTS

Preface vii

1. I Didn't Want to Be a Teacher 1

2. Almost Heaven and Unexpected Opportunities 13

3. A Series of Inspirations 23

4. A Lot of Jobs I Didn't Want 33

5. I'm Going to Graduate School Too?.................................47

6. My Engineering Life 55

7. I Thought a New Place Might Help................................63

8. Some Unbelievable Luck.................................71

9. Outside Opportunities for Sustenance 85

10. I Could Actually Graduate 93

11. You Did What? And We're Moving Where? 103

12. From Austin to Auburn 119

13. What Do You Mean I Can't Just Teach? 129

14. Chasing Tenure and Promotion....................................141

15. Making It Fun Whenever I Could 151

16. My Research Life...163

17. My Service Life 171

18. Short Courses and Summers Away 187

19. My Excessive Service Life...197

20. My Sabbatical Life..207

21. Back to Campus and Winding Down 219

22. An Unexpected Turn of Events....................................229

23. My Retirement Life 237

24. Reflections and Beyond Retirement.............................245

PREFACE

I wrote this memoir for my adult children. When they were growing up, they knew their father was a professor and their mother was a pharmacist. But they really didn't know how or why we got into those professions. Nor did they know very much about what our jobs were like. To help fill some of those gaps, I wanted to provide them with a written history of my life and professional career, and a little about our early life together as a family, some of which they never knew or may have forgotten. Hopefully, they'll pass this history on to their own children someday. I thought it would be something important to leave behind for each of them.

I also hoped that my kids would like it. After reading a late draft, they told me they did, so in that regard this project is already a success. Even though it was a huge undertaking, I enjoyed writing it and learned a lot in doing so. It was fun looking back on my professional life now that I'm retired. I found that my memory about events which occurred many years ago was quite good. The most challenging part was trying to reconstruct my thought processes during those events. It was especially fun, though, looking through and selecting old photos to include.

After I finished writing, it occurred to me that my extended family, friends, and even some of my former students might find this book interesting. I hope everyone enjoys reading it as much as I enjoyed writing it.

1

I DIDN'T WANT TO BE A TEACHER

I should say, I didn't *always* want to be a teacher. As a child, I had no interest in becoming a teacher when I grew up. It wasn't because I had anything against the profession, as my own father was a teacher. It's just that I wanted to explore the unknown and cut a new and adventurous life for myself. The thought of teaching wasn't exciting to me at a young age, like it might have been to other would-be teachers. My desire to teach came much later, and it was more of a calling than a conscious choice. In getting to that point, many people inspired, influenced, and supported me; some were educators, some were coaches, and some were neither. I may have even borrowed (or stolen) something from those who provided inspiration along the way, which led me to becoming a teacher.

Like many young boys, I started out wanting to be a major league baseball player. There wasn't much else to do besides play baseball living in the tiny town of Yukon, Pennsylvania. I was a catcher, because on my first day of Little League, the manager asked who wanted to catch and nobody answered. I thought if no one wanted to do it, I could play sooner if I volunteered. So, I did. My older brother, Ed, was also a catcher, so I knew how tough of a position it was. I never enjoyed catching, I endured it just to play. I eventually got to be decent at it and I was a good hitter. Throughout Little League and Pony League, I continued catching, although I tried other positions a few times with an incredible lack of success.

One unpleasant experience that taught me a lot occurred at what turned out to be my last Pony League game. Our manager wasn't very good because he knew little about baseball. My team was getting trounced, and he was unhappy with our performance. In the middle of the game, he left the dugout and went out to the right field bleachers to sit with a friend, leaving us to manage ourselves. None of the players liked that he left, and we bumbled through the rest of the game and lost badly. As we were packing up our gear afterward, he returned to the dugout and started yelling at the team for not playing well. I became upset, not only because we lost, but also because our manager had deserted us.

After he ended his tirade, I looked at him and said, "We may have lost, but it was better than leaving to go sit in the bleachers."

Our manager responded, "Well then, if you don't like it, you can turn in your uniform after the game." And I did, thus prematurely ending my Pony League career. It was the first time I remember speaking out about something I disagreed with, and perhaps it was an early sign of the rebel I'd become later in my life. That experience taught me to question authority and that not everybody in a position of leadership knew what they were doing.

I returned to playing baseball in my high school years, but I became more interested in basketball. My older cousin, Edward, who lived next door, helped me hang a wooden backboard and goal on a pole in the alley behind our house and taught me how to shoot. I practiced year-round, wearing nylon pallbearer gloves in the winter to keep my hands from freezing. I learned to be a good shooter, at least in my mind, and I ended up being far better at basketball than I ever was at baseball. My thoughts then turned to becoming a professional basketball player, but since I was short and slow, that wasn't a viable option for me, either. I soon realized I needed to turn my sights in a different direction.

Growing up in the 1960s, I developed a strong interest in space travel. I became part of "a generation lost in space," as Don McLean called it in his 1971 song, "American Pie." Living through NASA's Mercury, Gemini, and Apollo programs had a lot to do with it. After I watched the moon landing in 1969, I developed an interest in pursuing a career in aerospace engineering. Since I liked math and science in school, it seemed like a natural fit. My brother, being six years older than me, had already graduated from West Virginia University (WVU) with a degree in electrical engineering. Ed used his education to pave the way for him to become an Air Force pilot, which he did in 1968. My mom thought my becoming an engineer was a good idea too, because she imagined I'd be able to find a job after graduation.

My mother, Ann, grew up during the Great Depression Years of the 1930s and her family struggled just to put food on the table. Her father, a Croatian immigrant, worked hard in the Pennsylvania coal mines to feed his six children, so she wanted me to have a career where I'd always have a job. Her viewpoint of life when I was a child was that once you had a good job, you should keep it as long as possible. I understood her thinking, although it created some friction between us in later years. My mom knew the value of hard work. She cleaned people's houses for many years and later worked in a garment factory, which she loved and missed after she retired. Sewing was not only her job, but it also became her lifelong passion.

I enjoyed math and science because I had some excellent teachers at South Huntingdon High School, in Ruffsdale, Pennsylvania. It was a small school, and my graduating class was less than a hundred students. I was fortunate to have Mr. Horace Neal for algebra, trigonometry, and college algebra. He was a knowledgeable and patient teacher who helped me learn how to approach and analyze problems. In my sophomore year, Mr. Frank German taught me geometry and to challenge myself academically, which helped build confidence in my abilities. He was also the head track and an assistant football coach. His personality was that of a hard-ass, which was what I needed in a teacher at age sixteen.

One of the best teachers I had in all of my schooling was Mrs. Mary Sweeney, who taught chemistry and physics during my junior and senior years. She was energetic, intelligent, demanding, and taught on a high level. Mrs. Sweeney expected hard work and focus from her students, but she made it fun, too. During my time in her classes, she was also working on her doctorate in chemistry, which she earned soon after I graduated.

I was fortunate to have had such wonderful teachers for math and science, and I admired them. But rather than inspire me to want to teach, they inspired me to want to learn math and science, which itself was an incredible gift to receive at such a young age.

One non-math/science teacher I appreciated was Mr. Jim Mason, who taught American history. He wasn't an outstanding teacher, but he made class fun. The thing I remember most about him was each day when he came into the classroom he'd spend a few minutes discussing things other than history. He was always friendly and never failed to mention the basketball game the night before, the upcoming football game on Friday. He taught me how important it was to be personable in class every day.

As I mentioned, my father, Henry, was a teacher. Although, he was more of a musician who ended up teaching music. Music was his life, first as an avocation and later, also as a vocation. His primary instrument was alto saxophone, but he played tenor sax and clarinet too, all very well. He found music at a young age and joined any and every band he could find. During World War II, he was a member of the U.S. Army Air Corp band and spent time stationed in Mississippi, Louisiana, and Chicago. After he married my mother and the war ended, he attended the Conn School of Instrument Repair in Elkhart, Indiana. He planned to open a music store with a friend in Wheeling, West Virginia where he'd handle the instrument repair portion of the business. However, before he began that pursuit, a South Huntingdon Township School Board member approached him to ask if he'd be interested in becoming the band director at the high school. They didn't have a band and wanted to start one to play at football games. My father hadn't gone to college, but in those days, the state laws were such that a degree in education wasn't necessary. A person could teach if they earned a Standard Certificate instead by passing a set number of college courses to become qualified. He thought if he accepted the job, he'd still have time to pursue his own music playing in local bands. So he enrolled at Seton Hill College in Greensburg, Pennsylvania, to take enough classes to get his teaching credentials before school started the next fall.

After being named band director at the high school, he found out that they also wanted him to set-up the instrumental music programs in the junior high and elementary schools. His primary responsibility was to give individual music lessons to students, beginning in the third grade, and form concert bands for each school, besides the high school marching band. It was a big job, and my father quickly discovered he loved teaching music and putting bands together. He continued to pursue his own music, and as a hobby, he fixed musical instruments in the basement of our home to earn extra money.

My brother and I both took music lessons from my dad beginning in the third grade, and we played in the concert and marching bands throughout school. Ed was an excellent musician, but I wasn't. He played trombone, baritone, organ, and accordion growing up, while I struggled to play trumpet. It became clear early on that I inherited little musical talent from my father. I loved music, and for a short period, I entertained the idea of studying music in college. Although I knew my ability was too limited to find success playing music. I thought since I wasn't good enough to perform, I'd end up being a music teacher, and I still didn't want to teach.

The thing I recall most about my father's teaching, and what I admired, was his phenomenal patience. He was more patient with students than I thought possible. He wanted everyone to learn to play their instrument well, which wasn't always achievable. But he worked very hard at it and got amazing results. As much as I admired his teaching ability, I still wanted to do something different. I'll never forget his dedication and patience, which was what made him an excellent teacher.

It was fun to grow up in a musical family. My father often played in several bands, which included swing, jazz, brass, and even German Oompah bands. The bands came and went, but one constant was the dance band he belonged to most of his life. That band, called Joe Silvo and his Orchestra, had between seven and ten members, at different times, who played together every weekend for as long as I can remember. When I was young, our home was often full of musicians jamming in the basement, and I attended many parties and picnics with the band members and their families. One thing I enjoyed most was after repairing an instrument, my dad would test it by playing jazz riffs everyone could hear throughout the house. He'd play for hours, even though he knew after only a few minutes that the instruments he repaired were fine. He just loved to play. It was always lively around our house because of the music, and I had a fun childhood.

My mother and father both came from large families and that made it fun, too. My Aunt Edith and Uncle Mike lived next door, and they had nine children, seven sons and two daughters. They were more like brothers and sisters to me than cousins, although the youngest was seven years older than me. The boys taught me a lot about sports and cars, and a little about girls.

Dad's pride and joy was his 1950 Conn 28M Connstelation alto saxophone, which he purchased new and played throughout his life. It's the same horn that our oldest son, Corey, eventually used in his junior and senior high school bands, and later, our youngest son, Darby, played on a few of his records.

When I was eight years old, Joe Silvo's band played a stage show as backup for the vaudeville/comedy group The Three Stooges at a nightclub in Irwin, Pennsylvania. Since I loved their silly comedy when I was a kid, my dad took me along and we went backstage to meet the Stooges before the show. They were very nice to us and hilarious, even when they weren't onstage. I still have the autograph they gave me that night. I was very popular in the third grade for a few days when I showed off that autograph at school.

The arts always intrigued me, but I never had much artistic ability, although in high school I found I liked to write. One reason was that I had an excellent English literature and composition teacher, Ms. Cassandra Vivian. She made the students in her classes write a tremendous amount. We wrote paragraphs, poems, essays, book reports, and short stories of all types, both fiction and non-fiction. She sparked an interest in writing in me. I didn't enjoy reading my work out loud or speaking in front of the class, which was another sign that teaching wouldn't be an ideal profession for me.

Ms. Vivian used to get very annoyed at one of my friends, Wally, and me. She always allowed us to choose our own topics to encourage our creativity, which wasn't the best idea for the two of us. We were on the basketball team together and loved the sport, so the subject of everything he and I wrote was basketball, which I admit was a planned effort. We learned how to write a little, and Ms. Vivian learned a lot more about basketball than she ever wanted to know.

Wally and I both pushed Ms. Vivian to her limits, me in particular. One day in class, we were discussing the ancient riddle that asked, "What's the sound of one hand clapping?" Trying to be funny, I took my right hand and began 'clapping' with that single hand, i.e., slapping four fingers against my palm making a semi-clapping noise. Ms. Vivian stopped lecturing and scolded me for being a disruptive clown. My lifelong friend, Mike Cochenour, who I call Big Mike, still reminds me of that incident whenever we get together nowadays. I wasn't proud of my childish behavior, but I should note that it came many years before Bart Simpson did the same thing on the television show The Simpsons, circa 2015, so there's that at least.

Regardless, I learned a lot about literature and composition from Ms. Vivian, and I found I enjoyed writing more than reading. Since I had a pleasant writing experience early in life, I gained confidence in my ability and I looked forward to doing more of it someday. I always wanted to write a novel, and I recently tried it. However, I used a nom de plume, so I wouldn't embarrass my family, or Ms. Vivian, if they ever read it. I will say that my novel includes nothing about basketball, which I'm sure she'd appreciate. Writing is much more difficult than I thought, but it's given me an artistic outlet that I've long desired.

The outstanding teachers I had inspired me to learn and do well in school, but none inspired me to want to teach. I also had some poor teachers, and perhaps they were inspirational too. But becoming a teacher didn't enter my mind until I was in college. I focused my studies on math and science, and my brother and mother encouraged me to consider engineering. I knew I had to choose a field where I could get a good job. We never had much money growing up, and I'd have to support myself once I graduated from college. So the prospect of employability was an important factor for me. My father never made a very high salary, which I'm sure was also a deterrent for me becoming teacher.

When I was a young boy, I became infatuated with visiting college campuses. I visited many nearby, and whenever we traveled as a family, I always urged my father to stop so I could look at the schools we passed along the way. I loved seeing them for reasons I didn't quite understand, although it may have been because I liked college sports. Or perhaps it revealed my early attraction to higher education. Regardless, visiting campuses became a lifelong hobby for me.

I did well enough at basketball in high school that I believed I could earn a college scholarship, even though I wasn't quite six feet tall. Knowing I couldn't afford to attend an expensive school, a scholarship could open some doors that might otherwise be closed to me. I practiced and played basketball as much as possible and became a good shooter. I averaged over twenty points per game my senior year and once scored forty-two points to set a new scoring record for my high school. My basketball coach, Jim Farrell, was an outstanding coach and teacher. He was knowledgeable, patient, and knew how to motivate his players. He made us work hard to get the best he could out of our team. We didn't win any championships, but playing for him was a wonderful learning experience.

At the end of my senior season I was selected to play in an All-Star game between players from Westmoreland County and Fayette County. Rules in place at the time were such that anyone who played in the game became ineligible for spring sports at their school. That meant I'd have to give up playing baseball my last year in order to participate in the game. It was worth it to me because I was sick of being a catcher anyhow. So even though I was a starter on the baseball team, I chose to play in the All-Star game and give up baseball altogether, hoping I'd get more attention from college coaches. I remember scoring two points in that game, but giving up baseball was still worth it to me. I enjoyed the rest of my senior year NOT playing baseball.

I received a handful of scholarship offers from small schools in the local area and in the northeastern U.S. Many were state teacher schools but none had engineering programs. My most interesting offer was from Westminster College, a tiny liberal arts school in New Wilmington, Pennsylvania, a little north of Pittsburgh. It would have been fun to play basketball at Westminster, although I'd have had to major in mathematics, chemistry, or physics, and not engineering. Even then, the job prospects in those degree fields were bleak. I thought I'd need to go to graduate school or another undergraduate institution afterward to get an engineering degree before ever finding a job. That route seemed to be a long one, so I declined the offer. I'd already abandoned my fleeting thoughts of playing professional basketball anyhow. And I was always more interested in attending a large school since I lived in a small town all of my life.

When Ed was a student at WVU, I visited him many times and loved the campus and Morgantown. Being only about 50 miles from Yukon, my parents and I attended football and basketball games and I enjoyed my visits there. Besides, it was a much larger school than Westminster, which I liked, and they had several engineering programs. Ed studied electrical engineering, but WVU also offered a degree in aerospace engineering. After he married his wife, Jean, before his last year of college, she worked as a secretary in the Industrial Engineering Department while Ed finished his degree. Through her, I became even more familiar with the College of Engineering at WVU. And it didn't take me long to become a fan of Mountaineer sports, especially basketball.

The summer before my senior year, I attended a basketball camp run by the WVU coaching staff. The camp took place at Bridgewater College in Bridgewater, Virginia, and lasted a full week. It was a terrific experience, and I connected with the West Virginia coaches during my time there. Working with them helped me develop an even stronger interest in the university. Although they never recruited me to play basketball at WVU, they at least got to see me play a few times during that week. My most memorable part of the camp was meeting John Wooden, the famous basketball coach at the University of California, Los Angeles (UCLA) who won ten national championships in the

1960s and 1970s. He was a guest speaker at the camp and told many interesting stories. He talked a lot about his philosophy of teaching basketball and how it served the players better if he was a strict disciplinarian. That made a distinct impression on me. Overall, it was a wonderful camp, and it helped prepare me for my last year of high school basketball. I still have autographed photos of Coach Wooden from that camp.

By the end of my senior year, things were clearing up for me. I decided I wanted to attend WVU and study aerospace engineering. I felt I was ready to give up playing sports and focus on just being a student. An added plus was that it was cheaper for me to attend WVU as an out-of-state student than to attend an in-state school in Pennsylvania. But I thought I needed to take one more trip to Morgantown, just to be certain. My mother and I drove down one morning in the spring to look around campus again and find housing for me for the fall, which we did.

Although I was ready to give up basketball, I knew West Virginia had a freshman team, and I wondered to myself if I could play one more year as a walk-on player. In those days, most schools had a freshmen team, or junior varsity, since NCAA rules didn't allow student athletes to take part in varsity sports until their sophomore year. They only gave out five scholarships each year, but needed at least twelve players on the team. I thought it would be fun to play a year at WVU, even if I saw little action. I knew if I did, that I'd be fine with giving up athletics altogether and focusing on school. With that in mind during our visit, I took my mom over to Mountaineer Field House, where the basketball team played, just to 'look around'. As we were walking through the building, I saw that Head Coach Sonny Moran was in his office, so I dragged my poor mom in to say hello.

I knew Coach Moran from summer camp, and he may have recognized me when I walked in, although I wasn't certain he did. But he welcomed us, and we had a pleasant chat. During our conversation, I mentioned I was planning to enroll at the university in the fall and I thought I might like to try out for the freshmen team. Coach Moran asked how I did in my senior year, so I gave him a quick summary of my performance. At that point, he called down the hall to invite Chuck Windsor, the Freshmen Basketball Coach, to join us.

Coach Windsor remembered me from camp and was very gracious to us when he arrived. As we talked more about my senior season, they both encouraged me to come to the open tryouts in the fall. They asked for my contact information so they could let me know when the tryouts were going to take place. I amazed my mother by what I did that day. She hadn't seen me be so forward before, to just walk into the Head Coach's office unannounced and ask about being on the team. I think she enjoyed seeing me pursue something that I really wanted. I surprised myself a little by doing that, too.

With the possibility of trying out for the team in the fall, I spent yet another summer practicing to improve my game. I played in a basketball league in Greensburg, Pennsylvania with my long-time buddy, Melvin, who I called Bart after his father and older brother. Bart also played on my high school team and practiced with me in previous summers. He was shorter than me, but an outstanding defensive player. Our team had two games a week at one of the city's playgrounds, which made for a fun summer. Bart and I both improved by playing in that league.

I also got my first ever job in the summer of 1969, after my high school graduation. A family friend hired me to work for his company, which did landscape maintenance at the Westinghouse Electric Corporation Research Center in Churchill, Pennsylvania. Each morning, I rode in the back of a covered pickup truck for about an hour with five or six other guys to get to work. It was the research center where Westinghouse developed the camera to broadcast from the surface of the moon during the upcoming Apollo 11 mission. I liked to tell people I worked at the lab where they made the moon camera, but always followed up by admitting my job was only picking weeds outside.

The Apollo moon landing inspired me even more to become an aerospace engineer. I returned to Morgantown for freshman orientation later that summer and bought all my textbooks so I could peer at them for a few weeks before classes started. There were many reasons I was eager to get to college besides the academics and trying out for the freshmen basketball team. One reason was that I already liked beer and the drinking age in West Virginia was only eighteen for beer with 3.2% alcohol, which made it very weak and watered-down. It was nothing like the Stoney's Beer that I grew up swiping from my dad's refrigerator in the basement. Still, it was one more thing to look forward to about living away from home.

2

ALMOST HEAVEN AND UNEXPECTED OPPORTUNITIES

I couldn't wait to get to college. Since I didn't have a car, my parents drove me down the weekend before classes started and helped me move into my dorm room. I'm sure mom and dad felt much sadder about leaving me there than I did. Like most eighteen-year-olds, I was looking forward to the freedom of being away.

My new home was in 404 Columbian Hall, on the university's main campus and only a short walk from Mountaineer Field House, which would be convenient just in case I'd be spending time there. I filled the weekend with getting settled, making friends, exploring the town and campus, and enjoying being on my own with no parental supervision. I also bought my first legal beer at a downtown bar called Luigi's, which was more of a hangout for locals than a college bar. Luigi's was empty in the afternoon, and I had a beer without being carded.

The most significant event that weekend, although I didn't realize, was meeting the guy next door. Jim Goldsworthy became a lifelong friend until his premature and unexpected passing when he was in his early fifties. Jim was the best friend I could hope to have, and he was an education major who wanted to be a teacher. We became inseparable in the months and years ahead. Jim was one of those rare friends who, even after not seeing each other for a long period, we could continue the conversation we had the last time we spoke. Jim liked beer as much as I did, so we had a lot of fun and adventures together. It turned out that on Jim's first day in Morgantown, he also went to buy a beer at Luigi's.

I started out with a pretty difficult academic load. After passing an advanced placement test for math during my Freshmen Orientation, they allowed me to bypass both college algebra and trigonometry and enroll in calculus. My other classes included chemistry, English composition, philosophy, engineering seminar, and physical education, which all freshmen had to take in those days. Calculus was my first college class, a four credit-hour course scheduled at 8:00 a.m. on Monday, Tuesday, Thursday, and Friday of each week. It didn't take me long to realize my calculus professor was terrible! She didn't explain things well and was one of the worst teachers I'd ever had. She talked to the chalkboard, and most of us in class were lost.

When it came time for our first exam, I thought if I pulled an all-nighter to study, I'd learn everything I needed to know. I tried it, but that sure didn't work for me. In fact, it was a huge mistake! Not getting enough rest likely contributed to my very poor performance. When I received my grade, I got a 29! Getting an F on my first exam was an awful way to start. I vowed to never try to study all night again, and from that point forward I always stopped studying at midnight, whether I knew the material or didn't.

My calculus professor had announced on the first day she was pregnant and her baby was due near the middle of the semester. Everyone in class hoped for a better replacement teacher when our professor went on maternity leave, thinking nobody could be any worse. Then one Tuesday morning, we showed up to find a substitute who told us that our professor was in the hospital having her baby. The replacement gave a great lecture, and I felt much better about my prospect of learning calculus! Everyone thought, or at least hoped, that the rest of the term would go well since we now had a better teacher. However, our joy was short-lived! There was no class on Wednesday, but when we arrived on Thursday morning, expecting to see our substitute from Tuesday, we found our regular professor was already back. She ended up only missing one day of class to have a baby! It reminded me of those stories about pregnant women in Russia who'd be working out in the fields, stop and give birth, then continue to work. It was all very disappointing.

I somehow muddled through the semester and passed the class, but didn't feel good about my experience. In the following semesters, I found a different and better professor for Calculus II and III. It wasn't much fun to start poorly. My math professor's poor teaching had a considerable impact on me, but I wouldn't recognize it until years later. That experience taught me I wasn't always going to have good teachers. I also learned the key to doing well overall was to understand the material regardless of the teacher. Throughout my academic career, I sometimes had to rely on myself to learn instead of relying on my professor.

Chemistry, unlike calculus, was a breeze, as it was mostly a review for me. Mrs. Sweeney had prepared me well in high school, including the required lab work. My chemistry class was in a large lecture hall with tiered seating, and a couple of hundred students were enrolled. It had a moveable chalkboard system where the lecturer could raise and lower the boards so those in the back could see the material better. She did something while lecturing that I hadn't seen before or since. She spoke fast during her lectures, and she'd often write on the board with her right hand while erasing at the same time with her left hand. Her teaching style required students to pay close attention and take many notes. She was one of the best instructors I had in college, and I enjoyed her class. I also took her for my second chemistry course in the spring semester.

My other classes were fine, but I found that the teacher I had for English Composition wasn't as good as Ms. Vivian at my high school. She didn't make writing fun, and I felt uninspired to write well or write much at all until later in my life.

When I enrolled at WVU, none of my close friends or anyone else from my high school attended there with me. Most of them ended up attending the University of Pittsburgh (Pitt), Penn State University, or one of the small state colleges in Western Pennsylvania. But not knowing many people in an unfamiliar environment was one thing I looked forward to most when I started college. I was eager to make new friends in a different place. The only other person I knew who started at WVU the same time as me was my friend Annie. She was from a neighboring high school a few miles from mine, and we met and dated for a short while the summer before our senior years. We quickly found that dating didn't work for us, although we became trusted friends during our time in college and are still friends today. At WVU we often tried to fix each other up with our friends, but those arrangements never worked out well either.

Annie was a little homesick at school, so she'd call me about once a week and I'd talk her through her loneliness. In those days the dorms had pay phones in the hall and very few students had private phones, including me, and it was many years before cellular phones. Each time the phone rang, the nearest person would answer it and go to fetch whoever was being called. Annie or my mother were about the only people who'd ever call me, so I didn't receive any important calls, until one surprising afternoon about a month into the semester. Someone knocked on my door and told me I had a call, so I walked down the hall to answer it, expecting to hear a women's voice. But when I picked up the phone, it was a male and the following conversation ensued.

"Hello, this is Dave," I said.

"Hello, Dave, this is Coach Windsor from the basketball team. Do you have a few minutes to talk?"

"Sure coach, I have plenty of time," I replied.

"Well, we've started our informal team workouts with the scholarship players. We want to invite you to join the team as a walk-on now, if you're still interested in playing. You did well enough in high school, you won't need to try out with the others to make the team. We'd like for you to get started early, if you want to."

Somewhat shocked at what I was hearing, I said, "That's great, coach, of course I'm still interested, and I'd love to start now!"

"Okay, that's wonderful," Coach Windsor replied. "Come over to the Field House tomorrow after your classes, and we'll set you up with a locker and some equipment. You'll be able to join-in the pickup games with the other freshmen and the varsity players that happen every afternoon. I think you'll enjoy playing with them. And welcome to the team!"

"Thanks, coach! I'll see you tomorrow," I said.

Coach's phone call thrilled me. I doubted I could compete with the scholarship players, especially the ones on the varsity, but I couldn't wait to get started anyhow. I called home right away to tell my parents what just happened. They were both very excited for me.

When I arrived at Coach Windsor's office the next afternoon, they gave me a locker and workout gear and I met most of the players. After I changed and went to the court, I got into a pickup game pretty quick. There were a lot of varsity players in the game, many of whom were All-Americans in high school, and all were taller, quicker, and much better than me. It didn't take long to realize I was over-matched, which wasn't a surprise. But it was fun anyhow, and I enjoyed the challenge. The best part was being involved with a team again. The pickup games occurred a few days each week until organized practices began in the middle of October. When they did, I received a benefit of being on the team I didn't know about. I got to eat dinner at the Athlete's Training Table in the Mountainlair, the West Virginia Student Union building. So each day after practice, I got a free dinner, which meant a lot to me since I was on a tight budget.

The official team tryouts took place a few weeks later, and the coaches selected enough players to fill out the roster. They were all outstanding athletes and very nice guys. One player only lived a couple doors down from me in Columbian Hall.

Before the season started, the coaches invited me to play in the annual Blue-White game. This was an exhibition where both the varsity and freshman players were split into two squads and scrimmaged against each other. It was an event to help generate fan interest in the upcoming season and was played after one of the home football games that fall. Playing in that game was very special for me even though I only played a few minutes and didn't score any points.

It wasn't long before the regular season games started and my first semester was ending. I was very busy trying to do well in school and take part in athletics, which was difficult. I did okay considering everything I had going on. It was nice to have a break from everything over the holidays.

My second semester was even more intense than my first because now I was also taking physics, along with calculus, chemistry, English composition, and physical education, besides playing basketball. My typical days were to attend classes in the morning and early afternoon, using any breaks to study or grab lunch. Then I'd practice with the team from 4:00-6:00 p.m. each day. Afterward, I'd have dinner at the Training Table before going back to my dorm around 7:30 p.m. to study. When we had home games, the freshmen started at 6:00 p.m. before the varsity game at 8:00 p.m., which I always stayed to watch. Then I'd get back to the dorm about 10:30 p.m. and start studying. Away games required a long bus ride or short flight and meant a bigger time commitment. On those days, I'd get to my room around midnight and I was too tired to study. Then I had to wake up early for class the next morning and begin my routine over again.

Being on the basketball team was an enjoyable experience, even though I didn't get to play very much. I did score nine points one night, which was the highlight of the season for me. I wasn't on the same level as the scholarship players, and I knew it. However, I did a few things well, which made me get noticed once in a while. I just didn't have the skill set to make much of a mark in all the areas required. With such an enormous time commitment, I began looking forward to NOT playing sports anymore after the season concluded. Although, being on a major college team even for that one year was a dream come true for me. And I remain friends with a few of the players on the team all these years later. Our team photo is one of my prize possessions to this day.

One highlight of season for me was to get to play, or at least warm-up, in the Pittsburgh Civic Arena when we played Duquesne University. I'd watched many high school, college, and professional games at the Civic Arena before and always wanted to play there. To make it even better, my parents were able to attend that game.

Coach Windsor had a big impact on me, not only basketball-wise but also in a teaching sense. His coaching style was one where he was always supportive and encouraging of his players, and he taught with patience and respect. He treated us as adults and never got upset or raised his voice when we made mistakes. He viewed every player's mistakes teaching moments for the entire team. Coach Windsor was more of a father figure to a group of teenagers than he was a hard-line coach. He and I stayed connected during my remaining years in college, and he wrote me a letter of recommendation to help me get a job when I graduated. I respected Coach Windsor and appreciated his coaching and teaching styles, even toward a player we both knew didn't have a future in the sport after that one year.

One interesting and foretelling event occurred one night during the season. At one of our sold-out home games, while we were warming up, our team manager pulled me aside to give me a message. He told me that my 'Uncle Dunbar' was at the ticket office out front and needed a ticket to the game. Not having an 'Uncle Dunbar', I knew who it was: Frank Dunbar was a mentor of mine in my high school days who I hadn't seen since I graduated. "Dunny," as we called him, was in his early forties, and was a disheveled fly by-the-seat-of-his-pants kind of guy who always supported us basketball players in high school. His ambition in life was to help young players become successful and to become a teacher someday, which he later did. He was the only person I knew who'd show up unannounced at a sold-out game and want a free ticket to get in. Each player received two complimentary tickets to every home game, and I hadn't used mine that night. So I told the manager to take a ticket out of my locker and give it to my 'uncle' and tell him I'd join him for the varsity game. It was nice to see him again and catch up.

Dunny was the person most instrumental in my being recruited by some schools, and Westminster College in particular. I disappointed him by not going there, but after we watched the varsity game together, he revealed his alternative plan for me. He had become friends with the basketball coach at Carnegie-Mellon University (CMU) in Pittsburgh, and they wanted me to transfer there, where I could study engineering and continue playing. The opportunity flattered me and I thought about it, but not for long. I decided against transferring for a few reasons. First, I loved WVU and had made many friends, and I was off to a good start in school. I knew Carnegie-Mellon was an elite university and very competitive, and I wasn't sure if I'd be a good fit there or not. I already realized how difficult it was trying to play sports and major in engineering, and I was tired of doing both. Plus, CMU didn't have an aerospace program. So I didn't transfer and looked forward to my remaining years at West Virginia without playing an organized sport. My decision disappointed both Dunny and the CMU coach, but they both understood my reasons for declining. I'm not sure I ever saw Dunny again after that night.

My formal basketball career ended in our final game of the season against our archrival, Pitt. It was an historic night for a different reason though, as it was the final game ever played in the Mountaineer Field House. The WVU Coliseum opened the following year and became the new home of West Virginia basketball. It was a huge honor to take part in that final game.

During the spring semester, my now best friend Jim Goldsworthy convinced me to pledge the fraternity he joined the previous semester. So even with my limited time, I pledged Sigma Phi Epsilon, because of Jim, although I never bought into the whole Greek organization culture in college. Adding pledging a fraternity to my already full schedule didn't leave me much time for anything else. Physics was already kicking my butt, so the semester became even more demanding with my additional social responsibilities. I looked forward to finishing up and going home for summer break.

One funny thing happened in my physical education class that semester. I was taking swimming, and the instructor was the WVU swim coach. He was teaching us how to do the sidestroke. I was not a strong swimmer, and the sidestroke was hard for me.

As I was splashing around trying not to sink, he yelled down at me, "You're supposed to swim in it, not drink it!" It was an interesting way of motivating me not to drown. Maybe the old story about basketball players not being good swimmers because they're too muscular was true. At least I liked to think that was the reason.

Before I left campus, I met with my aerospace engineering adviser to discuss my program of study. During our meeting, he told me that since our country's space program was winding down, the jobs in the aerospace industry were drying up, at least for the foreseeable future. In fact, only one person from the current graduating class found employment, and that was the top student. I got scared. This news caused me great concern. Afraid that I wouldn't be able to get a job after graduation, I changed my major to mechanical engineering. Although it wasn't as interesting to me, the jobs available when I graduated would likely be more plentiful than jobs in aerospace engineering. I also rationalized that I could find some aspect of mechanical engineering that I liked, and if the aerospace industry rebounded, I could still work within aerospace with my background. I was less excited about my new major than my old one, and I'd end up regretting my decision for years to come.

The part of aerospace engineering that I found most interesting was orbital mechanics, or the study of how natural and artificial bodies moved in space. Although I knew I wouldn't get any exposure to orbital mechanics in my new department. I changed my major with my head instead of my heart. I suppose it was a wise decision, but not a change I truly wanted to make. Changing majors would, however, play a crucial role in my having a future as a teacher, which I still hadn't yet considered.

I took part in my fraternity's hell week and initiation at the end of the semester before leaving for home. The best thing about pledging was I'd get to live in the fraternity house the next year instead of a dorm.

3

A SERIES OF INSPIRATIONS

I couldn't find a summer job after my freshman year in college, and nothing much was happening around Yukon to hold my interest. It was the first summer I didn't spend practicing basketball in many years, and it wasn't fun being idle. I taught myself to play the saxophone to pass my time, dated some, went out with friends in the evenings, and played golf a little. Overall, it was a long, dull, unproductive break from school and I couldn't wait to get back to Morgantown.

Since basketball and pledging were both over for me, I'd have plenty of time to focus on schoolwork, and perhaps have a little fun too. I also began thinking more about what I might like to do in mechanical engineering. I was taking more calculus and physics courses, although I finished chemistry. Physics was hard for me, and I expected it to be even more difficult in the coming year. I'd already experienced many types of teachers. I seemed to remember the good and the bad ones, but not the average ones as much.

In my sophomore year, I began taking fundamental classes in the mechanical engineering department. To my surprise, I liked some of them a lot, the basic mechanics courses such as statics, dynamics, and mechanics of materials, in particular. I continued to experience a wide range of teaching quality. I thought the best teachers were ones who connected with the students on some level and could simplify hard topics and make them understandable for everyone. The teachers I didn't like came to class unprepared and talked over the student's heads. I got more out of my classes with outstanding teachers. The opposite was true for me in those with "less good" ones.

After taking physics in the fall semester, I began paying more attention to how professors taught. I noticed how they connected with students, what I thought worked for them, and what didn't work at all. Teaching still hadn't struck me as something I might want to do until one interesting day. My physics professor was Dr. Stanley Farr, someone who Ed also had when he was a student. The class was in a large lecture hall that had tiered seating for about a hundred students. Dr. Farr was an excellent and entertaining teacher. He made his classes fun, even though the material was difficult. Then on the day before WVU's football game with our old rival, Pitt, he did something very unusual and hilarious. In the middle of his lecture, he noticed some students walking past in the hallway. He stopped lecturing, went out into the hall, and came back with a student he lured into the classroom with him. He asked her if she'd lead the class in 'Beat the hell out of Pitt' cheers to help everyone get ready for the big game the next day. She played along with his little prank and began the cheer. At one point she even climbed up on a large table down front, and her cheering got everyone pumped up. This lasted for a few minutes and by the end, everybody was hollering and laughing, including the girl standing on the table leading the cheer. When she finished and climbed down, we all applauded her for being such a good sport. And Dr. Farr cheered along with the class. It was a gesture on his part that helped him connect with the students for an enjoyable experience. Afterward, I remember thinking that being a professor could be a fun job. In a strange way, Dr. Farr may have been the first to inspire me to think about teaching someday. I ended up doing well in Dr. Farr's class, and I later found out he was a member of Sigma Phi Epsilon fraternity when he was an undergraduate at WVU.

Over Christmas that year, Ed, his wife Jean, and my two-year-old nephew, Mark, came home from Texas for the holidays. Since Ed graduated in engineering and Jean had worked in the Industrial Engineering Department, they were interested in hearing about my experiences at WVU. I remember Jean talking about her job as the departmental secretary and saying how she thought college professors had the best jobs! I trusted Jean's opinion, and because she knew many of the professors, her viewpoint about their job piqued my interest even more.

One class I was looking forward to taking in the spring semester of my sophomore year was mechanics of materials, which was a first course in structural analysis. My professor had written the book we used, and it was a very good one. But this guy would come to class every day, sit down at a desk in front, and read stories from the Daily Athenaeum, the WVU student newspaper, to the class. He'd spend about half the hour reading to us, then ask if anybody had questions on that day's material he was supposed to be covering. Sometimes he'd work a problem or two from the textbook, but he never worked them all the way through for us to see the entire solution. I had to teach myself the material and didn't learn as much as I hoped to in that class. I'll always remember that professor, but not in a good way. Most of the time I spent in his class, I thought I could probably do better than him teaching young, eager minds.

Another very poor teacher I had that semester was a graduate student who taught thermodynamics. There were twenty-five students in class, and he told us on the first day that twenty percent of the class was going to receive each of the five grades. So there would be 5 A's, 5 B's, 5 C's, 5 D's, and 5 F's, regardless of how well everybody performed during the semester. I didn't think his grading scheme was fair at all. A student could learn a lot and still get an F if his or her average was in the bottom five of the class. To me it was just being lazy, and he shouldn't have been teaching anything. The fact he was just a graduate student was not an excuse. I expected to have quality instruction and felt cheated. He didn't measure up to the other teachers I'd taken, even the bad ones. It was another experience that sensitized me to the quality of teaching students receive in college. I was fortunate to come out of that class with a B and felt sorry for the five students who failed.

My teacher for differential equations the same semester was excellent. He was a delightful man, and the class was large, perhaps seventy-five students. The thing I remember most about him was that, besides my learning the material, he curved the final grades at the very end of the semester a tremendous amount. I thought it was a fun thing for a professor to do, surprising students and making them leave with a good feeling about the course. That I benefitted from his generosity often influenced how I assigned final grades myself during my career. Many of my former students may have benefitted in the same way I did because of my differential equations professor. Those who didn't should probably have worked just a little harder.

During the summer after my sophomore year, my father passed away unexpectedly from a heart attack at age fifty. It was a tough time for me, and I considered dropping out of college to work and help my mother. But she wouldn't hear of it. She knew the value of getting an education because she never had the chance to even attend high school. She wanted me to graduate and get a good job so I could support myself and perhaps a family someday. I knew she was right.

If I had quit college, it would have been a huge mistake for me and my entire life would have been different. So I'm glad she encouraged me to return to school. I did the best I could in my studies, and I still liked not playing basketball. Although I played intramural sports and I enjoyed being a member of a social fraternity. By that time, I was halfway through my degree program and began thinking about what my future would look like after graduation. After my father died, I purchased my first automobile, a 1969 Ford Mustang coupe. I loved that car and should've kept it forever, but I traded it in after I graduated.

When I changed my major from aerospace to mechanical engineering, they assigned me a new academic advisor. He also taught a required class in computer programming. The computer language used in those days was FORTRAN, and most of the course involved writing programs to solve various types of engineering problems. Being a beginner at programming, it took me a while to learn that skill. There were many times when I couldn't get my program to work and had to seek help from my professor/adviser. He was a nice man, but always started our meetings off the same way.

Before he even looked at my program, he'd say, "I already know what's wrong."

"What's that?" I'd respond each time.

"Well, you made at least one stupid mistake," he answered. And he was always right! After I became a professor, I used the same line on my students for many years when they couldn't get their programs to work. I was right every time too!

The classes I took in my major were all designed to give me the knowledge I might need to work as an engineer. They were quality courses and well taught, although I wasn't interested in all of them. My goal was still to finish my degree and find an interesting job somewhere. That plan began to change in the fall semester of my junior year when I had Professor Hasan Tahsin Gencsoy for a course in the kinematics of mechanisms.

I always arrived early to class because I wanted to be ready when it began. I often had to stand in the hallway near the classroom to wait for the previous class to finish and leave before I could enter. When they did, I walked in and always found a seat in the second row on the right side, facing the front. The classrooms in our department were short but wide, with maybe four or five rows of desks, with seven or eight seats in each row. Everyone was seated close to the chalkboard, which extended the entire width of the room. A podium usually sat to the left of the board for the professor.

There were only about twenty-five juniors in mechanical engineering, so we had all of our classes together. Most of the students were males, which wasn't unusual for engineering classes in the early 1970s. So the small classroom was nearly full every morning.

When Professor Gencsoy walked in, he immediately took control of the room and commanded our attention. A thin man of medium height, he was in his late forties with thin and graying hair. He dressed in a long sleeve shirt and necktie and dress slacks and always wore beautiful neckties and belts. He spoke with just the slightest hint of his Turkish accent, as he came to the United States in 1945 to attend the University of California, Berkeley. Later he received his master's degree from WVU before going to work for IBM. He didn't have a doctorate but held many patents in machine design. Professor Gencsoy was a distinguished and classy man. We all soon learned he was very knowledgeable and an excellent teacher.

Professor Gencsoy impressed me from the beginning because when he first read the class roll he pronounced my name correctly according to my Italian heritage. Without hesitation he pronounced it "Chi-chi," as opposed to our family's Americanized version of "See-sigh". He continued to call me Mr. Chi-chi the entire time I had him for class. I never attempted to correct his pronunciation of my name. I imagine if I had, he wouldn't have honored my request anyhow, because his pronunciation was correct and mine wasn't.

I enjoyed Professor Gencsoy's teaching style. His approach was more practical than theoretical, and his explanations were very clear. The figures he drew on the chalkboard, although sometimes complicated, were meticulous, colorful, and understandable. When he worked through problems on the board; he seldom finished all the calculations. Instead, he taught us how to attack the problems and set up the solutions more than talking us through the minor details of crunching the final numbers to get the answer. But he explained the hardest parts. When he got to where only plugging in the numbers remained, he'd always say, "And... boom, boom, boom, problem finished!" I tried to do that same thing in a few of my classes during my career, but I could never pull it off with the same flair.

By the time I graduated I took five classes from Professor Gencsoy. The courses covered basic and advanced topics in kinematics, dynamics of machines, and mechanical design. I enjoyed each class, and I developed a strong interest in the structural aspects of machine design. I became fascinated that Professor Gencsoy could teach so well and didn't need to have a doctorate to do so. He inspired me to learn, but I also began thinking about the possibility of being a teacher like him someday. I realized how much I gained from his teaching and thought that maybe I could do the same for other students.

When I arrived at my classrooms and waited in the hallway for the earlier class to finish, I stood near the departmental bulletin board. As I did, I always read the fliers for open faculty positions that were posted there. Reading through those job listings at other universities each day piqued my interest in teaching even more. I loved college and thought working at one would be fun. From reading those ads, I found that faculty jobs seemed to be plentiful but that a doctorate was the minimum requirement, along with some professional experience. I also learned that professors didn't just teach; they also had to perform research in their area of specialization. That didn't interest me as much as teaching, but I thought seriously about teaching as a potential career for the first time while looking at those ads. But knowing that I'd have to get a Ph.D. first was a daunting thought. I wasn't the best student in my class by far, so my academic record didn't predict the possibility of success for me in ever getting a doctorate. I assumed that having the goal of becoming a professor someday was an unreachable one for me.

I became very familiar with the advertisements of vacant faculty positions around the country and learned about the academic programs at other universities. I looked for jobs that didn't require a doctorate, although there were very few of those. The more I read, though, the more my interest grew in teaching because of Professor Gencsoy. But I realized it was a long shot for me.

I had to study a lot, as engineering wasn't easy for me. I studied almost every night and weekend, although I made it a point to never study on Friday nights. That was a night I always saved for myself to relax and unwind, go out with my friends, and just get away from academics so I wouldn't burn out. It was a plan that seemed to work well for me. Although the further along I got in school, the more I went out other nights during the week too. A lot of those times I went out with Jim Goldsworthy, but I still studied at least some each night. When I prepared for exams, I somehow developed a knack for identifying the important information and learned to predict what material the professor would ask. And I was often right in my guesses, which served me very well throughout my schooling. I also developed skills at being able to simplify difficult topics so I could understand them better. One thing I learned was that much of the material presented in class and in textbooks was superfluous and beyond what a student needed to focus on for the exams. That knowledge became valuable to me as a student, but also as a professor. I believe that was my strength as an educator.

I didn't have confidence that I could ever earn a Ph.D. in engineering, since I wasn't the top student in class. Not having that confidence made me think that goal was out of reach for me. But in reality, the opposite was true. Being from a small town and being raised by parents who lived through the Great Depression, I never received encouragement that I could do anything I wanted in life. I remember one time in junior high school when I became interested in going to college at the University of Notre Dame. I even sent away for a catalog.

When I mentioned it to my mother, she responded, "You can't go to Notre Dame, you're from Yukon, and nobody from Yukon goes to Notre Dame." Although I never bought into her viewpoint, I wouldn't have been able to afford it anyhow. Later I realized that Notre Dame would have been a terrible choice for me. Besides, there were other kids in town that attended West Virginia, my brother Ed being one of them. That was something my mom felt was within my grasp. Attending Notre Dame wasn't. In the back of my mind, I may have thought that earning a Ph.D. was something else that was out of my reach.

Ed helped my parents overcome their concerns about our career choices with his lifelong dream of becoming a pilot. His choice was a foreign one to them, but he persevered and ended up flying for his entire professional life. He first flew in the Air Force, where he was an instructor and a test pilot for twenty years. Then he was a captain with Delta Airlines for fifteen years before retiring. He finished his career with the Federal Aviation Administration, where he was a test pilot once more until he retired again at age 72. His drive and determination paved the way for me to aim high, too. So I did just that.

The summer before my senior year in college, my friend Big Mike and I took jobs at a steel fabrication plant in Greensburg, Pennsylvania. It was hard physical labor, and I had to develop a strong work ethic to survive each day. But after about a month, I was offered a junior engineering position which I applied for months earlier. It was at the same Westinghouse Electric Research Center where I worked a few years before doing ground maintenance. This time, however, I worked inside in the Fluid Dynamics Laboratory and didn't have to pick weeds outside. My job was building and disassembling testing rigs, although I also worked with the engineers to help run fluid flow tests. It was a fun job and one in which I learned a little about the research world. It was far better than working in a steel plant or picking weeds in the summer heat.

Before I graduated, I investigated going straight to graduate school to get a master's degree. I didn't think I could qualify for an assistantship, and I couldn't afford to pay my own way. Assistantships were much less prevalent in those days. I'd heard that most engineering companies would pay for graduate study for their employees so their engineers could get a master's on a part-time basis while working full time. That became an affordable back-up plan for my future, to get a job with a company that had such a program and was near a school with a graduate program in engineering. By the time I finished my mechanical engineering degree, I had already become infatuated with being a professor someday. That was because of Professor Gencsoy and those fliers on the bulletin board.

I played a lot of intramural sports for my fraternity during my last three years in school. They even voted me the Outstanding Athlete during my senior year. I'm not sure I deserved that recognition because I only played football, basketball, and softball. I think I won the award because I suffered a broken nose in one of our basketball games not long before I graduated. To make it worse, it came from an errant elbow thrown by one of my teammates while diving for a loose ball. Ironically, my injury occurred in the Mountaineer Field House, on the same court where I played freshman ball three years earlier, so that place played another part in my life. I had to wear a small facemask to class until I had my nose fixed during outpatient surgery at the WVU Medical Center several days later. My wife tells me I was a lot better looking before I broke it.

I lived in the fraternity house for my last three years of college. My roommate for the last two years was John Catselis, who was a year younger than me and majored in civil engineering. John was a fun and very bright guy, who was always up for a good time, sometimes even at the expense of his studies. John didn't have to study much and got through his classes with minimal effort. He didn't even bother purchasing the books he needed for some of his courses. One semester I went with him to the bookstore right before final exams. John stood in the aisle and read the textbook he hadn't bought for one class to get ready for the final. I learned a lot about student capabilities from him. John and I also lived together for two more years after he graduated from WVU and took a job in Pittsburgh. He's still a fun guy to be around.

My time in college went by much too fast. Even though I didn't break any records grade-wise, I graduated in four years without ever attending summer school or having to repeat a class. I remember thinking I'd like to spend longer in school and delay going out into the real world, although I couldn't. I needed a job. But I still thought how great it would be to live in a college town again someday.

4

A LOT OF JOBS I DIDN'T WANT

WVU had an outstanding College Placement Center (now called the Career Services Center), which helped soon-to-be graduates find work in their field. In 1973, jobs in mechanical engineering were plentiful, as I had hoped, while there were still very few available in aerospace. It turned out that changing my major was a good idea for many reasons, the most important one being that job opportunities for me would be better when I graduated. I was thankful, as that was my goal all along.

Interviewing for jobs through the placement center was easy and similar to the process at other major universities. They'd publish a list of companies scheduled to visit campus to conduct preliminary interviews and the degrees they were interested in hiring. Students could sign up for on-campus interviews as long as their degree matched the company's needs. Based on the results of the preliminary interview, companies could offer applicants follow-up interviews at their facilities. Accepting such an interview would require traveling to their company's location and missing a day or two of school. Candidates may or may not receive a job offer afterward.

I built my resume to express an interest in finding a position in the areas of mechanical/machine design or structural analysis, subjects I liked the best, thanks to Professor Gencsoy. I also included a statement that I hoped to pursue a master's degree on a part-time basis while working full time. In the personal section, I mentioned I had been on the freshman basketball team in college, something they asked me about in almost every interview. Many interviewers also commented on the pleasant things Coach Windsor said about me in the letter of recommendation he wrote. I believe playing basketball opened some doors to employment opportunities I may not have had otherwise. Those experiences also played a future role in my teaching career. I didn't receive a basketball scholarship, but playing the sport still proved beneficial to me throughout my life.

I signed up for at least fifteen on-campus interviews through the placement center. My GPA wasn't 4.0, and I didn't graduate at the top of my class. My grades were decent, not great, but I interviewed very well. After my campus interviews, ten or twelve companies invited me for on-site interviews at their facilities. Those visits required me to fly to most of the locations, but I could drive the rest. A few of the places I traveled to for interviews were Pittsburgh and Philadelphia in Pennsylvania, Akron, Ohio, Schenectady, New York, Canonsburg, Pennsylvania, and Fredrick, Maryland. I also had a cousin who worked at Schenley Distillers, which was near Pittsburgh. He tried to get me hired there, but they had no open positions at the time I was graduating. Too bad! In addition, I applied to jobs in Atlanta, Georgia, and Fort Lauderdale, Florida, but I didn't have any luck finding opportunities in those cities. I hoped to find a job in a warmer climate, and I loved Fort Lauderdale from my visits there during spring breaks. It was unfortunate for me those places didn't work out because I would have enjoyed milder weather. Visiting Florida for those breaks gave me a small taste of what I'd been missing out on.

After all of my interviews, I received eight or nine solid offers. During my on-site interviews, I found some jobs weren't interesting to me for various reasons. Either the work wasn't challenging, I didn't like the location the salary was lower than others, or there wasn't an opportunity to further my education. Deciding what job to accept was difficult. At first, I narrowed my list down to four companies: General Electric in Philadelphia and Schenectady, Babcock and Wilcox in Akron, and McGraw-Edison in Canonsburg, near Pittsburgh. I also received a job offer from Schlumberger in Houston, Texas, to work in the oil industry, which was booming in 1973. They offered me a job but didn't invite me to visit their facility. I thought there must have been something they were hiding that I wouldn't have liked, so I declined their offer. Besides, working in the oil industry didn't enthuse me much at all.

The work at each of the four jobs I considered was interesting on some level. And they all offered an opportunity for me to pursue a master's degree in mechanical engineering, but none of those potential schools had an aerospace program. The starting salaries were comparable and between eleven and twelve thousand dollars per year. That amount doesn't sound like much now, but in 1973 it was the going rate for recent engineering graduates. It was more than my father ever made as a music teacher, so it sounded like a lot of money to me. The biggest differences in the jobs were the locations. I wanted to be in, or near a big city. Philadelphia was a large city, Akron was a mid-sized city, and Schenectady and Canonsburg were small cities, although Canonsburg was close to Pittsburgh, which was also large. Canonsburg was nearest to my home and I was very familiar with Pittsburgh, since I grew up about thirty miles southeast of the city. The other places were unfamiliar to me, as I'd never been to any of them before my interviews. If truth be told, I wasn't excited about any of the jobs. I was already more focused on where I wanted my career to end up, not where it would start. It was not the right mindset for me to have at the start of my career. I didn't want any of those jobs, but I didn't have any other options. Looking back, I should have gone straight to graduate school and stayed at WVU for a master's degree. Being young and stupid, I thought I'd have a lot of money if I took a job. Boy, was I wrong.

After much contemplation and uncertainty, I accepted the position at the McGraw-Edison Company in Canonsburg, over Babcock and Wilcox in Akron. McGraw-Edison (now Pennsylvania Transformer Technology) was a facility that manufactured electrical power transformers and circuit breakers. They hired me to work in the general area of the mechanical design of linkages and mechanisms used in their oil and gas circuit breakers. It was about as far from the aerospace industry as I could get, except for maybe the liquor industry with Schenley Distillers. It was not a good employment choice for me. Now, I wished I'd have investigated government positions in the intelligence community. It would have been more interesting and much more challenging, and I could have lived in the Washington, DC area.

I know I accepted the position at McGraw-Edison because of the location, which was the wrong reason. It would have been wiser to choose a job for the work instead of the location. But Pittsburgh was familiar to me, and I wanted to be closer to home because my mother was living alone. Another factor in my decision was that I already had friends in Pittsburgh and several others were heading there for jobs after college, which also wasn't a good reason for me to move there. I often ponder how different my life would have been if I'd have taken one of the other jobs.

After graduation, I went home to spend a few weeks with my mother before moving to Pittsburgh, where I planned to live. The day after I received my degree and returned to Yukon, my mom said to me, "Now that you're an engineer, can you fix the refrigerator? It hasn't been working right."

I answered, "Mom, I didn't learn how to fix refrigerators in college."

Then she said, "You mean I spent all that money on tuition for you to get an engineering degree and you can't even fix a refrigerator? What did you study down there, anyway?" We both laughed, and I still think she was only joking. At least I hope she was, otherwise she had wasted a lot of tuition money. But to this day, even after two more degrees, I still can't fix a broken refrigerator.

In June 1973 I moved to the South Oakland section of Pittsburgh and lived with my buddy, Big Mike, who had just graduated from Pitt. I sublet a bedroom in his apartment for the summer from another one of my high school friends who graduated and took a job in Ohio. I planned to commute forty-five minutes to Canonsburg for work each day, driving against rush-hour traffic both ways.

It was great fun sharing an apartment with Mike. We lived in a third-floor walk-up on Ward Street, a few blocks from where the old Forbes Field used to be. Forbes Field was where the Pittsburgh Pirates played before they moved to Three Rivers Stadium in 1970. It was within walking distance of the restaurants and nightlife of the college scene around Pitt and CMU. It wasn't too different from being in college, except I had to go to work every day. The bad part about living in South Oakland was that we lived just across the Monongahela River and up the hill from the Jones & Laughlin Steel Plant. Each morning I'd go out to my car to find it covered in rust-colored soot from the smokestacks of the steel mill. Pittsburgh was a very dirty city in those days; but it's much cleaner and more beautiful now. We had a fun summer, a great social life, and we met a lot of interesting people. Mike was just starting his career as a special needs teacher, which was one of the most demanding jobs I could ever imagine. But he loved his job and was excellent at it.

Mike and I enjoyed living together and planned to look for a different apartment for the fall, away from the soot and the crowded streets of Oakland. When we did, we found a terrific three-bedroom a few miles away in Shadyside, one of the more trendy parts of the city for young people. A college fraternity brother of mine, Fred Leif, took the third bedroom in our new apartment since he was also moving to Pittsburgh. Shadyside was a much nicer and a cleaner than South Oakland, although it was a little farther drive to work for me each day.

Fred worked for the Baltimore & Ohio Railroad, as did his dad and older brother, Glen. He worked odd shifts, and they called him in to work whenever they needed him, sometimes in the middle of the night. One eventful Friday, after Mike and I were out on the town and may have been over-served at several bars, a phone call from the railroad dispatcher woke me around 3:00 a.m. He wanted to reach Fred, to tell him he needed to go to work. When I answered our phone and they asked for him, I said hold on while I get him, my intention being to wake Fred to take his call. Instead of following through with my intention, I set the phone on my nightstand and lay back down and fell into a deep sleep with the phone off the hook. So of course, Fred never received the message about going to work.

After a short while of getting no further response, the dispatcher hung up and called Fred's brother, who lived in Washington,

Pennsylvania, to inform him that Fred was unreachable. Glen, knowing it was important that Fred receive the message, tried to call several times but couldn't get through because the phone was still off the hook in my bedroom. So Glen drove well over an hour to our apartment in Shadyside to give Fred the message after pounding on the front door until he woke up. (I didn't.), and Fred made it to work. When I awoke the next morning and saw the phone lying on the table next to my bed, I remembered what happened during the night. Fred told me the entire story when he got home from work the next day. I felt awful! I apologized many times to both Fred and Glen for my actions. In fact, I still apologize for that night whenever I see Fred now.

Working as an engineer was a lot different from being in school, and I didn't like it nearly as much. The McGraw-Edison Power Systems Division was a manufacturing facility, and I worked on developing their new line of high voltage oil circuit breakers. My responsibility was to design the release mechanisms required to break the circuit when a voltage overload occurred. The engineering staff was small, and my mentor traveled a lot and provided little guidance. I found it to be overwhelming when I started. It surprised me to realize not much of what I learned in school was useful in my job.

One very important piece of advice a family friend gave me before I started working was to make friends with the company staff. He said that regardless of their positions, show everybody, even the janitors, as much respect as I show my bosses. That was brilliant advice, and I took it! One person I became friends with was a drafting technician, which was a position comparable to what would be a computer-aided designer nowadays. He was middle-aged and a very nice guy. We worked together when I needed engineering drawings created, but we also spent a good bit of time talking about non-work issues. He was easy-going, funny, and always happy to provide help or a joke whenever I needed one. It turned out that his friendship would be beneficial to me much sooner than I ever expected.

Not long after I started working at McGraw-Edison, I arrived at work one Monday morning in August to find a picket line of union workers blocking the entrance. The plant workers had gone on strike for higher wages. The point of the picket line was to keep people from going to work so the plant couldn't function without the union workers. I didn't know if I should go into work or not, as I wasn't a member of the union and was not on strike. So I called my boss, who was already inside, and asked him what I should do. He told me since I was part of the engineering staff, I needed to come to work if I wanted to continue to get paid. But if I didn't enter, I wouldn't receive my salary. He said it was my decision to cross the picket line or not. I needed the money, but I didn't want to offend my friends and fellow workers who were picketing by not supporting their actions. Having grown up around unions, I knew strikes were important to the workers, so there wasn't any way I'd cross their line and disrespect them, even if it meant not getting paid.

As I approached the plant entrance and the picket line to evaluate the situation, the first person I saw was my drafting technician friend holding a "Strike" sign. He called to me to come over and said that he'd allow me to enter if I wanted. I told him I thought I needed to go to work, and he understood and let me in. He knew that letting me into work wouldn't compromise their position on the strike, and I was glad he felt that way. So I went to work that first day, along with the other engineers, the professional staff, and of course, the company administrators. I appreciated my friend understanding my position and letting me into work.

One big thing about going to work during a plant strike was, there wasn't anything to do. The engineers couldn't do anything without the union workers, which included all the drafting technicians, along with the factory and assembly line workers. Company management told us that even though there was little work for us to do, we'd still get paid as long as we showed up. But it wasn't much fun going to work when there was nothing to do. And I wasn't learning anything by not working. The plant strike lasted for almost six months, from August until early spring, before the union and the company settled on a new collective bargaining agreement. It wasn't a good work experience for a junior engineer. Besides, nobody wins when there's a strike.

To make matters worse, not long after the strike ended, my mentor was killed in an automobile accident while conducting tests on new electrical equipment in the Netherlands. He left a wife and two young daughters. That horrible event rocked and saddened our small department, and the entire atmosphere at work became sad and solemn. Although I didn't know his family well, they asked me to serve as a pallbearer at the funeral.

By that point in my first year of working, I was disillusioned enough with McGraw-Edison that I looked for opportunities elsewhere. I only ended up working there eleven months, although it seemed like much longer under the circumstances. Perhaps if I had accepted one of my other offers, my first job experience would have been a better one. At least I gained some insight into job hunting and first jobs that might help me give advice to my students someday. For that reason, I was glad to have worked at McGraw-Edison Company. But it was a job I didn't want and shouldn't have taken. My poor decision was one I would draw upon in the future, so at least it was a valuable experience in that regard.

Ann and Henry Cicci, 1946   Third grade, 1959

Joe Silvo Orchestra, circa 1960

Aunt Edith and my cousins next door, 1963

Junior high school, 1961

High school senior, 1969

Shenandoah Sports Camp, 1968

South Huntingdon High School Basketball Team, 1968-69
(Wally is to the left of me and Melvin is on the far right.)

Ed and Dad at Reese AFB, TX, 1970

WVU Freshmen Basketball Team, 1969-70

Last game in Mountaineer Field House, 1970
(Courtesy of West Virginia & Regional History Center)

On the Mountainlair Plaza with Jim Goldsworthy,
Morgantown, WV, 1970

WVU graduation, 1973

5

I'M GOING TO GRADUATE SCHOOL TOO?

One good thing about working at McGraw-Edison was their tuition reimbursement program, which would cover my tuition to take graduate courses toward a master's degree. The only requirement to receive reimbursement for the tuition I spent on a course was to earn a grade of B or better. Any grade below that in a graduate course is not good anyhow.

There were two options for graduate study in engineering in Pittsburgh: Pitt and Carnegie-Mellon (CMU). Both universities were in the Oakland section of Pittsburgh, next to each other and close to my apartment in Shadyside. Both had master's and doctoral degree programs in mechanical engineering, but neither offered one in aerospace.

The program at Pitt required a thesis, but the one at CMU had a non-thesis option. A non-thesis program would be a better choice for me since I was working full time and it would be difficult to complete a thesis going to school part-time. I also found that CMU was trying to build their graduate program by attracting working professionals, so they offered many of their classes in the late afternoons and evenings to make them more accessible.

I was skeptical about being accepted at CMU since it had a world-renowned engineering school. To help assess my chances of admission there, I called the mechanical engineering department head about two weeks after starting at McGraw-Edison. I asked about the possibility of my attending graduate school there and I described my background. I told him I wanted to attend take classes on a part-time basis while I worked full time. He encouraged me to apply and was optimistic about my chances of being admitted. So I did. Now I must add that having attended WVU, where Pitt was its biggest rival, I was not enthusiastic about ever going to Pitt anyhow. That gave CMU an enormous advantage from the beginning. Going to WVU helped me build a pretty strong dislike of Pitt, so I struggled to think of enrolling there unless there were no other options. Besides, I also felt somewhat connected to CMU ever since the basketball coach tried to recruit me to transfer from WVU after my freshman year. I also had two close friends who were amazing trumpet players, and they both attended CMU as undergraduates on music scholarships. I felt like that gave me another connection to the school. CMU had a beautiful, serene, and traditional looking campus as opposed to Pitt's large urban campus surrounded by city streets, traffic, a lot of noise, and very little grass.

Driven to get a master's degree at the best school I could, I applied to CMU, not expecting that I'd get in. I assumed that the department head was just being nice and didn't want to let me down over the phone. However, within two weeks of applying, I received a letter from the CMU Graduate School informing me of my official acceptance for graduate study. Being accepted at CMU surprised and excited me! I'd be starting classes in the fall semester of 1973, which was less than two months away. I knew it wouldn't be easy, but I planned to work hard and do well. A degree from CMU would be invaluable to me in my engineering career regardless of what type of work I did.

The non-thesis master's degree program at CMU required thirty-two semester hours of coursework, or ten courses. It also required students to pass comprehensive written examinations in two technical areas. I wanted to specialize in structural analysis and control systems since they didn't teach orbital mechanics, so those would be the two exams I'd need to pass. Because I worked full time, I thought I could finish the coursework in six semesters over a three-year period. They didn't offer graduate classes in the summers, so I planned to take two courses in each of four semesters and one each in the remaining two semesters.

Before I knew it, school started in the fall. It was great to be back on campus taking classes again. I registered for an introduction to solid mechanics course called strength of materials, and a theoretical solid mechanics course focused on elasticity. The class times were from 4:30-6:00 p.m. and 6:30-8:00 p.m., respectively, on Mondays and Wednesdays. My boss at McGraw-Edison graciously allowed me to leave work early on those days in order to make it back to Oakland for class.

CMU was a smaller school than West Virginia, with only about 8,000 students compared to almost 20,000 at WVU. It was in a big city rather than in a small college town, and their sports were on a much smaller level. I attended a couple of CMU football games, but, regretfully, no basketball games. There was a different basketball coach by then, and I had no connection to the program that sparked my interest to go to a game.

I didn't know what to expect from my courses at CMU or how they would compare to my undergraduate ones at WVU. I wasn't sure how good the teachers would be, since CMU's strong reputation was more of a research institution than of a teaching one. But it didn't take long to find out.

The professor in my elasticity class was from China and didn't speak English well. I sat in the front row and it was difficult for me to understand much of anything he said. It was tough just listening to the lectures. There were about twenty students taking the course, and everyone was having trouble understanding the professor. He knew the material and tried hard, but his teaching was not conducive to learning, at least not for me, because of his language barrier. The course was hard, and he taught it at a very high level, which made it even more difficult for me.

By the time I started classes, the strike at McGraw-Edison was underway and I had nothing much to do at work, although I continued to show up every day.

When I asked my boss what I should do while I was there, he said, "Well, you're in school, aren't you?" When I confirmed I was, he replied, "Then just study or do your homework, that'll be fine with me. But if you want to keep getting paid, you need to continue to show up. Nobody can do anything until the strike's over anyhow. Just come in and do your schoolwork."

So I was getting paid for doing my homework, which was a pretty good deal for me. McGraw-Edison had a decent technical library, which helped me find some references I needed to study. But school was hard. The level of academics was much more theoretical and less practical than at WVU. I had to spend a lot of my free time, besides my time at work, studying. It was common for me to spend two nights a week in class, and two more nights and all of Sunday on my schoolwork. I loved being back in school and on a campus again so soon. Since I didn't live far from campus, I often studied at either the Hunt library or the Math and Science library at CMU. Another place I'd study was the Chatham College (now Chatham University) library, which was even closer to my apartment. It was an undergraduate liberal arts school for women in the Squirrel Hill part of town. Being single, I enjoyed studying in their library sometimes too.

Since I was twenty-two years old, I spent much of the rest of my free time going out and socializing with many of my college friends who lived in town. There was always something fun to do with them. Mike, Fred, and I had a very nice apartment, so we had a lot of parties. But my primary focus was on school, even though I was having fun living in a big city.

I made it through my first semester of graduate school and learned a lot. In the spring, I took the second part of the same two courses from the fall with the same professors. This time my Chinese professor taught plasticity, which was even harder for me than elasticity. By that time I could semi-understand his lectures, but it still wasn't an enjoyable learning experience. They hired him for his research abilities and not for his teaching skills, which is the case at so many universities. He left the university after the spring semester so future students didn't have had the same bad experience as I did.

I soon tired of the ongoing strike at McGraw-Edison and commuting to Canonsburg every day. Even though they allowed me to study during work hours, I began looking for another job. When the strike ended in the early spring of 1974, I had already accepted a position at Westinghouse Electric Corporation, Bettis Atomic Power Laboratory in West Mifflin, Pennsylvania, which Westinghouse ran for the U.S. Department of Energy. It was a shorter commute, and the work was more interesting. Plus, the tuition reimbursement program was the same as McGraw-Edison's, and there was no labor strike. I started at Westinghouse in May 1974 right after the semester ended and I was reimbursed for my tuition.

That summer Fred and Mike moved out of our Shadyside apartment and my college roommate, John Catselis, and another fraternity brother, Rich Adams, moved in. John worked as a civil engineer for the Pennsylvania Department of Transportation, and Rich was a bank examiner for the federal government. It was great fun sharing an apartment with those two. That fall I injured my back playing flag football and needed to have surgery. While I was in Shadyside Hospital, Rich was involved in a terrible automobile accident. I missed about a month of work, and Rich was off even longer as we recuperated at home together. Even though I still attended class, I didn't enjoy being so idle and was happy to get back to work after I recovered.

My position at Bettis was that of a structural analyst working on power plant components for the U.S. Navy's nuclear-powered submarine and warship fleet. That was much more interesting to me than power circuit breakers, and the work was closer to my focus in graduate school. Bettis had many more employees than McGraw-Edison, and it was a research and testing laboratory, not a production facility. A lot of junior engineers and scientists worked at Bettis, and there were many organizations and clubs to take part in. During my time there, I played in the softball, basketball, bowling, and golf leagues, and joined the ski club to learn how to snow ski. I took skiing lessons on Tuesday nights at the Hidden Valley Ski Resort in Somerset, Pennsylvania. Bettis was a very social environment. A group of us went out for lunch and to happy hours after work a few days each week. It was an enjoyable place to work, and I built many close friendships.

I continued taking two graduate classes each semester, all in the evenings, and experienced a wide range of teachers. There weren't any professors I'd classify as outstanding teachers, although many of them were brilliant researchers. Most of the ones I had weren't as good at teaching as my professors at WVU. I took notice of both what I liked and didn't like about their teaching methods. My grades continued to be Bs or better and I got reimbursed for the tuition costs. However, that changed when I took the final class I needed for my master's degree.

My last course at CMU, called advanced engineering analysis, was the only required course in my program of study. It was an applied math class focused on mechanical engineering applications. They only offered the class from 11:00 a.m.-12:15 p.m. two days a week, and never in the evenings. Because of that, all working engineers taking the class had to leave work during the day and drive to campus to attend. I left work at 10:30 a.m. and didn't get back until 1:00 p.m. Parking was always a problem during the daytime at CMU and I seldom got lunch on those days. So I didn't have a great attitude about the class, anyway.

To make matters worse, the professor was terrible! He explained things poorly, came to class unprepared, and didn't teach methodologies or approaches to solving the problems we studied. He also gave little guidance on the problem-solving techniques he expected us to use. I often felt as though he was just bumbling along and wasn't interested in spending the time to teach well. He'd taught the course many times before, and I didn't think he cared much anymore. As a result, the students suffered, myself included. I learned a lot about how not to teach from him, and I vowed never to be that guy! It was my only disappointment about attending CMU.

I didn't do well in the class, although I'm sure I could've done better if I had worked harder. It was my worst class and performance, and I received a C for a grade. Even though such a poor grade hurt my GPA, it didn't affect my graduation at the end of the semester. The worst part wasn't that I didn't learn as much as I should have. It was that I wouldn't get reimbursed for my tuition of over $600 for that one course, which was a lot of money to me in 1976. To this day I feel cheated because the professor was so bad. I think I received an outstanding education at CMU, but I still hold a grudge for the terrible experience I had in his class and the money it cost me. It still irks me he came to class unprepared every day and didn't teach the students much of anything.

After I passed my comprehensive examinations, I graduated with a Master of Science degree in mechanical engineering in May 1976. I felt honored to have attended such an elite school. They held the graduation ceremony during the week and I had to miss it because of work. I regret not attending that event. My mother was very proud of me, and she would have enjoyed seeing me graduate.

Getting my masters was a tremendous accomplishment for me. I never forgot the fact that Professor Gencsoy only had a master's degree. Although, it was a different time now, and it was unlikely I'd be able to find a teaching job without having a doctorate. But I liked the work at Bettis, so I put my hopes of being a professor someday on hold for a while longer. I didn't consider continuing on for a Ph.D. at CMU. I drew weary of working days and going to class and studying most of the evenings, and I needed a break from school to focus on other aspects of my life. Besides, I met a woman the previous fall and began spending a lot of time with her. I didn't want to use my free time to study, at least not then. The woman I met, Christine, was an elementary school science teacher, and she loved it. She joined the Bettis ski club and the bowling league with me, and we learned to ski at Hidden Valley together. We enjoyed both, but bowling was especially fun because there was a lot more beer drinking than bowling. It turned out that I had the highest bowling average in our league and Chris had the lowest, so we balanced each other out.

When I met Chris, she was working on her master's degree too, but she was going to Pitt. (I often teased her how it couldn't have been very hard to get a master's over there.) She was scheduled to finish her degree about a year after me. Most of her classes were in the Cathedral of Learning, a beautiful, forty-two story, Late Gothic Revival skyscraper on the Pitt campus. It was just across Schenley

Park from my department at CMU. I used to (and often still do) tell her that, according to WVU fans, there were two more appropriate names for that building: the Tower of Ignorance, and the Height of Stupidity. Chris never saw the humor in those names and still doesn't when I continue to call it by those names to this day.

My interest in teaching continued, and perhaps even got stronger after my experiences at CMU. It was my impression that the instruction should be better in both undergraduate and graduate classes. I continued to read ads for faculty positions in the American Society of Mechanical Engineering (ASME) magazine I received each month. Every once in a while an ad would appear for a job that didn't require a doctorate. Most of those were at undergraduate institutions, junior colleges, community colleges, or foreign institutions. I still enjoyed looking at the ads to see which schools were hiring faculty members, what they were looking for, and what their programs were like.

When there was an advertisement that didn't require a doctorate, I'd apply for the position. I received an offer of a full-time teaching job once, sight unseen, as an assistant professor at the University of Puerto Rico Mayaguez. I'd never been to Puerto Rico, and they didn't offer me an on-site interview, and the pay was very low. Because of those reasons, I declined what may have been the only teaching position I could have gotten without a Ph.D.. There was just too much uncertainty about moving to a Caribbean island and risking the ability to change jobs without a doctorate later. But I felt honored to receive the offer from UPRM. (Go Bulldogs!) It surprised me to learn that UPRM has separate Bulldog mascots for the men (Tarzans) and women (Janes) sports teams.

Even though I had a master's degree in engineering, I considered other career options. I didn't think I wanted to just be a regular engineer my entire life if I couldn't teach. I thought about going to other professional schools, such as medical school or law school. Looking back, if I had made either of those choices, it would have been a huge disaster.

6

MY ENGINEERING LIFE

I enjoyed working at Westinghouse Bettis, much more than at McGraw-Edison. The projects were interesting, and it was a fun workplace environment. The professional staff at Bettis was large, perhaps 1,500-2,000, and I was part of a group of structural analysts. Although, after receiving my master's degree, I began looking for other opportunities where I would have more individual responsibility and receive a higher salary. Besides, in July 1977 I was lucky enough to marry the beautiful and brilliant Christine Smith. I thought we could use more money to save up for a house and perhaps start a family.

In the fall of that year, I received an opportunity too good to turn down, a consulting position at Swanson Engineering Associates Corporation (SEAC), in Peters Township, Pennsylvania. John Swanson, who developed the software analysis program ANSYS in 1970, founded SEAC. Swanson Analysis Systems, Incorporated (SASI) was the company that maintained and marketed ANSYS, while SEAC was a small group of engineering consultants that served as practical problem solvers, using ANSYS. SEAC gave me a nice raise to hire on, but a big drawback was that the company was near Canonsburg, which would mean a long commute again each.

However, SEAC's primary mode of operation was to provide consultants to other companies. The plan was for me to work as a contract engineer, i.e., short- and long-term assignments, on-site at various other locations in the western Pennsylvania area, rather than my working at company headquarters. After Chris and I married, we moved to another apartment in Shadyside, close to where I lived when I was single. She was teaching elementary school in Hampton Township north of Pittsburgh. If I had worked at SEAC's main office, our two work locations were about forty-seven miles apart. Fortunately, I only had to commute to Peter's Township for the first couple of weeks I worked there.

SEAC soon sent me on a long-term consulting job at, of all places, Westinghouse, but it wasn't Bettis this time. Instead, it was their nuclear division in Forrest Hills, Pennsylvania, which was only about eight miles from where we lived. I spent several months working at Forrest Hills and then moved to their Monroeville nuclear division, which was about ten miles away, to work for another six months.

I moved to yet another Westinghouse nuclear division for my next assignment, this one in Cheswick, Pennsylvania, and only about twelve miles away and northwest of where we lived. These positions all involved structural analysis of nuclear power plant components. SEAC provided solid work opportunities, and I received a bonus for working at our client's facilities. Ultimately, none were related to aerospace, and of course, they weren't teaching jobs. It was fun working in a variety of locations and with a lot of different people. I became very good at start-ups and adapting to new work environments.

I joined the American Society of Engineering Education (ASEE) to investigate teaching opportunities and graduate programs around the country. When I did, I learned something new and interesting. I found schools hired people with master's degrees to work as instructors while they pursued their doctorates. So I began contacting schools that had graduate programs in structures and/or structural analysis, rather than orbital mechanics, to inquire about doing that. I received many responses to my inquiries. Although I got a lot of rejections, I also received offers for on-campus interviews from four schools. Those were Mississippi State (MSU), Texas A&M (TAMU), Georgia Institute of Technology (Georgia Tech), and WVU. TAMU even offered me a position without a visit. I again became very intrigued at the possibility of returning to school and being able to teach while pursuing a doctorate.

I began interviewing for instructor positions in the spring of 1979. I flew to Starkville, Mississippi, to investigate the opportunity at MSU, and to Atlanta, Georgia, to look at Georgia Tech. After those visits, I took car trips to WVU in Morgantown and TAMU in College Station, Texas. All four visits were interesting for very different reasons.

I'd never been to Mississippi. Starkville was a tiny college town, and my host for the trip, the department head in mechanical engineering, picked me up at the airport. On the way to the hotel I witnessed a crop-dusting plane doing its work, which was something I never saw in Pennsylvania. I didn't like MSU for several reasons. The program was small, there weren't many course offerings I'd be interested in, and I couldn't see myself living in Starkville. It was too small and too rural for me after living in Pittsburgh. Everyone was friendly there, and they tried hard to entice me to accept their offer. The worst part of the trip was when I arrived at the airport about an hour before my flight home I observed my plane taking off without me. Eastern Airlines had moved up the departure time and failed to inform me about the schedule change. The next fight out to anywhere was four hours later, and it took me through Memphis, Tuscaloosa, and Birmingham, before changing planes in Atlanta to get back to Pittsburgh. I was glad that the Golden Triangle Airport in Columbus, Mississippi, had a snack bar that sold beer. I spent my long wait drinking and basking in the aura of rural Mississippi, and I got home around midnight. It was many years before I returned to Mississippi and even longer until I ever made it back to Starkville, something I viewed as a good thing.

My visit to Georgia Tech went well, but it was a little on the bizarre side. It's a renowned engineering school, it had a fantastic program, and I always liked Atlanta. So I was optimistic, at least at first. The people were all very gracious and welcoming, except one. During my interview, the department head took me to meet several faculty members. One professor had an ongoing feud with the head and he spent the entire time criticizing him, the department, the university, and Atlanta. He told me it was the worst place in the world and I'd be crazy to take a job or attend school there. That discussion turned me off to Georgia Tech. I hesitated to go anywhere with the obvious internal problems this one individual showed me, imagining there may have been other faculty members that were also unhappy. It wasn't clear why they wanted me to talk with such a disgruntled employee during an interview.

Later in the spring, I drove to Morgantown to reacquaint myself with WVU and learn about their graduate program. The best part of that trip was getting to see Professor Gencsoy again. I believe he may have remembered me from six years earlier, because he still called me Mr. Chi-chi. The problem was, he told me he was going to retire soon and I wouldn't be able to study under him for my degree. If I couldn't work with Professor Gencsoy, I didn't want to return to WVU. It would have been fun, but different from undergraduate days. And sometimes you just can't go home again.

Of the four opportunities I had, the one I considered most seriously was TAMU. The program was better, larger, and the pay was going to be higher than the others. I had loved Texas since Ed and Jean moved to Lubbock after college for Ed's pilot training. In the summer of 1979 Chris and I drove all the way to College Station, Texas, to look at the program further. What we saw impressed us, and we both liked it a lot. By this time Chris was contemplating leaving her teaching job so we could start a family, and we thought if we moved there, we'd want to have a small house. So during our visit, we looked at some houses and found one we loved! It was a three-bedroom, two-bathroom home with an atrium in the entryway. Real estate was much cheaper in Texas in 1979, and the price of this house was only $50,000. We made an offer and felt that if the owners accepted it, we'd pack up and move to Texas. We offered the full asking price with no contingencies attached. However, our realtor called that evening to tell us that the owners rejected our offer and took their house off the market. They must not have been very serious about selling. Not getting the house was disappointing, but Chris and I both viewed it as a sign that a move to College Station wasn't the right thing to do. I ended up turning down the opportunity to attend TAMU. Little did we know, it was going to be for the best. But looking back, I can't imagine going through the rest of my life as an Aggie.

We drove back to Pittsburgh with the intent on developing an alternative plan. The highlight of our drive home was to spend a night in Arlington, Texas, about three hours north of TAMU. I learned that the Texas Rangers were hosting the Toronto Blue Jays in baseball that evening. We went to the game hoping to see an old friend of mine I played high school basketball against who was now the shortstop for the Blue Jays. It was nice to get to chat and catch up with him before the game. The next day we looked around the city of Arlington and found it to be a place we liked very much. It turned out to be an omen of things to come.

Not long after returning to home, we learned Chris was pregnant. We were both very excited and realized it might not have been a great time for me to quit my job and go back to graduate school anyhow. Perhaps the 'sign' we received in College Station was a message to us. So we developed an alternate plan for our careers and for starting our family.

After Chris became pregnant, she got interested in nutrition and dietetics. To learn more about those subjects, she began taking some evening classes at the Community College of Allegheny County (CCAC), now called the Allegheny Campus. It was on Pittsburgh's North Side, near where Rivers Stadium used to be. I hate to admit doing this, and I still deny it when Chris mentions it even now, but I took another class too, at Pitt of all places! I always wanted to take a graduate level course in dynamics and didn't have a chance at CMU, but I found a class that was being offered over on the 'dark side' in the fall of 1979. They taught it one night a week for three hours. When I talked with the mechanical engineering department to ask about taking the class, I was told that I had to be a graduate student there before I could enroll. I suppose they never heard of 'special student' status. So I applied to the graduate school, and they granted me admission as a Ph.D. student. I still claim it was a scam to get more graduate students on their books because nobody wanted to go to Pitt when CMU was just across the park.

The class material was very interesting, although the professor was very dull and had zero personality. I enjoyed learning some advanced concepts in dynamics, but I didn't enjoy the course much (nor did I enjoy having anything to do with Pitt). But the textbook we used in that class was great. It was Methods of Analytical Dynamics by Leonard Meirovitch. Two chapters in the book had the titles Problems in Celestial Mechanics, and Problems in Spacecraft Dynamics, both of which were subjects that interested me for years. Although, we didn't cover that material in the class and that disappointed me. I read and studied those chapters myself, which piqued my interest in those topics even more. That material was a part of the field of orbital mechanics, which was what I wanted to study for so many years but never had an opportunity.

That was the only class I ever took at Pitt, even though they listed me as a doctoral student in the department. I don't know how the future might have unfolded if I continued in their program, but I'm glad I didn't for a lot of reasons. I still don't readily admit that I attended Pitt for even that one class!

Not long after I began working at SEAC, I got my Professional Engineer's (PE) license, which was something useful for a consulting engineer to have. The requirements to get a license were to pass two examinations. I passed the Fundamentals of Engineering (FE) Examination before graduating from WVU. Then, after working for four years as a practicing engineer, which was another requirement, I passed The Principles and Practice of Engineering (PE) Exam in 1977. Since I was always good at taking standardized tests, I prepared little for them. In fact, I only slept for two hours the Friday night before my FE exam, and it wasn't because I stayed up late to study.

Those exams were both open book when I took them. All you had to do was take a suitable set of reference books with you and know where to find the topics you might need. I brought a small box of references to both exams, but there were others who showed up with shopping carts full, something I found very amusing. In actuality, it wasn't necessary to have very many books, as a few good ones were enough to do well. You just had to know which books were the good ones and how to use them. I passed both exams on my first attempt, partly because I was skilled at determining what material was important and what wasn't. Having a PE license was another credential that looked good on my resume but didn't turn out to be of much use to me during my career.

Once I had a master's degree and a PE license, I was more qualified as an engineer. I continued to look for an opportunity to teach, even though I didn't have a Ph.D. My first chance came courtesy of the Pennsylvania State University (PSU) McKeesport Campus (now called Penn State Greater Allegheny). They hired me to teach a PE review course in fluid mechanics for civil engineers. It was only part-time, one evening a week for a month offered to engineers in downtown Pittsburgh. The material was easy, so a lot of preparation wasn't necessary. I drove into the city after work and taught a group of practicing engineers to help them prepare for their own PE exam. Finally getting to teach was an exhilarating experience, and it fueled my desire to want to do it even more.

There's an interesting side story to my PSU experience. The Director of the Continuing Education and Outreach Program, Tom Modrak, who hired me, was also a part-time scout for the Pittsburgh Steelers. He worked his way up to become the Head of Scouting for the Steelers and later, the General Manager of the Philadelphia Eagles from 1998 until 2001. After that, he became the Vice President of College Scouting for the Buffalo Bills until 2011. Tom gave me my first opportunity to teach, and I'll always appreciate that he did.

My position at Cheswick was an open-ended one and renewable every six months. Knowing that, Chris and I moved a little closer to both of our jobs. Besides, our building on South Aiken Avenue in Shadyside didn't allow children. We found an apartment in Etna, just across the Allegheny River from the East End of Pittsburgh, in the same complex, Shaler Highlands, where Chris lived when we met. After moving, my commute to work was eleven miles, and Chris's was only about seven miles. She scheduled her maternity leave in April and didn't plan to return to her job until after summer break. Therefore, we focused on our child's arrival and I tried to forget about ever being a teacher. Although that fire continued to burn after my experience with the PE review course.

The first great joy of our lives, our son Corey Dylan Cicci, arrived in April 1980, and thrilled us both. It was fantastic being new parents! Chris enjoyed being home with Corey, and I continued to work at Cheswick for SEAC. I gave up on ever getting a Ph.D. now that I was a father. Still, I was becoming more disenchanted with my job working on nuclear power plant structural components. The long winters and overall gloomy weather of western Pennsylvania also exhausted me. It didn't snow too much, but because of its location, we never had many sunny days, even in the summer months. The skies were often gray, and it rained much of the year. Besides, I still wanted to work in the aerospace industry, so I looked for opportunities somewhere away from the north. Deep down, I hadn't given up the hope of being able to teach, something I knew would never happen as long as we lived in Pittsburgh.

I knew it would be hard to leave SEAC. It was a great company to work for, and the people there were wonderful. I couldn't have asked for a better or more caring organization. My decision to leave became even more difficult when they made me an offer to become a Principal of the company, which was comparable to becoming a Partner in a law firm. Knowing I wanted to move to another part of the country, I turned down their offer. When I did, I told them I didn't want to stay in Pittsburgh long term, so it wouldn't be a huge surprise when I resigned later. Although they did their best to get me to stay with the company, including offering me an immediate pay raise. After I left, we remained on good terms throughout my career. They even funneled some work my way later, which was a big help to us when we needed it. I'll always appreciate how well they treated me over the years.

It was hard to leave Pennsylvania for another reason. I felt like I'd be deserting my widowed mom, who was still living alone in Yukon. She and I talked about my leaving many times. She understood why I thought I needed to go and supported my decision. I think leaving was harder on me than on her. Looking back so many years later, leaving Pittsburgh was the best thing Chris and I could've done for our future.

7

I THOUGHT A NEW PLACE
MIGHT HELP

I searched nationwide for a job where I could work in the aerospace industry and find educational opportunities for Chris and me: from California to Florida, and everywhere in-between that had a mild climate. I thought moving to a new city would improve my outlook. I hoped so. We both wanted to live in a place with better weather after living all of our lives in the north. I regretted not accepting one of the instructor positions. Turning those down was a pragmatic decision, and perhaps I was wrong in doing so. But if I had accepted one, I would never have been able to study orbital mechanics, which was also still a goal in my life.

After searching over many months, I found a job that might work for us both. It was the position of Engineering Specialist at Bell Helicopter Textron (now Bell Textron, Incorporated) in Fort Worth, Texas. I'd be working on the structural dynamics of rotorcraft. We always liked the idea of moving to Texas, and we could live in Arlington, a place we already explored and thought we'd like. The best thing we found in evaluating the prospect of relocating was the proximity to educational institutions for us both.

Besides Texas Christian University (TCU) in Fort Worth and Southern Methodist University (SMU) in Dallas, there were programs we liked at the University of Texas at Arlington (UTA). UTA was a large state university midway between Fort Worth and Dallas and close to where we wanted to live. UTA had an aerospace engineering department and offered a doctoral degree. They also had a significant enrollment of working professionals, so they taught many of their classes in the late afternoons and evenings. It appeared we had a promising situation where we could start a different life with new opportunities. So even though it was hard to leave Pittsburgh and my job at SEAC, off we went to Texas!

I started at Bell in March 1981. We purchased a house within a couple of months and settled into life in Texas. We loved our newfound home. I applied for admission to the Ph.D. program in aerospace engineering at UTA and began taking classes that summer. Bell was an interesting place. It was a large engineering and production facility; the work was challenging, and the people were friendly. My primary project was analyzing the vibration problems that plagued the original tilt rotor plane, the XV-15. It was exciting starting a job in a new city, in the aerospace industry, and in a warmer climate. Still, I was more interested in pursuing my Ph.D. than in going to work each day.

I didn't know what to expect from the courses at UTA. It shocked me that the very first one I took was amazing. It was a math class in numerical analysis taught by the acclaimed mathematician Dr. Donald Greenspan, who moved to UTA after a distinguished career elsewhere. Dr. Greenspan was a wonderful teacher and was crystal clear in his explanations of difficult concepts. And we used the book he wrote for the course. I loved his class and did very well. Much of it involved programming numerical analysis techniques in FORTRAN, which I hadn't used since WVU. I was very careful not to make too many stupid mistakes this time around, although there were still some.

I learned a tremendous amount from Dr. Greenspan. There were two things I remember about him in particular. The first was he always wore a pair of half frame reading glasses that rested on the tip of his nose while he lectured. The second was that he didn't like anybody showing up late for class. To fix that problem, he'd lock the door behind him as he entered so tardy students wouldn't disrupt his lecture. It wasn't long before everyone learned they needed to arrive early. I'm proud to say he never locked me out of class.

By the start of the fall semester, they also accepted Chris for admission to UTA so she could continue taking courses related to nutrition and dietetics.

I enjoyed taking classes in the core areas of aerospace engineering. I enrolled in boundary layer theory, or viscous aerodynamics, when the academic year started in the fall of 1981. The course proved to be a tremendous amount of work for a three-credit hour class. It included project after project after project. And they were all long and tedious, requiring an enormous amount of computer programming. Everybody in class was looking forward to the end of the semester and the course being over. On the last day of class for the semester, when we thought the projects were over, the professor handed out a final project. He made it due on the day of the final exam the following week. It was an enormous relief when I finished that exam and turned it in along with the final project of the semester. But I learned viscous aerodynamics well, and a lot about what professors shouldn't do to their students.

During my year of taking classes, all the graduate students had to attend a departmental seminar one evening each week. They invited outside speakers to discuss various aspects of aerospace engineering. The speaker at one seminar during the fall was Dr. Donald Brand. He was an engineer in the Dallas-Fort Worth area who had also taught a few classes at UTA in the past. His engineering specialty was orbital mechanics, so his talk was very interesting to me.

I told Dr. Brand that I also wanted to study orbital mechanics, and he told me point blank I was at the wrong school! He said I'd never get to learn much orbital at UTA, and it would be very difficult to work or teach in that field after I graduated. Dr. Brand also said I needed to go to the University of Texas at Austin (UT) if I wanted to work in orbital mechanics. UT was where he got his Ph.D., and he told me they had the best program in the country for orbital mechanics by far. We spent a lot of time talking about the UT program that night. I came away from our conversation enlightened and excited. I knew nothing about UT, but Dr. Brand gave me the names of some contacts and told me I ought to take a trip down to have a look. As great as it sounded, I didn't think there was any way I could ever go to school there. I wanted to investigate it further anyhow, just to learn more about the best educational program in the field.

After my conversation with Dr. Brand, I became disenchanted with UTA because I now knew I wouldn't be able to study much orbital mechanics. Another thing that bothered me was that I read an article talking about finding a faculty position in engineering. I learned that the large majority of professors hired only attended a handful of prestigious research universities. UTA wasn't one of those. It hit me that even if I earned a Ph.D. from UTA, I might not find a teaching job, or at least not somewhere I'd wanted to be, or teaching what I'd like most. That idea was very discouraging. Earning a doctorate and still not getting a faculty position would have been quite disappointing. Then what? It would have shattered my dreams.

Working at Bell Helicopter wasn't enjoyable either. It was an enormous company and from what I could tell it wasn't run well. I thought the first level engineering managers were fine, but the management above that was awful, which became very clear to me one day at work.

In the spring semester of 1981, I wanted to take a class in flight dynamics, but they only offered it during the day. I asked my immediate supervisor, Jim, if it would be okay if I took off work for a couple hours twice a week to attend class. I also told him I'd stay late those days to make up for the time I was in class. He thought the arrangement would be fine, since the class would benefit both Bell and myself, but he'd have to clear it with his boss, my second-level supervisor, first. I was still at my desk after work one afternoon when Jim went into the supervisor's office to talk to him about my situation. Since everyone else had already left and the office was quiet, I could hear their conversation.

Jim explained the situation, and his boss flew off the handle. He started screaming and saying how he didn't want anybody leaving work just to go to class and that my request was unacceptable and he wouldn't approve it. Jim tried to reason with him, but he was adamant and kept screaming. This old guy was an ex-military type who only had a bachelor's degree in engineering and didn't value advanced education. It looked to me like he was trying to manage professionals the same way he commanded troops, which can't be done effectively. He shouldn't have been managing anybody and showed his ineptitude and shortsightedness that day.

Afterward Jim came to talk to me about what happened, knowing that I heard every word of their conversation. He told me I should take the class anyhow as long as I made up the time and he'd cover for me with his boss. I appreciated Jim for supporting my education very much. That experience left a horrible taste in my mouth about the lack of progressiveness of Bell and the people they had in charge. Perhaps it was another case of a company promoting the incompetent. Working for someone so narrow-minded and unaccommodating didn't appeal to me at all. It made little sense to me that a company with a tuition reimbursement program would have supervisors who didn't value education.

Another interesting class I took that spring at UTA, this one being after work, was a math class called interval analysis, taught by Dr. Ray Moore. Dr. Moore was an excellent teacher and very laid back. He also wrote the book we used in the course. When he described how he'd run the class on the first day, he didn't mention the grading scheme at all. When someone asked about the exam structure, Dr. Moore replied that there wouldn't be any exams, nor would there be a final exam. Everyone then assumed that our homework would determine our final grades. In response to another question about the homework, Dr. Moore said that there'd be some assignments, but we didn't have to do them if we didn't want to. He also mentioned that he wouldn't take role each day either. Then he stated we should focus on learning the material, and not to worry about grades because everyone in the class would get an A anyway. It was an interesting way to conduct a class. Although I learned little, and I would rather have done homework and taken exams to have learned more, I did like Dr. Moore's teaching style.

Based upon my discussion with Dr. Brand, I thought it would be valuable for me to visit UT to find out more about their program. So in February 1982 I called Dr. Paul Nacozy, an orbital mechanics professor in the Department of Aerospace Engineering and Engineering Mechanics (ASE/EM). We scheduled a meeting on a

Friday a couple of weeks later, and he arranged appointments for me with a couple other faculty members during my visit to campus.

Before making our trip to Austin, I also called Dr. John J. McKetta, Jr., an old friend of my father. Dr. McKetta was a chemical engineering professor at UT, who went to my high school long before me. He grew up in a neighboring town, Wyano, which was even smaller than Yukon, and also where my friend Big Mike lived. Dr. McKetta still had family there and visited them often, but I had never met him. My father always told me that if I ever made it to Austin, I needed to look him up, and so I did.

I soon learned that Dr. McKetta wasn't just a professor. During his career at UT, he served as department chair, dean, and chancellor at various times. In addition, he was an energy advisor to five different U.S. Presidents. Dr. McKetta also wrote the first ever encyclopedia of chemical engineering, along with twenty other books, and he was a member of the National Academy of Engineering, the Hall of Fame for engineers. So he really was far more than a professor.

Dr. McKetta was friendly, down-to-earth, and never forgot his roots. In fact, he kept a coal miner's helmet on the corner of his office desk to remind him of his days working in the Pennsylvania coal mines. He always claimed that experience drove him to want to get an education so he wouldn't have to work in the mines his entire life. When Dr. McKetta retired from UT later, he donated all the salary he received in over fifty years back to the university. They've since renamed his former department at UT the John J. McKetta Jr. Department of Chemical Engineering, for his many contributions.

During my phone conversation with Dr. McKetta, I mentioned we were going to be visiting Austin, but I didn't tell him the reason for our visit. He invited Chris, Corey, and me to his house for brunch on the Saturday morning after my appointments on Friday. It was a gracious gesture, but that was just the type of people he and his wife, Pinky, were. He was more than happy to invite three total strangers into his home to share a meal and get acquainted.

My interviews in the department went well and were very interesting. I spent a good amount of time with Dr. Nacozy and the Graduate Advisor, Dr. David Hull. They both gave me great insight into the program and details of the degree requirements. Based on my interests, they took me to meet Dr. Byron Tapley, who was also an orbital mechanics professor and Director of the Center for Space Research on campus. I had a lengthy discussion with Dr. Tapley, who, in his mid-forties, was already a world-renowned researcher. His specialty was a field called 'estimation theory,' which was a specialization within orbital mechanics. He appeared to be interested in me because I earned a master's degree from CMU; I had professional experience, even though my experience wasn't in aerospace; and because I wanted to teach. During our talks, I learned I had competitive scores on the Graduate Record Examination (GRE), but my undergraduate grades might not have been as good as the other students there. When I shared my concerns about my undergraduate grades to Dr. Tapley, he told me a very personal story.

He said, "Dave, grades aren't the most important sign of a student's potential for success. My grades were never that great either. In fact, when I was in high school, the guidance counselor told me I should get a job and not even think about going to college. But I went to UT anyhow. Then as an undergraduate, my grades weren't very good and my advisor told me I should get a job and not even think about going to graduate school. But I went anyhow. And, when I was getting my master's degree, they told me I shouldn't even think about getting a Ph.D.. But I did that too, and here I am today."

Dr. Tapley's story impressed me, and I was even more moved that he'd tell it to me. His research area was one I thought I'd enjoy too. It involved determining the orbit of satellites to a high level of accuracy. It was numerically intensive, something I already enjoyed after taking Dr. Greenspan's course at UTA. During our discussion, Dr. Tapley said that he thought I could also help with teaching while I was there, which sounded great to me. So after our conversation, I was optimistic about my chances of being accepted into the program, even if I could never see my way to go there. That would be an enormous step for me, with many obstacles to overcome in order to take that step.

Chris and I both enjoyed our visit to the department and seeing UT's large and exquisite campus. Austin was an amazing city. It was the state Capital, it had an Air Force base nearby, and it was home to a large and wonderful university.

As I mentioned earlier, I had never met Dr. and Mrs. McKetta in person. Dr. McKetta, who was in his mid-sixties, loved connecting with people from back home. They welcomed us to their large ranch house on Lake Austin, which was part of the Colorado River dammed up to form a lake. They even had a boat channel leading from the lake to a boathouse inside their residence. It was an incredible house they had built after moving to Austin many years before.

During our discussion at brunch, Dr. McKetta asked why we were in town. When I told him I was interviewing at the graduate school there, he wanted to hear all the details about who I talked with the day before.

When I mentioned Dr. Tapley's name, he said, "I know Tapley very well. In fact, I hired him when I was the dean of engineering. Let me go get him on the phone right now." He attempted to call Dr. Tapley, but couldn't reach him. I don't know what he said to Dr. Tapley when they talked later, but I believe Dr. McKetta spoke well of me to him. And I'm forever grateful that he did.

I liked the program at UT enough that I applied for admission when we got back to Arlington. I still didn't believe it was possible to attend since I would have had to quit my job. Going to school full-time would've been very hard for me to do since we had a one-year-old. I wasn't even sure if I'd get admitted to such a prestigious university and the top program in the country for orbital mechanics. So, I didn't think I'd ever have to make that hard decision.

8

SOME UNBELIEVABLE LUCK

It didn't take long to receive a letter from UT granting me admission to pursue a Ph.D. in the Aerospace Engineering/ Engineering Mechanics (ASE/EM) Department. They even offered me a teaching assistantship to help pay my way. I never imagined that I'd get to attend such a great university as UT. Receiving the opportunity to study orbital mechanics at the best program in the country was beyond my expectations. It was a dream come true for me! I just wasn't sure if I could, or should, go!

UT offered me a position as an Assistant Instructor which paid $650 per month. I appreciated it, but the thought of giving up my salary at Bell, which was about $30,000, and taking such a drastic pay cut was daunting. I had a wife and child to support, and I felt like it wasn't something I'd be able to do with those obligations.

But I married very well! Chris supported me going back to school and told me I needed to accept the offer. She said we'd come up with other ways to make money while I worked on my degree. With her positive attitude, I told myself I had two choices: I could either accept their offer to pursue a Ph.D. in something I always wanted, or forget about it and put teaching out of my mind forever. And I knew that wasn't possible. A force I couldn't control was driving me to teach, so I quit a job I didn't like to return to school, which I expected to love. But I wouldn't have done it without a supportive wife. I appreciate her influencing my decision more than I could ever tell her. I rationalized that I'd try it for a year and see how it went. If I didn't like it or couldn't do the work, I could find work many places with my credentials, or even go back to Bell, if I had to. That idea comforted me. After I accepted UT's offer, Chris also applied to UT to continue pursuing a new career. So in the fall of 1982, we were headed to Austin for another big adventure!

When I told my mother that I was going to quit my job to go to graduate school full time she thought I was crazy. She couldn't fathom why I'd do such a thing, especially when I had a family. I understood her thinking, but it was something I had to try. She relented after I explained why I wanted to do it, and Chris told her she agreed it was a good idea.

The savings we accumulated after our marriage went into our house in Arlington. We had little money to fund this adventure, but wanted to keep the house just in case, since we liked it so much there. We rented a small apartment in Austin and traveled back to Arlington on weekends and holidays. Perhaps it wasn't the best plan, but at least it was a plan. I knew it would be a long road ahead and it wouldn't be fast. Even with a master's degree, I was looking at three years as a minimum and likely longer. But I felt I was up to the task. Although we needed more than $650 per month to live and go to school.

If I stayed at Bell until classes started, we could have saved a little money, but I had a better idea. I called Alan Errett, a principal at SEAC, thinking I could make more working on an engineering contract at SEAC if they needed some help. He graciously offered me a summer job working at yet another Westinghouse plant. This one was in Waltz Mill, Pennsylvania, about two miles from where my mother lived in Yukon. I could save more money working at SEAC than if I stayed working at Bell. Plus, I could live with my mom for free and even ride my bicycle to work. And Chris and Corey could come up for most of the summer to enjoy being with Grandma while I was at work. So off we went back to Pennsylvania, but only as a temporary stop so we could go to Austin a few months later and not starve. I drove up first, and Chris and Corey flew up the next week.

We had fun that summer, but it's hard living at home again when you're an adult with a family. I made a lot of money to get us started in Austin, so it was worth it. The work was interesting, my mother loved having us there, and it was nice spending time with her again. But by August, it was time to head back to Texas.

Before we left, we had one very interesting experience that summer when Chris and I attended a Kris Kristofferson concert in Uniontown, Pennsylvania. I'd been a fan of Kris's for many years and saw him perform previously in Pittsburgh. It turned out that a guy on the sound crew for the show was the son of a close friend of Chris's father, so we went down front before the show to say hello. Pete was happy to see us both and invited us backstage after the show to meet the band. Chris and I enjoyed meeting Kris and the other band members, and they were all gracious and friendly to two strangers. We even had a beer together, and Kris happily signed an autograph for Corey.

Our Austin apartment was in the East Riverside Drive area, a few miles south of town and near the Colorado River. Chris had already been accepted for study too, and we could ride the free shuttle bus to campus, trading off watching Corey when one of us was in class.

Chris and I registered for classes and had our IDs made at the Frank Erwin Center a few days before fall semester began in 1982. We took Corey to registration with us and for fun they made him a UT ID too, even though he was only two years old. They welcomed us into the Longhorn family from our first day.

UT was enormous even then with over 50,000 students. The graduate program in ASE/EM was also large, with over 100 enrolled. It was a little overwhelming, but we both felt great to be college students again. Plus, I was going to get to teach!

Besides taking nine credit hours of classes, my fall semester assignment was to help with undergraduate instruction. They assigned me to assist a professor in EM 314, a course in engineering mechanics with 120 students. My responsibility was to conduct problem sessions three evenings a week. I met with four sections with about thirty students in each one. I'd go over problems and answer questions for two hours per section. They were really formalized tutoring sessions.

I enjoyed teaching those classes, but it took a lot of time since I was spending all day at school and I didn't get home until late three nights a week. I couldn't be with my family as much as I wanted, which made even more work for my exceptional wife.

The course was tough for undergraduates and was used to weed out those who didn't belong in engineering. In fact, about 30% of the students failed each time they taught it. As I expected, I loved being in front of a class. I drew on many of the things I experienced with my outstanding teachers in my past. It seemed to work out okay, and I think the students liked me as an instructor.

My first semester back was tough academically, and it took a while for me to adjust to taking a full load of classes. But I did all right, and I enjoyed studying orbital mechanics. The hardest course for me was a high-level analytical methods class, i.e., math, which had about forty students. The professor was from the engineering mechanics side of the department, and the course was geared more toward them than the aerospace students. She wasn't a wonderful teacher, and it was her first time teaching the class. Many of us struggled, but we made it through.

I also took a course my first semester called Supervised Teaching. It was a class to teach people how to teach. It discussed educational methods, objectives, and effectiveness. The class proved invaluable to me and made my eventual career in academia much easier.

Chris did great in her classes, too. She enjoyed being back in school and exploring different career options. When she had class, she'd bring Corey to campus and he and I would hang out. Our favorite activity was to go over to Texas Memorial Stadium and play on the football field. Corey loved to run from one end zone to the other and pretend to score a touchdown. His legs were so short, it took him a very long time to cover the hundred yards. I'll always remember those special times we spent together at the stadium.

In talking with her advisor about what courses she wanted to take, Chris mentioned her interest in studying nutrition. The advisor thought, with her background, it might be better for her to pursue a more challenging path. She advised Chris to take organic chemistry and come back, and depending on how she did in that very hard course, they could talk about her options. Well, my amazing wife did well in organic even with a small child and a husband that did little around the house!

When Chris returned to her advisor with her grade, she was told she needed to aim higher and perhaps look at going to medical, dental, pharmacy, or veterinarian school. Of those choices, pharmacy was the most attractive to Chris. So she began taking the prerequisites she'd need to follow that path someday. She'd have to take several more courses in the sciences, but was up to the challenge and looked forward to a career change. Her plan was to go to pharmacy school after I finished and, depending on where we'd be, try to find a program nearby. Neither of us thought we'd be at UT long enough for her to attend there. At least we hoped not.

In the spring semester, they assigned me to be the instructor in two back-to-back sections of a course in statics, which I taught three afternoons a week. Being in charge of the classes was very stimulating, and I found I loved teaching even more. I also thought I could excel at it someday if I worked hard.

I learned a lot teaching those two classes. It helped me throughout my entire career, not only in how to teach but also how to deal with students and their many issues and troubles. In fact, something occurred during the very first exam I gave that followed me for decades. My exams had four or five problems with one problem on the front of each page and nothing on the backs of those pages. Students could use the backs if they needed more space. After I returned their graded exams the next class day, I always went over them and provided the correct solutions. When I did that for the first time, a student came up afterward and complained that I didn't see his calculations on the back of one page. I doubted I would have missed his work and felt certain he just wrote it there while I was going over the solution. However, I couldn't prove it, so I regraded his exam and gave him more points for what he claimed I didn't see. After that, and for the next thirty-five years, whenever I graded exams, I'd draw a red line on all the back pages to make sure I didn't miss anything.

Those two courses were the only ones I ever taught at UT. I switched over to be a Research Assistant for Professor Tapley the next year. Doing so was very beneficial to me, because getting paid to do my research would allow me to finish my degree sooner, even though I'd have rather kept teaching.

Our initial plan was for me to try graduate school for a year to see if I liked it. I found I did like it and also did well in my classes, which made me want to keep going. So we adjusted our plans for me to continue. We rented out our house in Arlington and leased one in Austin, but we still needed more money to support our family.

That summer, I accepted another contract engineering job, again for the money, but this time through a Texas company that placed me at what was then General Dynamics Corporation (now Lockheed Martin) in Fort Worth, Texas. It was a six-week long assignment, and I worked on software development for F-16 flight simulators. After those six weeks, I returned to Austin to spend the rest of the summer studying for my written doctoral qualifying examinations, which were a huge hurdle in the Ph.D. program in Aerospace Engineering. The exams covered the first year of course work and they scheduled them for the week before classes began in the fall. In 1982, those dates were August 22-26. I studied eight hours a day every day for two months after I got back from Fort Worth, so I'd be ready.

Doctoral students had to pass written qualifying exams in three technical areas. Everyone had to sit for the math exam, plus we had our choice of two others. I chose celestial (orbital) mechanics, and optimal control/estimation theory. Besides passing those exams, there were additional requirements for a Ph.D.. They included an oral examination in your area of specialization during your second year, followed by the defense of a dissertation on your research.

The requirements were like those at other institutions, but the expectations at UT were very high. I ended up taking fourteen courses, or forty-two credit hours, which were beyond my master's degree and my work at UTA. I always thought the toughest part of the program for me would be to select a research topic. It had to be something new that added to the base of knowledge in your field. Professors didn't just hand out topics; it was up to each student to find an acceptable one. Many students couldn't get past the point of selecting a topic and never finished their degrees.

One thing many of my classmates and I did during that first year was learn how to juggle. It was a pleasant diversion when we needed a break from the intense studying. I never excelled at juggling, but it was fun learning. I thought it was something all graduate students did, but it may have just been a UT thing. It was valuable training for standing in front of a classroom and entertaining students. Years later I purchased some juggling balls that were replicas of the Sun, Earth, and Moon. I brought those balls to class a few times and juggled for my students, but I doubt my juggling skills impressed them.

We found out early in the spring of 1983 that Chris was expecting our second child in August, smack in the middle of my qualifying exam week. They only gave those exams once each year. If a student failed or missed the exams for any reason, he or she would have to wait another full year to re-schedule them. So it was very poor planning on our part. I didn't want to miss our child's arrival, but I also couldn't miss taking those exams. That being the case, we invited Chris's parents to stay with us during my exam week to help and cover for me if I couldn't be at the hospital.

We, or I, got very lucky! My in-laws were scheduled to arrive on the Friday before my exams began, and Chris went into labor in the middle of the night on Thursday. The second great joy of our lives, Darby Austin Cicci, entered the world at noon the next day, the same time my in-laws were landing at the airport. I had Chris's father paged in the terminal and left a message for them to take a taxi to our house and relieve the baby sitter who was watching Corey. I was glad that I didn't miss Darby's arrival. Not long after his birth, I thanked my lovely wife, told her she did a superb job, and that I'd see her in a week. She understood, and everything worked out fine. Her parents watched Corey and brought Chris and Darby home from the hospital while I was at my office tending to my exams the next week.

The qualifying exams were hard, and math, which I took first, was the hardest. They gave us copies of the exams from previous years to help us study, but the math exam wasn't similar at all to any of the earlier ones, and my classmates and I were extremely surprised and disheartened. Feeling like I didn't do well on the first test took the pressure off, so I was much more relaxed for my two remaining exams.

I thought I nailed my other two, but once I finished, I assumed I failed the qualifiers because we had to pass all three to be successful. Several of my friends felt the same as me.

They were to decide the exam results the following Friday afternoon during a faculty meeting. We were all nervous and waiting in our offices. At one point, I walked out into the hallway to get some water and saw Dr. Nacozy walking in my direction on the way to his office. He'd just left the faculty meeting, and with nobody else around he came up to me and told me it looked good for me.

I said, "Are you kidding? I didn't think I did very well on the math exam."

He only repeated, "It looks good," before heading to his office. I wasn't sure what he meant by his comments, but I appreciated him giving me that information.

After the meeting concluded, we were each called to the Graduate Advisor's office and given the results separately. I was told I did great on two exams, but my score on math was marginal. So the faculty voted to give me a 'conditional pass' rather than a clear pass or a failure. Several other students received the same outcome as me. We were told that the faculty didn't feel the math exam was a representative one for aerospace students because it covered material much different from preceding years, and they wanted to make accommodations for the inconsistency. The results of the exam showed that the average for engineering mechanics students was much higher than for aerospace students. I believed the difference resulted from the poor teaching of our math professor and her bias in teaching material that was more geared towards engineering mechanics students while mostly neglecting aerospace-related material.

The condition on our passes was that we needed to take two more math classes to strengthen our abilities, which we were thrilled to do. I believe Dr. Tapley helped us get through the process because we all aced the estimation portion of his exam and he felt we were qualified to continue in the program. Since his opinion carried a lot of weight in the department, the rest of the faculty agreed. If I had failed those exams, I would have had to wait an entire year to retake them, which I'm not sure I would have done.

It turned out to be a momentous time in my life. I passed the qualifying exams (even though it was a conditional pass) and I got an incredible new son!

An unexpected pleasure of our move to Austin was an opportunity to re-connect with my cousin Mike Cicci and his family who lived in San Antonio. I hadn't seen them in many years, and it was very nice getting to visit with them occasionally. They even came up to Austin when Darby was baptized at Saint Louis Catholic Church. It was nice to have family members so close again.

Not long after Darby was born, Dr. McKetta invited us to an afternoon cookout at his home. It was a small gathering, which included two of his sons and their families, and Dr. Tapley and his wife, Sophie. I think Dr. McKetta thought it would be a good idea for Dr. Tapley to meet my family. It pleased me he did. Dr. McKetta was a well-known jokester, which I was just learning about. During the party, he picked up Darby, who was still newborn bald, and held him up next to Dr. Tapley's head, who was middle-aged bald. Then he said loud enough so everyone could hear, "Look, they're related!" Everybody laughed, even my very serious advisor.

Over the next two years, I needed to satisfy my math requirement, take several additional classes to finish my coursework, pass my Ph.D. oral exam, select a dissertation topic, and get started on my research. By then I knew I wouldn't finish my degree in three years, so I set my goal at five years. Dr. Tapley continued to support me through a grant from the NASA Jet Propulsion Laboratory (JPL), and he gave me immense freedom to choose my topic and plan my research.

I took two classes in the math department to clear my conditional pass. The professor I had for linear algebra was an excellent teacher but had the most annoying habit. He'd come to the classroom early, perhaps fifteen minutes before the scheduled starting time, and fill up all the chalkboards with notes. So when students arrived, we'd already be far behind, which we didn't appreciate. Another issue I didn't care for was his grading scheme on exams. He gave positive points for a correct answer, negative points for an incorrect answer, and zero points for not attempting to solve the problem. It was a game to figure out how many problems to try or skip in order to get the number of points you needed for the grade you wanted to receive. I remember ending up with the exact point total to get an A in the course. I thought the whole grading scheme was pretty silly for graduate students and not something I ever considered using.

Taking a Ph.D. oral exam is an interesting and anxiety-filled experience. You stand at a chalkboard before your committee and they ask you questions for three hours. They'd spend about an hour finding something you don't know, and then pummel you on that topic for the rest of the time. Their goal was to find out how much you knew and how you could think on your feet and reason through topics you didn't know very well.

I prepared for months learning and re-learning everything I could about my specialization. When my exam time arrived, I felt confident about what I knew. I think I did well, but I got a little confused about gravitational potential functions, which they drilled me on for quite a while. I survived and passed and put that step behind me. Taking an oral exam on that level is outstanding preparation for teaching in that you have to think fast and express those thoughts to your audience. The most important part is to not try to bluff your way through any answer. Nobody knows everything, and it's better to admit you don't know something than to pretend you do. It's very clear to your committee when you're bluffing, and that's the worst thing you can do. It was an enormous relief when it was over.

One of my friends at UT had a terrible oral exam experience at Stanford University. During his exam, he was so nervous that he fainted. They called the paramedics and his exam was re-scheduled. Then during his second attempt, he fainted again. After that, he left Stanford and came to UT to start his Ph.D. program all over from the beginning. But he graduated and became a respected scientist at NASA JPL.

I had some outstanding teachers at UT, and Dr. Tapley was one of them. His lectures were fast moving and non-stop, and he'd fill the chalkboard with equation after equation, using no notes. It was very impressive and, being the eminent expert in estimation theory, he knew the material backwards and forwards.

Dr. Tapley was famous in his field, which provided both plusses and minuses for his graduate students, especially me. The plusses were that his gigantic reputation and amazing network of connections would help me in finding a faculty position and building my career within the orbital mechanics community. The minuses were that he was so busy he had little time to devote to his many students. I had few opportunities to meet with him to discuss my work and for him to provide direction. He canceled our meetings often because he was out of town or too busy to see me. There were advantages and disadvantages to the lack of guidance I received, however. The advantage was that it helped me develop independence as a researcher and taught me not to rely on others. The disadvantage was that it slowed down my progress toward graduation.

Dr. Tapley was also notorious for keeping his students around a long time before they'd graduate, many years in fact. There were a few cases where his students worked on their degrees for ten or twelve years or longer. During our infrequent meetings, I often reminded him I had a family and couldn't stay that long. After a few years of my telling him that, I think it registered. But I'm very thankful to have had such an incredible mentor, and we remain friends to this day. However, his unfamiliarity with the details of my research because of his lack of time would pose a significant problem for me before I graduated, which I'll describe later.

One funny thing happened with Dr. Tapley. Several of us were taking his advanced topics course. It was near the end of the semester and we all had to give class presentations on a topic of our choice. He'd been traveling and re-scheduled our class for one evening after he got back into town from a trip. All of us students showed up for our evening class, but Dr. Tapley never arrived. We waited and waited and no Dr. Tapley! Somebody called his home to check on him, and his wife said he forgot about the class and fell asleep. She woke him and he showed up a little later, feeling quite bad about sleeping through our class.

Dr. Wally Fowler was the most personable professor I ever had. He was outgoing and friendly and always had a joke ready to tell. I couldn't count the number of times he'd walk up to me and say,

"Dave, did you hear the one about…" He knew I wanted to go into academia and did everything he could to help me.

Perhaps the most famous professor I've ever had was Dr. Victor Szebehely, the eminent expert in The Restricted Problem of Three Bodies. He wrote the first and most comprehensive textbook ever written on the subject in 1967, called The Theory of Orbits. Dr. Szebehely started the orbital mechanics program at UT when he brought most of the existing department with him to Austin from Yale University back in the 1960s. He was a friendly, grandfather-type gentleman who always had a pleasant word for students. I took two classes from him in which we used his textbook. He graciously inscribed my copy with the note: 'To David A. Cicci, who soon will know much more. Victor Szebehely, December 1984.' His autographed book remains one of my most prized possessions. He once gave a very interesting homework assignment in class. A certain table in his textbook had numerical errors in a few entries, and it was our task to find and correct them. To do so, we had to reproduce the entire table in the book, something that proved to be an outstanding learning experience.

Overall, the UT orbital mechanics program was unparalleled. It was easy to see why it was the best in the country. Besides the amazing faculty and terrific courses, we had a never-ending supply of wonderful guest speakers, which included many astronauts and NASA officials, from JPL and Johnson Space Center in particular. I even got to meet Buzz Aldrin one day. I don't think I could have received a better education anywhere.

One thing I continued to do during my years at UT was to stop by Dr. McKetta's office occasionally to say hello. He was always interested in how I was doing and how my degree program was progressing. I'd usually get to school about 7:30 a.m. and drop in on the walk from the parking lot to my building. He'd always stop whatever he was doing to chat with me, and he never failed to ask about Chris and the boys and my mother back in Yukon.

Graduate school was fun, challenging, and very stressful for nearly all my classmates. There was a lot of pressure to do well and be successful, especially for me since I had a family to support. Many students struggle with the level of stress and I was no exception. But I got through the anxious times even though sometimes I doubted I would.

9

OUTSIDE OPPORTUNITIES FOR SUSTENANCE

I got paid as a Research Assistant during the rest of my time at UT, although I never made very much money. The most I made was $800-$850 per month in my last year. The amount wasn't enough to support a wife and two small children, even in Austin, Texas in the 1980s. As I mentioned earlier, I married well. Chris was always willing to do whatever she could for our young family to help support us. She never doubted that I'd finish my degree, although I sometimes did, and she knew someday there'd be a better life ahead for us all. Deep inside, I hoped she was right. I know I never would have graduated to become a professor without her support.

We were fortunate to find many opportunities for financial support outside the university. Early on, I learned about programs where two corporations provided forgivable loans to graduate students interested in careers in education. Both the General Electric Foundation and the Ford Foundation had such programs at UT to encourage students to pursue teaching as a career. Since that was my goal all along, it was a perfect situation for me. Both foundations would forgive loans at 25% for every year spent in full time teaching after graduation. I borrowed as much money as I could, around twenty thousand dollars total, while I was in school. When I became a professor, I didn't have to pay any of it back after only four years. Those programs were an enormous help. I appreciated General Electric and Ford for providing those opportunities to us when we needed them.

Chris and I also took part-time jobs whenever we could find them to earn extra money. I drove a taxi for a short time, but made little doing that. I did the same thing in Pittsburgh years before but didn't make much money there either. Both experiences have contributed to comedic relief for Chris ever since, and she still laughs at me when I mention it.

I spent another summer working in Pennsylvania for SEAC and living with my mom in Yukon. This time I worked in their office in Peters Township and commuted each day, which was about a forty-minute drive. Chris and the boys came up to spend a few weeks, but didn't stay the entire summer. We had fun while they were there. I made a good bit of money again, thanks to Alan Errett and the others at SEAC for hiring me once more.

Over Christmas break one year, I worked for a company doing fundraising for the Austin Police Department. My job was to drive around town to pickup checks from people who pledged donations over the phone. Once they received a pledge of a donation, somebody needed to pick it up before the donors changed their minds. I was the 'bagman' who arrived to retrieve the checks. I got to know Austin very well driving all over town, and I enjoyed traveling around fetching those donations to help the police.

One job we both did for a briefly was working as note-takers. A company paid us to sit in classes with large enrollments, like introductory biology, chemistry, or psychology, and take notes during the lectures. Then we'd give our handwritten notes to the company, which would have them typed and sell them to people who didn't attend class those days for various reasons. I believe that most of the time it was because the students just didn't want to go to class, but it wasn't our place to judge why they purchased them. They could have only wanted to use our notes to supplement their own, to be sure they got everything. But I doubt that was the case. Anyhow, we each received twenty dollars per lecture for our notes. I only did one class, but Chris did several and was much more clever than me. She figured out a way to get paid for the notes she took in classes for which she was enrolled. So she got paid to attend class. It was brilliant! Besides, she took amazing notes because she got all As in the courses in which she sold her notes. So the students who purchased them got a great deal.

A minor job we did together was pose as models for a water purification system advertisement. Our next-door neighbor worked in marketing and asked if he could photograph Chris and me wearing jogging clothes while we were drinking purified water. It was a fun thing to do, but we only did it to help him. He paid us fifty dollars each for posing, plus we got to keep the outfits. We still have that advertising pamphlet as a souvenir.

I also tutored students in engineering mechanics courses. Dr. Nacozy referred one of his students to me who wanted to hire a tutor. I never tutored one-on-one before, and I didn't know how much to charge. A little research into what other tutors were charging helped me set my rate at eight dollars per hour. I tried it and found tutoring to be enjoyable. I thought I could turn tutoring into a small business to earn more extra money, so I posted fliers in all the classrooms around campus where engineering mechanics classes met. The fliers had tear-off strips at the bottom with my phone number so anybody interested could take one and call me. It turned out that I received so many calls and got so much business that tutoring was taking most of my time. I kept raising my price to keep the number of students down. It seemed each semester I had to increase my rate otherwise I'd have too much business. By the time I graduated, I was charging twenty dollars per hour to tutor, and I still had plenty of students. The undergraduates at UT had a lot of money. One day a student who came for tutoring told me he hadn't been in class for a few days because he'd been duck hunting in Mexico. He direly needed help and didn't mind paying for it!

Chris also took care of other people's children. One of her duties was to transport their kids to kindergarten at Good Shepherd Episcopal School in West Austin, close to campus, and return them home later. In doing so, she got to know the teachers and administrators at the school. When it came time for Corey to start kindergarten, they accepted him as a student because Chris knew them all. Good

Shepherd was on the exclusive side, and most of the children there were from affluent families. Not ours, but most of the others. Often the family maids transported the kids to and from school. Corey realized this at his young age, and one day when Chris picked him up, he asked why our maid never brought him home from school like the other kids. At least Corey didn't know we were poor.

One interesting temporary job Chris took, and I helped with, was making questions for a medical trivia board game. We made up hundreds of them. It was fun and easier for her than me. The biology class that I got paid to take notes in helped me in creating questions. We don't know if they ever used ours in the game or not, but doing it was an enjoyable experience.

By the time Corey started kindergarten, Darby was ready for pre-school. Being a former teacher, Chris got a job teaching the two-year-old class at Tarrytown Baptist Church, and Darby was in her class. Besides her getting paid, Darby could attend school for free. We took turns watching the kids during that time. I'd drive Corey to school and Chris would pick him up at noon, or she'd drop them both off with me on campus when she had class. Sometimes, we'd trade off other ways. I got to spend a lot of time with my young sons at the park having lunch or just exploring Austin or the UT campus in those days. We still talk about those times often.

The next year, Chris moved to teach pre-school at St. Matthews Episcopal Day School, which was closer to where we lived. This time, Darby was in a different three-year-old class. so he could learn from someone who wasn't his mother. Corey was starting first grade at a new elementary school in north Austin he could walk to from our house.

The small taste of teaching I experienced during my first year made me miss it, so I got another part-time job. This one was teaching college algebra at Austin Community College (ACC). I started in the spring semester of 1985 and my class met on Monday and Wednesday evenings for 75 minutes a night. It was very easy for me because they held the class in the building next to mine on campus to be convenient for the ACC students who were also UT students. I continued to teach this same class every semester until we left Austin. I often said that was my best job ever, and I meant it. To this day, I miss teaching that class and I'd do it again in a heartbeat if I had the opportunity.

College algebra was easy for me, but not for most of the students I had in class. I mastered the subject in high school and continued to use it every day, as most engineers and engineering students do. Those who took the class from me weren't math or science majors. They were education, business, nursing, or liberal arts majors, disciplines that required little math. In fact, for most of my students, college algebra was the only one they had to take in their entire degree program. I found out that many of the students were not good in math. It was very challenging for me to get through to some of them, which helped me become a better teacher.

My algebra classes had between thirty and thirty-five students, and at least 80% of them were eighteen-year-old freshmen. They were outgoing, personable, energetic, and entertaining. But I made it fun too. I assigned plenty of homework problems and some were due every period. A regular part of my class was to have students come to the chalkboard and work through problems while explaining their solution. A few were nervous and didn't enjoy doing it, but most of them had fun with it and enjoyed the experience. It made for a very relaxed class, and I believe the students felt comfortable in such a casual environment. Before exams, a group of kids sometimes showed up at my office door with a pizza and cokes to lure me into an empty classroom to help them study. I helped them as much as I could, and I did my best to get everyone to pass the course. I didn't give many failing grades. Teaching those classes taught me how to help students learn, even when they may not have been interested in doing so.

I was a very particular teacher. I was picky about attendance, not being late, how students did their homework, how they explained it, and how they worked the problems on the exams. I had a set of rules I liked them to follow to maximize their learning experience and minimize my frustration. But even though I was particular, I was friendly and informal, and I tried to get to know my students. I began each class by asking if anybody had questions, either about class, the homework, or something else. One day when I did, a student who was sitting a few rows back raised her hand with a very unusual question.

When I called on her, she said, "Mr. Cicci, are you married?"

Surprised, I answered, "Why yes I am, but why would you ask me such a question?"

Not knowing what she was going to come up with next, she responded, "Because you're so picky I can't imagine that anybody would marry you!"

Rather stunned, all I could say was, "Well, someone did!" The entire class laughed at both her question and my answer.

I enjoyed teaching those algebra classes, and it was where I believe I learned how to teach. I had to, or some students never would have been able to get through the course. It was an exceptional training ground for me. Along with all the tutoring I did on the side, I felt I cultivated my skill of being able to simplify and explain hard concepts. I think those experiences stayed with me throughout my teaching career, although some of my former students may disagree with that statement. I'm thankful I taught at ACC, and it saddened me to leave that job, even though I only got paid about $1,200 per semester to teach that class. But that was a lot of money to us and I had fun too! I prided myself in my ability to simplify hard topics and explain them so people unfamiliar with the subject could understand them. One day when I was working on completing my dissertation, Dr. Roger Broucke, a faculty member on my Advisory Committee, came to my office.

He said, "David, come with me."

Not sure of what he wanted, I followed him to a vacant classroom across the hall.

He sat at a desk in the front row, and said, "Okay, now explain estimation theory to me so I can understand your dissertation." And I did. I wrote on the chalkboard for an hour, equation after equation, and described what they meant, how to use them, and how estimation theory worked.

After I finished, he said to me, "That was wonderful. Nobody has ever explained it to me like that before. Now I feel I understand it for the first time. Thank you!"

"You're very welcome, Dr. Broucke," I replied.

"I was happy to have the chance to explain it to you." Dr. Broucke told me several times after that how I explained estimation theory to him better than anyone else ever did. He told the same thing to Dr. Tapley.

We never had much extra money during our time in Austin, but we never felt poor. Well, perhaps we did a few times. With two small children we needed little money, because there were a lot of free things to do in Austin for kids. We didn't go out to bars or restaurants much, but when we did, we traded babysitting with friends. I know we missed amazing music and nightlife in Austin in those days, but we didn't feel deprived of anything. My one brush with a famous person in Austin came one morning when I was driving down the expressway to campus. A beat-up old pickup truck passed me and the driver smiled and waved. That driver was the country singer Willie Nelson, a long-time Austin resident.

Our time in Austin was fun. On Friday nights, we always ate out, often at Pok-e-Jo's BBQ near our house, or we went out for a pizza. We rented a delightful house on Saxony Lane in northwest Austin that had a small garden. One summer we bought a pop-up camper for $650, even though we didn't camp often. Corey and Darby used it as a playhouse in the driveway more than we used it for camping. We sold it several years later in Alabama for the same amount we paid for it. The kids had a lot of fun in that camper.

The boys raised mini-lop rabbits for a couple of years. They started out with two and ended up with twelve. I did a dumb thing one Easter and brought home two baby ducks. We kept them in the garage until I built a pen and tiny pool for them in the backyard. Once they were full grown, which didn't take long, we donated them to the petting zoo at St. Theresa's Catholic Church where we attended. Unfortunately, they met their untimely death at the beaks of the unwelcoming ducks on the day they moved in. We took our last two rabbits with us to Alabama. They survived the trip, although they didn't last long afterward.

Tuition at UT was very cheap, about $200 per semester at its highest. That wasn't much of a hardship with the loans I took out from General Electric and Ford. We were both very lucky to attend a great university for so little money. The kids got everything they needed, we never wanted for anything, and I think they enjoyed our time living in Austin. Chris and I have only been back once or twice since we left. Darby, however, visited many times as a touring musician when his band played at the annual South by Southwest (SXSW) Music Festival. Ironically, the SXSW Festival began during our very last year in Austin in 1987.

10

I COULD ACTUALLY GRADUATE

After getting past the written qualifying exams, my doctoral oral exam, and finishing my coursework, I needed to find a research topic. I always feared that would be the hardest part of my program, but that didn't turn out to be true for me.

I had to choose my dissertation topic myself, although Dr. Tapley suggested a general area for me to consider. It was up to me to decide what exactly I wanted to do. Of course, whatever topic I picked, he had to approve. I received some brilliant advice from Dr. Nacozy one day. We were discussing dissertation topics, and he told me to pick something I loved because by the time I finished, I'd hate it!

I remember the exact day I found my research topic. The general problem I wanted to address was to find a novel way to improve the accuracy of determining spacecraft orbits when limited data was available. I explored various ideas for months and tried many theories. Most of the ones I attempted were specific to orbital mechanics, but sometimes techniques common in other fields had unique crossover capabilities. I read tons of engineering research articles and grew weary of the process. Then I spent a few more days perusing old business and statistics journals in the Perry–Castañeda Library (PCL) at UT. As I skimmed through one article a huge light bulb turned on above my head. The technique I was reviewing used a numerical method I envisioned could be modified to work for spacecraft orbits. Studying the method for a week or two verified that it functioned as I hoped it might, and I presented the idea to Dr. Tapley. He thought it had great potential, so my 'find' had the potential to be a treasure! After making some adjustments and revisions, and verifying them with mathematical proofs, I demonstrated that it worked well for orbits and it became the basis for my dissertation. So, the topic I fell into one sunny afternoon at the PCL was a major stroke of luck for me. I was even luckier to have found it fast, and it was something I enjoyed working on. I soon verified that the new technique worked even better than I hoped they might.

Once I got such positive results in my research, I felt confident I was going to finish my Ph.D.. Even better, it didn't look like it would take me a decade or longer to do so. I worked very hard. I was in my office by 7:30 a.m. every day, and I seldom left before 4:30 p.m., treating it as if it were a regular job. I took time off to watch Corey and Darby when Chris was in class, and I played racquetball or basketball at Gregory Gym a couple times a week during lunch. Mostly, however, I was at school working on my research. In my mind, you don't have to be a genius to get a doctorate, you just have to be reasonably bright, stay motivated, and work hard without becoming discouraged. Some of the brightest students who started UT with me never graduated. And most of us who weren't geniuses finished because of our focus and determination.

The further along I got on my project, the less interaction I had with Dr. Tapley. I talked to him when I needed to, but those meetings didn't occur often. I had to develop into an independent researcher in order to survive. Being an experienced engineer, I shouldn't have needed much direction from him, anyway. Those may have been his thoughts and the reason he allowed me freedom to do my research with little direction.

Chris continued to take classes and before we left Austin, she completed most of the prerequisites she'd need to apply to pharmacy school wherever we ended up. Otherwise, she'd develop a different career plan, and I appreciated her willingness to do so. But it became important to me to find a job where she could do what she really wanted.

I had a lot of excellent classmates at UT and made many friends. Two of them played an important role in me being able to finish my doctorate. From our first semester at UT, Doug Kirkpatrick, Lisa White, and I shared our experiences and helped each other through the rough patches along the way. We supported each other through every step of our programs.

Doug was a major in the U.S. Air Force, who came to UT on a three-year educational leave from the Air Force Academy, where he taught orbital mechanics. At the end of his leave, he'd return to the Academy and continue teaching full time while he finished his dissertation. It turned out that Doug grew up in Pittsburgh, close to where my wife lived with her family. Lisa was from Houston, Texas, and received both her bachelor's and master's degrees from UT, then came back after a few years of working. The three of us did everything we could to help each other along the way, and we competed through each step in the friendliest of ways. The best thing was that we all finished our degrees, albeit at different times.

Doug returned to the Air Force Academy after UT and worked on writing his dissertation whenever he found the time. One day during lunch, while he was alone in the office working, the departmental telephone rang and rang and rang. Since Doug was the only one around, he reluctantly answered the phone, even though he tried to avoid it. The person calling was a representative of Nike Corporation, who wanted to get a clever quote about why Michael Jordan could jump so high to use in an upcoming Nike advertising campaign. Doug declined to give them any statement, but they insisted. Being the nice guy he is, Doug relented and gave in to the caller's request and provided a short quip to explain Michael Jordan's extraordinary jumping ability. The caller thanked him for his help and hung up, which Doug assumed was the end of the conversation and his involvement. But it wasn't.

Several months later, Nike called Doug back and asked him if he'd be interested in traveling to New York to appear in a television commercial. He'd appear with Michael Jordan and Spike Lee and it would feature his quote. They wanted him to dress like a professor and recite the same line he gave over the phone months earlier, only this time on camera. After discussing it with his family, Doug agreed to take part.

In 1991, Nike made their iconic 'Do You Know' commercial. It featured Spike Lee (as Mars Blackmon) asking Professor Douglas Kirkpatrick, of the American Institute of Aeronautics and Astronautics, the questions, "Yo Professor, how does Mike defy gravity? Do you know? Do you know? Do you know? Do you know?"

In the commercial, Doug dressed like a geeky scientist wearing a pair of black-rimmed glasses, a short-sleeved white shirt and a skinny black necktie. He even had a pocket protector in his shirt pocket. He answered Mars with the statement, "Michael Jordan overcomes the acceleration of gravity by the application of his muscle power in the vertical plane, thus producing a low altitude Earth orbit." Then to the puzzled looks of both Jordan and Blackmon, Doug continued, "Do you know what I mean? Do you know? Do you know? Do you know?"

It was a funny commercial and very popular when it debuted, and it's still available to watch online. Nike even sold posters commemorating the commercial, showing Doug with Michael Jordan and Spike Lee along with Doug's quote, which I bought and hung on my office wall for years. I don't know how much Doug earned for appearing in that commercial, but he once told me it paid for the college education of one of his children. That stroke of luck couldn't have happened to a nicer guy!

By the fall semester of 1986, my research progressed to a point that I felt confident I'd done enough and could defend a dissertation on my work. Even better, Dr. Tapley agreed. So I began writing my document, the part I was looking more forward to than actually doing the work. I still went to my office every day to stay focused on my task, and I made progress daily. I found the most important aspect of writing was developing a good outline. Once I did that, the writing was easier than I expected. The *Introduction* was the hardest part to write because it required so many citations, and it was the last chapter I wrote. I worked at a leisurely but steady pace. Since I hoped to get a faculty position, I expected to start a job the next fall. I wanted to finish writing early in the calendar year so I'd have time for interviews.

That would allow me to have a relaxing summer so we could plan our move to our new home.

I completed my dissertation in the early spring of 1987, and I titled it, "Optimal A priori Covariance Selection for the Solution of Ill-Conditioned Nonlinear Inverse Problems." It was 251 pages long and included eight chapters, twenty-three tables, forty figures, and 124 references. I doubt anyone else has ever read it other than my wife and my Dissertation Committee, which had to approve it. My committee comprised Dr. Tapley, three of my other aerospace professors, Drs. Wally Fowler, Bob Schutz, and Roger Broucke, and an Astronomy professor, Dr. William Jefferys.

After I finished the document, I wanted to spend a thoughtful amount of time writing my Acknowledgements page. It was important to me to thank everybody who played a role in my success. I'm glad I did, as I was very proud of it! And since so few people have read it, I thought I'd publish it again here, so perhaps somebody would get to see it now. Here's that page as it appeared in my 1987 dissertation, which I hadn't written as well as I remembered.

ACKNOWLEDGEMENTS

The time has finally come for me to reflect on a most rewarding period of my life to recognize the people who have contributed so much towards my success.

I wish to thank Drs. Roger A. Broucke, Wallace T. Fowler, William H. Jefferys, III, and Bob E. Schutz for serving on my Dissertation Committee and providing useful suggestions on the research. Special gratitude is extended to my Supervising Professor, Dr. Byron D. Tapley, for the guidance, support, and freedom he has given me throughout my degree program and for granting me such an outstanding opportunity in the beginning.

I owe my colleagues in the Department of Aerospace Engineering and Engineering Mechanics a sincere thanks for superb technical assistance, in particular: Drs. P. A. M. Abusali, John Lundberg, C. K. Shum, Richard Eanes, David Hasan, John Ries, and Dahning Yuan. Additional recognition is extended to Doug Kirkpatrick and Lisa White who, in addition to contributing many hours of technical support, have shared in both the best and worst of times.

I am very grateful to The University of Texas at Austin for providing the facilities and the financial support received as a Teaching Assistant and Assistant Instructor, and to the Center for Space Research for providing funding as a Graduate Research Assistant in order to perform this study.

Many others deserve thanks for contributions of different forms: Dr. Donald Brand for persuading me to attend The University of Texas at Austin; Drs. Paul Nacozy and Victor Szebehely for providing inspiration and encouragement. Robert Kennard for contributing useful bibliographical information; Alan Errett, Dr. Steven Rodi, the General Electric Foundation, and the Ford Foundation for providing outside opportunities for sustenance; Christine Cicci for reviewing the original manuscript; John Gerlach for providing the expertise in word processing required to create this document; and my family and friends for contributing strong moral support the many times it was needed.

In addition, I would like to thank the many undergraduate students at The University of Texas at Austin and Austin Community College whom I have taught and tutored over the years, for helping me to feel younger than I am, and in some cases teaching me as much as I taught them. Finally, I will be forever grateful to Dr. John J. McKetta for opening that first door.

David Allen Cicci
May 1987

I knew my wife was disappointed when she read my acknowledgements because I only thanked her for reading my manuscript. I realize it was a very shallow recognition for everything she did for me along the way. But my minimal 'thank you' to her was a part of my larger overall plan to thank her.

They scheduled my dissertation defense for Monday, June 29, at 9:00 a.m. in the departmental library. As a show of respect, I invited Dr. McKetta, but he said he didn't think he could make it. Since defenses were open to the public, I also asked Chris to attend so she could share my experience. A few of my friends and classmates also sat in.

I distributed the document to my committee a couple of weeks ahead of my defense to allow everyone time to read it. In the meantime, I made overhead slides and prepared my presentation. Then I scheduled my final meeting with Dr. Tapley for 10:00 a.m. the Friday before. He needed to review my work and hear what I was going to present on Monday. But that didn't go very well.

During our meeting, I described my project to Dr. Tapley in great detail. After about an hour I arrived at the most crucial table, which compared the results I got with my new solution techniques to those using conventional methods. In doing so, I misspoke and stated that the numbers displayed in the table were the average errors for all the parameter estimates calculated.

Dr. Tapley looked at me surprised and responded, "Those aren't good numbers. The errors are much too large to be useful!" He continued, "The committee will never approve your dissertation with errors that large. You may have to fix this and re-schedule your defense for another time."

My jaw dropped, and I was in shock! How could I not have realized the results were so bad when I thought they were excellent? Not sure what to say or do, I went back to my office a complete wreck, wallowing in self-pity and full of enormous anxiety. I couldn't imagine what would happen if I failed to graduate as I hoped. Dr. Tapley's comments devastated me!

Thinking if I worked the rest of the day and all weekend, perhaps I could fix the problem or get new results somehow before Monday.

To make matters worse, we had planned a family camping trip at a nearby state park to take my mind off my Monday defense. But I knew I couldn't go camping in my current mindset. So I left my office to head home to tell Chris and the kids there wasn't any way I could go. I'd ruin the fun for everybody if I did.

During my thirty-minute drive, I replayed my meeting with Dr. Tapley in my head over and over. Just before arriving at the house, I realized I was wrong when I told him that the errors in the table I described were the average errors. In reality, they were the total errors, which I knew would change everything! Still frantic, I went into the house and told Chris what happened and that I needed to get back to school right away to catch Dr. Tapley before he left.

She wasn't happy and said, "But what about camping, the boys are all ready to go?"

I replied, "Well, I can't go now, maybe later."

Then Chris said, "Fine, but we're going anyhow. You can show up if you want to."

I responded, "OK, I'll try to make it after I talk to Dr. Tapley."

I climbed back into my car to return to campus as Chris and the kids got into her car to head to the campground with the pop-up camper in tow. During my drive I thought about what I'd say if Dr. Tapley was still there, which I doubted as it was now 5:00 p.m. and he seldom stayed that late. Everyone else in the department had left and his office door was closed, but his light was on. So I pounded on his door in hopes he'd appear. And he did! Surprised to see me, he opened the door and invited me in.

When I told him how I misspoke during our meeting and explained what I should have said, he responded by saying, "Oh, okay, it'll be fine then. I'll see you on Monday!" Never feeling more relieved in my entire life, I left and drove straight to the state park, only stopping to get some badly needed beer along the way. When I arrived, I helped my family set up the camper for the night. We had a fun, relaxing, and stress-free weekend, which was the perfect way to prepare for my defense.

In the aftermath of my near-tragic Friday meeting, I now felt confident I'd pass. On Monday, Chris and I arrived early so I could get ready for my presentation. After I did, the first person to walk into the room was Dr. McKetta, wearing an untucked linen Cubavera shirt, looking like he was on his way to the beach! Once I saw him, I knew everything would be fine. He wished me luck and told me not to worry, that I'd do great. I appreciated him being there and the moral support he provided me by doing so. Then my committee and a few of my classmates filtered in. After everyone found seats, Dr. Tapley introduced me and I began my presentation. I spoke for about forty-five minutes and after I finished, the visitors, including my wife, left and my examination continued with thoughtful and comprehensive questions from each committee member. I felt I gave appropriate answers to all of them. When they completed their questioning, Dr. Tapley asked me to step outside while they deliberated my fate.

After a short while, he called me back into the room and said, "Congratulations, you passed!" The only thing I had to do was make a few editorial corrections. Each member of my Dissertation Committee and Dr. McKetta congratulated me and my defense was over. It was a wonderful feeling!

When everyone left, Chris came in and I told her the news, which she had already surmised when she saw my committee leaving. We were both happy and relieved. I walked over, hugged her, and handed her a piece of paper.

I said, "Here, I didn't put this in my document yet and I wanted you to see it first." In my meager attempt to thank her for everything she'd done for me, the paper I gave her was my Dedication page. It became a permanent part of my dissertation, and I wanted to include it again here for others to see.

DEDICATION

To my wife Christine and my sons Corey and Darby,
whose sacrifice has been far greater than mine.
I promise to make it up to them.

Chris appreciated my gesture, and I hope she realized how instrumental she was in my success. My kids were too young to realize their contribution, but perhaps they will one day. And I'm still trying to fulfill the promise I made in that dedication.

My mother knew I was defending my dissertation that day, so I wanted to tell her I passed. But I didn't want to call her on the phone. I'd always planned to send her a telegram with the good news since she grew up when telegrams were commonplace. I also wanted her to have a keepsake of the event. So I called Western Union and sent her an old-fashioned telegram telling her my defense was over.

After she received the phone call from Western Union with the news, she called to congratulate me. I could hear the happiness in her voice. My mother never expected to have a doctor of any type in our family.

When I finished my degree after five years of study at UT, I believe I set a record for the fastest completion of any Ph.D. under Dr. Tapley. It was a great feeling, especially for an overachiever like me. Getting a doctorate was a tremendous amount of work, but it was all worth it!

It only took me a few days to make the editorial corrections that were suggested, get the required signatures, and submit my document to the university. Then I ordered twelve bound copies of my dissertation. I kept three for myself and my family; I gave one to each member of my committee, one to the department, one to UT, and one to my mother. The last copy went to Dr. McKetta to thank him for everything he did for me.

11

YOU DID WHAT? AND
WE'RE MOVING WHERE?

I began my job search in the early spring of 1987. After such a long road, I was, at last, in a place and had the qualifications to have the career I hoped for. But getting hired as a faculty member isn't easy. There are very few openings each year and even fewer in my specialization, and the competition is tough. Each vacancy in engineering attracts between seventy-five and a hundred applicants, most of which are well qualified. A person needs to stand out to the Faculty Search Committees at the places they apply to make an impression. Just wanting a faculty job doesn't mean you'll get one. I knew I'd be very disappointed if I didn't. I was realistic, and the odds against me were high. For that reason, I applied for some industrial positions as a back-up plan as well. We'd been poor for too long, and it was time to move on with our lives and have a regular salary and a normal life. Chris was also ready to find another career path for herself. It would have been perfect to just stay at UT as a professor, but that wasn't possible since universities seldom hire their own recent graduates.

I applied for many jobs, most of which were in academia, and I answered every faculty vacancy announcement I saw related to my area of expertise. The more generalized advertisements read 'dynamics and control', and the more specific ones included the words 'orbital mechanics' or 'astrodynamics'. There weren't a lot available in those areas in 1987. I even sent out applications to departments which didn't advertise openings to inquire about potential jobs. That turned out to be a waste of time since they required schools to announce all open positions. I received a rude letter back from the University of Miami. They stated their department didn't have any openings and also told me not to bother sending them any more uninvited inquiries. As if Miami could be that arrogant, considering their inferior engineering program. I received friendly and professional responses to all of my other applications, even if they were rejections. Miami's response wasn't friendly or professional.

I believed my credentials would compete with other applicants. Besides having a new Ph.D. from a preeminent research university, I studied under a very famous professor in my field, had nine years of engineering experience and classroom teaching experience, a PE license, and my references and letters of recommendation were outstanding. I felt as though I was in an excellent position to find a job I liked. But other factors played roles in the hiring process. Sometimes schools have 'preferred' candidates, and other times there are certain individuals that have inside tracks some other way. A good candidate also had to be lucky to get a job. I thought the entire search and interview process was very interesting and a lot of fun. It was also stressful.

I put together a wish list of things I hoped to find in a new position. My desirables included teaching orbital mechanics, working at a university that had a pharmacy school for Chris, good public schools for the kids, a warm climate, and affordable housing. I also would have liked to work at a large university with major college sports, although that was of lesser importance and was not important at all to Chris. She wanted some of those same items, but to her, being a former teacher, the quality of the public schools ranked highest. Because of that, she compiled a list of states where she didn't want to move. That list included Arkansas, Oklahoma, Mississippi, and Alabama since she'd heard so many negative stories about the school systems in those states. If I took a job in industry, an additional requirement for me would be to work for a company that supported the space program or other similar projects.

I answered ten or fifteen advertisements for faculty positions in my area or related ones. I also signed-up for five or six interviews for industrial jobs through the placement center on-campus in case I wasn't able to land a teaching job. I received invitations for interviews from four universities and two companies. The schools were the University of Florida (UF) in Gainesville, Florida, the U.S. Naval Academy (USNA) in Annapolis, Maryland, the University of South Florida (USF) in Tampa, Florida, and Auburn University (AU) in Auburn, Alabama. One company that invited me was Sverdrup Corporation, at NASA Stennis Space Center (now NRL Stennis Space Center), Mississippi, near Slidell, Louisiana. Unisys Corporation, formed by a merger between the Sperry and Burroughs corporations, in Clear Lake, Texas, also invited me for an interview. They were a contractor to NASA Johnson Space Center (JSC). I thought the most unusual and perhaps most interesting industrial job was with Sverdrup, which involved using satellite data to map the ocean currents for the Naval Research Laboratory (NRL). That job seemed to be an odd fit, but the work there closely paralleled my dissertation research.

I received offers from both companies I interviewed. Sverdrup impressed me for several reasons: I already knew the work; they had strong ties to my department at UT; I hit it off well with the person who would be my supervisor; and it was close to New Orleans, Louisiana, a city I loved. I turned down Unisys and kept the offer from Sverdrup as my back-up. As good of a job as it was, I knew it would come in a distant second to working at a university.

My first on-campus faculty interview was with the Department of Mechanical and Aerospace Engineering at UF. It was a very intense, two-day interview, which included non-stop one-on-one meetings with each faculty member in the department, presenting a requisite hour-long seminar, a brutal group interview with most of the faculty at once, and meals with the Search Committee. The group interview was in a conference room with about ten or twelve professors who took turns firing questions at me about engineering and other topics. One question I was not prepared for was, 'If you were on a train trip from New York to San Francisco, what non-technical books would you bring along to read?' Since I wasn't a big reader, I had to bluff my way through that answer. I came up with something about American history and the Civil War.

Then, after I finished bumbling through that answer, the same individual followed up with another one. 'Okay, then if you had to get back on the train and return to New York, what other non-technical books would you bring along to read?' It was more difficult stumbling through that answer.

My visit to UF was enjoyable, and I liked the job, the department, the campus, and Gainesville. I believe I would have accepted an offer had they made me one, but they never did. I thought it went well, but I guess it didn't go well enough. It was my first faculty interview, and perhaps the results would have been different if it wasn't. I learned a lot going through that arduous experience, and I'm sure it helped me in my following interviews.

My second faculty interview was at the U.S. Naval Academy. I'd never been to Annapolis and found the town and campus to be both charming and beautiful. They arranged for me to stay in a large old house on the Academy grounds where visiting officers stayed. My entire visit was very interesting, and I felt it went great. The job was teaching orbital mechanics, and the facilities were exceptional. At the time I thought I would have enjoyed working there, although I'm not sure if teaching at a military academy would've been a good fit for me. I never believed the academies had the best students, since they all had careers already planned for them. They didn't need to excel in the classroom, just do enough to get by.

The Search Committee must have felt my interview went well too, and within a few days I received an offer of a position. It pleased me, but I thought the salary was very low. After a good deal of research into the cost of living around Annapolis, I wasn't sure I could have supported a family of four on the money they were offering. It was, however, an opportunity to teach what I wanted in a beautiful location. And being a professor at the USNA was a very prestigious position. Another negative was that Chris would have to commute to either Baltimore or Washington, DC to attend pharmacy school, which wouldn't have been ideal. It would have been doable, but not a perfect situation by any means.

When I told Chris about the offer, she screamed. "A job!" And when I gave my mother the news, she was even more excited. Since she still lived in Pennsylvania, she'd be able to see her grandsons more often if we were to live closer. Chris would have been nearer to most of her siblings in Pittsburgh, which she would have liked very much.

I believe Chris wanted me to take the job at the USNA. She thought she'd love living in Annapolis, even though it would have been harder for her to attend school. After an enormous amount of contemplation, study, evaluation, and discussion with Chris, I turned down the offer, even though it was the only one I had in hand. When I told her and my mother what I did, I was not popular with either of them. I knew I disappointed Chris, and I also saddened my mom because Maryland was closer to her than any of my other job possibilities. The reason I rejected their offer was very logical to me. My salary there wouldn't have allowed us to buy a house, at least not right away, since the Annapolis area was so expensive. We may have been able to afford a remodeled garage, but that would've been about it. I refused to go from being poor in Austin to being poor in Annapolis. But nobody appreciated my explanation. I perceived myself as being ostracized for a period by both my wife and mother after my fateful decision.

My next interview was with the Department of Aerospace Engineering at AU, which was in a small, southern college town. Even though Alabama was on Chris's list of states she didn't want to move to because of the public school system, I accepted their invitation for several reasons. AU had an outstanding aerospace engineering department, and they told me I'd get to teach as much orbital mechanics as I wanted. Also, three of my classmates at UT were Auburn graduates, two with bachelor's degrees who were master's students, and one with a master's degree who was a doctoral student. I played intramural basketball with two of them, and I'd heard many tales of what a great place Auburn was from all three. During my first year at UT, I shared an office with one of those AU alums. He was another Air Force officer on educational leave, and he'd be the first one in the office each morning. I usually arrived soon after him, and when I did, I'd hear the Auburn fight song blasting from his cassette tape player every morning. That was my first introduction to the phrase, 'War Eagle!'

The head of the Search Committee was John Cochran, Jr. As an undergraduate, John was an all-conference football player at Auburn and also earned his Ph.D. in aerospace engineering from UT. He was an exceptional person and a brilliant scholar! After finishing his master's degree at AU, he was an instructor and completed his doctorate at UT in nine months. That was something nobody had done before or since. When he returned to Auburn as a professor, he went to law school and got his Doctor of Jurisprudence (JD) degree while he was teaching full time. The UT faculty all knew John and held him in high regard. They had many stories to tell about his brief stay in Austin and his record-breaking performance there. In his career at AU, John also served as the Acting Athletics Director for a few years in order to help clean up internal problems that arose from NCAA violations in the football program. After his success in athletics, he returned to continue his outstanding academic career in the aerospace engineering department.

When my friends and the faculty members at UT heard I had an interview at Auburn, they were all very excited for me. They even called ahead to put in a kind word for me before my visit. When I arrived in Auburn, they made me feel right at home.

My AU interview was 1½ days, and I thought it went better than all the others. My UT friends had told them about my basketball experience before I arrived. One AU faculty member, Malcolm (Mac) Cutchins, invited me to join in a game of noontime basketball with him and other faculty members from across campus, which they played regularly. Mac explained to me later that he found playing basketball with someone was a much better way to learn about them than through any formal interview. Nobody ever asked me to play basketball as part of an interview before, but I enjoyed the experience. I had an advantage though because my friends at UT gave me a heads-up on how to get on Mac's good side. They said, "Mac loves to shoot, so just pass him the ball and he'll like you." And that's what I did! Every time I touched it, I looked for Mac first so he could take a shot. That plan seemed to work, and we had an enjoyable game. It was funny to me I spent much of my young life playing basketball, and the sport was still involved in my life so many years later.

When we finished our noontime game, Mac took me to his home to have lunch with him and his wife. It was so nice that they did that. In fact, the entire trip couldn't have gone better. I was sorry that Chris wasn't there with me though, as it may have changed her opinion about living in Alabama. Everyone I met during my visit was friendly and made me feel comfortable and at home, especially the department head, Jim Williams. What impressed me the most was that everybody I talked with asked about my family. The department was very family oriented, starting with Jim. He told me that if I worked there, my family would be the most important thing and would take priority over any of my work responsibilities. The 'family first' attitude he and the other professors conveyed during my interview meant more to me than anything else we discussed. Another huge plus for Auburn was that they had a very good pharmacy school right on-campus that Chris could attend.

On an amusing note, my second day in Auburn was on April 1. It was a tradition that the campus newspaper at AU, The Auburn Plainsman, printed a special edition for April Fool's Day each year. The paper that day was full of jokes and fictitious stories. I took a copy home for Chris to read so she could get a small sense of the school and the culture there. I also brought back some AU t-shirts and hats for Corey and Darby.

My last faculty interview was with the Mechanical Engineering Department at USF. They wanted me to teach more controls than orbital mechanics, which would have been fine, but that wasn't my preference. I wouldn't have been able to focus on my specialization or establish a research program in the area I desired. USF had a beautiful campus and excellent facilities, I liked Tampa, and the cost of living was low.

After I turned down the job from the USNA, I received offers from both AU and USF, both around the same time. Receiving them made Chris feel a lot better. Since I had more offers now and we wouldn't end up jobless, I became a little more popular in my house. Of course, that didn't last long.

Having three offers to decide between was a luxury, but the decision wasn't easy because there were plusses and minuses about each one. The evaluation process I needed to undertake took some time, and there were many things to consider. Chris knew I was also very concerned about the quality of the public schools in Alabama. I had a major decision to make about my future and that of my family, and I had a lot of pondering to do before I could decide.

Early in 1987, Chris's parents moved to Sebastian, Florida, which was on the Atlantic Coast, only about a 2½ hour drive from Tampa. She spent some time in that area in the past and liked it. In addition, her best friend from college lived in Orlando, which was only about an hour's drive. I think she got excited about the possibility of my accepting the job at USF, although they didn't have a pharmacy school then—and the nearest one was two hours away in Gainesville. She claimed it didn't matter, and she'd find another career path if we went to Tampa, but she never convinced me that was true.

The opportunity to become a professor after all the work and so many years of waiting thrilled me. I didn't think I could've made a bad choice with the options I had. Since I held two offers from universities, I turned down the Sverdrup offer. As I suspected, there wasn't much of a comparison between it and the faculty positions. The AU job had everything I was looking for, except that it was in Alabama. I knew I'd like working there with the friendly and easy-going faculty and having a wonderful department head for a boss. Tampa was a better location, but the USF job wasn't as good of a fit for me. As far as Chris's options went, that AU had a pharmacy school provided a major advantage for Auburn. As much as I talked with her about it, she still had concerns about moving to Alabama after the bad things she'd heard about the public schools there. Another drawback, for me, was that Alabama was a very conservative, very religious, deep-red state, and I was a liberal democrat from the north and not religious. I was a Catholic and attended church, but that was more to set an example for our kids. I never bought into the whole organized religion game that's so prevalent in our country and in the south in particular. Between the two choices I had, I think Chris preferred me going to USF. I already turned down the job at the USNA, which I still believe would have been her first choice.

It was a tough decision, and one I had to make soon because my deadlines were approaching. With more thought than I ever put into anything in my life, I made my selection one afternoon at school, a couple of days before my deadlines. I called Jim Williams and accepted his offer of a tenure-track Assistant Professor position at Auburn University. Once I placed that call, I felt relieved, and I knew I made the right choice. Then I phoned USF to inform them and say thanks for considering me.

I felt good about my AU decision. But then I did something idiotic. When I got off the phone I told some of my classmates I accepted a job, and they twisted my arm into going out for some beers to celebrate. The problem was that I didn't tell my wife about the AU job first! I may have hesitated to do so because I knew her feelings about Alabama. But I realized I should have told her the moment I decided. Except that, like a dope, I didn't!

Later that night, after I got home from celebrating with my friends, I gave Chris the news. After having dinner and feeling no urgency, or perhaps fearing the response I'd receive, I said nonchalantly while we were watching TV, "Oh, by the way, I accepted the Auburn job today!"

Stunned at what I just told her, she looked at me and said, "You did what?" Then I vaguely remember her saying something like, "We're moving to Alabama and you didn't tell me?"

Then I replied, "Well, I wasn't sure you'd want to hear that news, so I waited until I got home."

She continued, "And somehow you thought it would be a good idea to go out drinking with your friends before you told me, and they knew before I did?"

"I'm sorry, I should've told you right away. But it was a hard decision, and I needed those beers," I blithered.

After my news sank in, Chris responded, "Well, congratulations! I knew that was the job you wanted all along. You made the best choice!"

"Thanks, sweetie, I think I did too," I said to her.

We spent the rest of our night talking about the possibilities and what was ahead for us, moving, and of course, the public schools in Alabama. The more we talked about it, the more comfortable Chris became with the idea. She wanted to know all about the city and what it was like there. I told her I thought there was only one street in town. What I meant was there was one main street with businesses and restaurants, not just one street, but 'one street' was all she heard. Then our discussion moved to Auburn's pharmacy school, and her mood lifted, and the more excited we both got. And it thrilled the kids we were moving to a new city, with new schools, and we'd get a new house. The only questions they had were if we could take our two remaining bunnies with us and if we could get a house with a swimming pool. The expectations of our young children were much lower than those of their parents.

Ed, Yukon, PA, 1975

Chris, Pittsburgh, PA, 1976

Our wedding, Wexford, PA, 1977

Mike Cochenour's wedding, New Kensington, PA, 1978

Jim Goldsworthy's wedding, McKeesport, PA, 1979

Expecting our first child, Yukon, PA, 1979

John McKetta, Austin, TX, 1982

University of Texas graduation, 1988

John and Pinky McKetta, Austin, TX, circa 2000

Byron Tapley, Austin, TX, 2006
(www.csr.utexas.edu)

12

FROM AUSTIN TO AUBURN

Since we planned to leave Austin in the summer, we sold our house in Arlington in the spring. It had been a rental for four years, and we wanted to purchase a home in Auburn. We took a house-hunting trip to Alabama two weeks before I defended my dissertation and well before classes were to start. In those days, AU was on the quarter system and the fall quarter began in September and ended in December. The winter quarter ran from January until March, and spring quarter from March until June. It was an academic calendar I didn't think I'd like since I'd only ever experienced semesters, and I confirmed those suspicions after I started teaching in that system. But the Auburn public schools began in late August, so we had to arrive early and get settled so the kids could enroll in school and start on time. Corey was entering second grade, and Darby was going to attend pre-kindergarten.

Our trip to Auburn excited the boys and me, but I could tell Chris was more apprehensive, not knowing what she'd find in Alabama. It was a twelve-hour drive, and we broke it up into two days, spending the first night in Baton Rouge, Louisiana.

The drive to Alabama was pleasant, but once we passed Mobile on Interstate 65 and headed north, Chris became silent. All we saw from the car were pine trees! Other than passing by Montgomery, there wasn't much at all to see between Mobile and Auburn except the forest. Hoping to change the mood, we stopped to have lunch at the only restaurant we could find, the Bates House of Turkey in Greenville, Alabama. If you didn't like turkey, it was the wrong place to stop since everything on the menu was turkey-based, even the lasagna. But we liked what we ordered. And everyone was friendly, which was a preview of the people we'd find upon arriving in our new town.

When we reached Auburn, we checked into the Best Western Hotel on South College Street, near to the interstate, then we drove around to see the city and AU. The city was just a small town, but there was more than the one street I recalled. It was quaint and pretty, and the campus was beautiful, even nicer than I remembered. We drove out to the mall and through a few neighborhoods to see what they were like. After our brief tour, the kids decided they liked it and Chris felt a little better.

We'd been in touch with a realtor, so we looked at about ten houses that were for sale. There weren't many homes on the market, and no new ones were available in our price range. We found one in the Whippoorwill subdivision, a few miles south of town in a rustic neighborhood. Although it was twelve years old, there were two acres of land and a swimming pool, so the kids liked it better than the others we saw. We made an offer on the house and it was accepted, so the trip was a success. Our realtor helped us arrange for a mortgage and did the required paperwork, so it was all quite easy. However, I still had to go back and defend my dissertation and finish school. If I failed, I'd ruin everything. But as I described earlier, I succeeded even though I had those few tense moments.

An even bigger success than finding a house occurred when we learned about the Auburn City Schools. We heard the school system was excellent, and much better than those in the rest of Alabama, because the university community demanded it and supported the schools very well. Years earlier, the city leaders instituted an extra school tax above the state appropriations to fund a quality educational system for the children in Auburn. That news relieved us both. Chris might have even taken Alabama off her list of places she wouldn't ever live.

Once we had an address, we registered Corey for the second grade at Wright's Mill Road Elementary School. We also found a pre-kindergarten program for Darby at Grace United Methodist Church. After accomplishing so much during our visit, Chris and I left Auburn feeling a lot better. We were pleased about the quality of the public schools and knowing where we were going to live. I may have even been off the hook for accepting a job in Alabama!

After returning home, we had about two months for me to defend my dissertation, plan our move, arrange for a moving company, pack, say goodbye to our Austin friends, and learn what we could about Auburn. We took one weekend trip to see our extended family members in San Antonio once more.

Before we got ready to leave Austin for good, we had a momentous Fourth of July celebration. Dr. and Mrs. McKetta invited us to their annual Independence Day party, which included a small celebration of my completing my doctorate. It was a gorgeous summer day, and we enjoyed a cookout and took part in the boat parade on Lake Austin. At one point Dr. McKetta gave me a gag gift of a pin which had the printed message, 'Trust Me I'm A Doctor.' He always did his best to make everyone laugh with his antics. Dr. Tapley didn't attend the party this time, so there were no bald jokes.

The night was even more memorable when we took the boys to their first-ever rock concert. We went to Zilker Park to see The Beach Boys perform their annual Fourth of July show. It was a year when they performed two shows on Independence Day: the first being in Tampa, Florida, in the late afternoon before they flew to Austin for their second show that evening. We sat close to the stage, the back of which was open to downtown. We could see the fireworks taking place behind the band as they played their fantastic beach songs. I took turns holding Corey and Darby on my shoulders so they could see better. It was the best Fourth of July celebration we'd ever had, a terrific way to celebrate the holiday and our time at UT, and to say goodbye to the wonderful city of Austin as a family. I still get chills when I think about that night, and we continue to talk about it even now.

Another highlight of our last weeks in town was having a farewell dinner with Dr. and Mrs. McKetta. After our meal they gave us a gift of some money with the strict instructions, "This money is for Chris, she's suffered being poor for long enough and she needs to spend it on herself." We thanked them for the gift and everything else they both did for us during our time in Austin. They made our time there even more special than it would have been otherwise. And Chris bought some nice things for herself with the money they gifted us.

Even though I officially received my Ph.D. in the summer of 1987, I chose not to attend formal graduation ceremonies until the next spring. I planned to return to Austin the following May after working for a year. My friends who also finished in the summer and fall were planning to do the same.

Before we knew it, it was early August and time to leave, as we had set up the closing on our new Auburn house for August 7th. We packed our two cars with our clothes and other necessities and two rabbit cages. One car even pulled the pop-up camper, and we were moving to Alabama, perhaps for good as we didn't what the future held. We talked about staying for five years, until I got tenured, and then finding a job somewhere that wasn't in Alabama. Chris would have finished pharmacy by then, and we could both look for new opportunities. That was our original plan, subject to modification, of course.

Leaving Austin was very hard. We loved it there, but we couldn't stay. We felt fortunate to have lived in such an incredible city for as long as we did. It saddened us to drive out of town, but once we crossed the Louisiana border, our mindset changed from Austin to Auburn. We became eager to get to our new home and begin our lives there.

Once again, we took two days to make the twelve-hour drive, this time spending the night in a Baton Rouge hotel with the rabbits. When we arrived in Auburn, we stayed at the Best Western again for a few days until we closed on our house. Then it was moving in and getting settled and readying the kids for the start of school. Of course, the first thing they wanted to do was go for a swim in our new pool, but we had to have it cleaned before they could. The city schools started a few weeks before AU, and it was nice to have that time to adjust and settle in before starting my job.

Chris planned to take a year off from taking classes to get the house in order. That plan changed when she met with the pharmacy school faculty to discuss her plans. She learned the coming spring quarter was the last time a mid-year class would begin the program. From then on, there would only be an incoming class in the fall. Starting in the spring meant she could complete her pharmacy degree in two-and-a-half years if she went through the summers, otherwise it would delay her graduation. So Chris planned to apply for spring admission but needed a few more pre-requisite courses before she could begin. Instead of taking time off, she jumped right back in and enrolled for the fall and winter quarters. She took inorganic chemistry and calculus, which were classes she needed to satisfy the admission requirements.

Since AU started the quarter so late in September, there were two or three football games scheduled each year before classes even began. Auburn's first game in 1987 was at home against UT. It was ten days before my official start date at AU, and we were still Texas fans after having attended games in Austin. We found four tickets for the game, dressed in our UT gear, and went to pull for the Longhorns. Auburn had a better team that year, and by halftime Texas was getting clobbered, 21-3. That's when we switched our allegiance over to Auburn and cheered for the Tigers during the second half. It was easier for Chris and the kids to make the change than for me, but I converted mid-game too and have been an avid Auburn fan ever since. AU won the game 31-3, so we felt great about the outcome for our new team. Still, Texas would always remain one of my favorite teams, along with West Virginia and, of course, Auburn.

In those days they called the City of Auburn, "The loveliest village on the Plains." It was small and quaint, with a population of only around 30,000, and beautiful. The neighboring town of Opelika added 20,000 more residents, and the student enrollment at AU contributed an additional 20,000, so the greater Auburn-Opelika area was almost a mid-size city. Auburn was a college town, and Opelika was an old railroad and mill town and the setting for the 1979 film,

Norma Rae. A shared hospital was between the cities. In downtown Auburn, there were two principal streets lined with small businesses and a few restaurants. They were family-owned ones, the kind that thrived in small towns across America. I thought there were too many churches monopolizing the area, but we were in the South. College Street ran north and south through town, and Magnolia Avenue east and west. The intersection of the two streets is the famous Toomer's Corner, and the university occupied the land southwest of that corner.

Many people would no longer consider Auburn to be a village or lovely. Today the population is over 76,000 and Opelika is nearly half that, so the area has more than doubled in size since 1987. The student enrollment at AU is now well over 30,000, so it isn't a village anymore. And as far as lovely goes, Auburn used to be beautiful, with those small shops and eateries on tree-lined streets. Over the years the city leaders bowed to the money of corporate America and filled the town with chain stores, chain restaurants, and large, hideous apartment buildings sprinkled throughout the area. The monstrosities seem to multiply yearly. There are more restaurants now, and being a college town, there are a lot of bars too.

One thing that stood out the most after we arrived in Auburn was how friendly everybody was, in particular the people who were born and raised in the South. It took us a while to adjust to how slowly everyone moved. For example, it wasn't unusual to be waiting in line at the grocery store while the cashier and a customer carried on a long conversation about how their families were doing and what they had planned for the weekend. Life was slower paced than even Texas, and much more so than life back in Pennsylvania.

And people were very religious, at least they acted like it. Chris and I were both raised Catholic, but Auburn only had one Catholic Church, Saint Michael's the Archangel. However, that didn't stop people from trying to convert us to be Baptists or Methodists, or something else. Many people, even strangers, would talk to us about their church.

Those talks often lead up to their statement, "You should come and visit our church. You'd like it there."

When we'd answer, we were Catholic and had already joined Saint Michael's, they seldom accepted that as a subtle, "No, thanks," as we intended.

Rather, they'd continue with something on the order of, "I understand, but you need to give ours a try. It's a wonderful church!" They never 'got it'. And we never gave their church 'a try'. Although they were always friendly throughout the whole punishing ordeal. I didn't appreciate those discussions much at all. I was never a big supporter of organized religion, and after many years of living in the South, I've turned against it even more.

Soon after we moved to Auburn, Dr. Leo Hirth, a professor in the Chemical Engineering Department, invited us to a cookout at his home. Leo was Dr. McKetta's very first doctoral student at UT. He wanted to welcome our family to town and to AU. Dr. McKetta had written Leo telling him about our moving there and that he thought we'd like each other. He also mentioned jokingly (I think) that he'd probably like Chris more than me. It was very nice that Leo and his wife, Marge, asked us over. When we arrived, we found they also invited others in town that had UT connections. It was a beautiful afternoon, and we enjoyed meeting more new people with Texas ties. We remained friends with Leo and Marge until they retired and moved to Florida to be near their kids. We valued their friendship and appreciated their warm welcome to Auburn.

Being a liberal, I knew I'd have trouble dealing with so many conservatives and religious people in Alabama. And there were a lot. But people from other places filled a university community, too. Many of our new friends in Auburn were on the faculty or otherwise connected to AU somehow. We gravitated to the more liberal and the less religious people we met. Some new friends were also from the North, a few of which we met at church not long after we arrived. We even met one couple from Pittsburgh. Bill Trimble was an AU history professor, and his wife, Sharon, graduated from the same high school as Chris! Remarkably, we shared some mutual friends back in Pennsylvania. Another couple, Keith and Maryanne Campagna, both pharmacists, got their pharmacy degrees at Duquesne University in Pittsburgh. Keith was even a professor in the pharmacy school at AU.

With our new friends and AU, we felt somewhat insulated from whatwe didn't like and as though we lived in a bit of a utopia. There weremany other good things in Auburn for us and only a few bad ones, which we learned to tolerate.

One thing we found we liked best was the location. We were only two hours from Atlanta and Birmingham, three and a half hours from some of the best beaches on the Gulf Coast, and six hours away from New Orleans. The cities of Montgomery and Columbus, Georgia were within an hour's drive, we could get to the mountains of Tennessee and North Carolina in four hours, and the great cities of Savannah, Georgia, and Charleston, South Carolina were only about five hours away. Even though Auburn was small and didn't have what some bigger places could offer, we had a lot available to us close-by. Auburn had wonderful and friendly people, which was the best of all, and made our transition to becoming Alabamians much easier than it would have been otherwise.

Another advantage of teaching aerospace engineering at Auburn was that the state had a thriving aerospace industry in Huntsville, which was two hundred miles north. Huntsville was the home to NASA's Marshall Space Flight Center (MSFC) and Redstone Arsenal, which was the center for the U.S. Army's missile development activities. There were also many government contractors nearby that supported the engineering efforts at NASA and the Army. With such a booming aerospace industry, there were many opportunities for research, consulting, and collaborations for AU faculty members.

The people we met in Auburn helped us to feel at home. With that and everything else we found after we arrived, we felt lucky we came to Alabama, even though it wasn't on our original list of places to go.

Not long after we moved to Auburn, my brother Ed retired from the Air Force and became a pilot for Delta Airlines. They based him in Atlanta, so he and Jean planned to move south from Fairfax, Virginia and build a house in Peachtree City, Georgia. Before they finished their house, Ed stayed with us for a few months between his Delta flights. Jean stayed in Virginia until my niece, Marnie, finished high school. Because Auburn was on Central Time and Atlanta was on

Eastern Time, it was a little inconvenient for Ed when he had to make early morning flights. He'd have to leave very early because of the time change so he could get to the airport for his flight. I stayed up much later at night then. Sometimes I'd be going to bed, and he'd be getting up to go to work and we'd cross paths in the kitchen. We used to laugh because to save time, he'd pour his cereal in a bowl the night before and cover it with plastic wrap. Then he'd just have to add milk in the morning. He may have saved about a minute each day doing that. It was great having him stay with us during that time and the boys enjoyed having their fun Uncle Ed around.

13

WHAT DO YOU MEAN
I CAN'T JUST TEACH?

I began working at AU on September 15, 1987, two weeks before classes started. I was very excited. After such a long road, I had the job I wanted at last. On my first day, I performed all the usual tasks of new employees: I filled out tax and insurance forms, and got my parking pass, office keys, computer, books, etc. In those days, the Department of Aerospace Engineering was on the ground floor of Wilmore Laboratories, which was an old red brick building in severe need of renovation. My office was on the second floor at the top of a wide set of marble stairs. The two-story structure didn't have an elevator.

On my first day, I learned that I'd be teaching two classes in the fall quarter: astrodynamics, i.e., orbital mechanics, and aircraft structures. It surprised me when Jim Williams asked me to teach the structures class, but they were short a faculty member in that area. Jim explained that because I had so much experience in structures, he'd appreciate it if I'd agree to help out. They planned to hire another professor the next year to cover those courses. I was fine with his request, but I was more excited about teaching astrodynamics than I was about aircraft structures.

My new office was rectangular, with windows at the far end opposite the door, extending from mid-wall to the ceiling. The view

from my office was a sidewalk and the back of Ramsay Hall, which
housed the College of Engineering offices. The gray government-
issued furnishings in the office were old. My desk was on the right wall
and a similar one held my desktop computer on the left side behind
my desk. Two gray metal bookcases were next to my computer. They
painted the plaster walls tan, which were peeling near the windows
from the dampness, and the floors were green tile. Brown and aged
fluorescent light fixtures hung from the ceiling and lit the room well.
My first office as a professor was old, worn, and very used, but I liked
it better than any other I had during my career as an engineer.

With two weeks to prepare before classes started, I got busy
making up my course syllabi and lecture notes, and everything else
I was going to need. Like the ones I'd taught at UT and ACC, I was
in charge of all aspects of my courses. Jim promised nobody would
interfere with the way I wanted to teach or how I conducted my classes,
nor would anyone tell me how I should grade. In the classroom, I was
the boss, something I expected to be the case but also appreciated.

It didn't take long to find out that preparing for two courses took
most of my time. I wouldn't accept not being an excellent teacher, so I
was going to do whatever was necessary to be one. Since I experienced
many poor teachers in my life that came to class unprepared and
offered little to the students, I promised myself that would not be me.
It was important to me to excel at being a professor, and it was a lot
harder than being an engineer.

My time working at UT and ACC helped me to establish
a teaching philosophy and style. I used the common authority, or
lecture style, when I taught. And when I asked questions to the class,
I allowed any student to answer instead of selecting random students
and putting them on the spot. Of course, I always welcomed questions
about the material throughout my lectures.

I wanted my classes to be informal so nobody would hesitate to
take part in the discussions. Although I was a demanding professor,
I believed I was a fair one. My intention was to teach in a way that
if anybody didn't learn; it was his or her fault, not mine. I had high
expectations, and I needed to convey that early in the course. I hoped
to be a teacher that my students could trust and turn to for guidance

about anything. My teaching talent was the ability to recognize the important topics and simplify difficult ones and explain them so everyone could understand. If I continued doing that, I could offer a lot to students and help them pursue their dreams of becoming engineers.

When the first day of classes arrived, I couldn't wait to get started and meet everyone. It was a very exciting time. When I walked into my first astrodynamics class, it represented the end of a very long and winding road for me. There were about twenty enthusiastic students, all seniors, eager to learn more about space. It enthused me to provide that knowledge.

I intended my classes to be tough; I assigned a lot of work, and I expected everyone to keep up. Most of them did, but some couldn't or wouldn't. I learned how to differentiate between students who were trying but having trouble grasping the material from those who were just uninterested. Although, if they couldn't understand it, I wanted to do whatever I could to help them learn. I had little patience with lazy students though, because I was never one. They were wasting my time and theirs if they didn't want to do the work. I always tried to challenge everyone to perform the best they could, but they needed to try.

Most of the students at AU were from Alabama, and only a few of them came from strong academic programs in high school. I believed the top students in my classes were as good as the top ones at UT or any other university in the country. But the lower end of the talent was below that at the better schools. Many unique challenges came with teaching at AU. I couldn't lecture to A students and let the poor ones get passed by, nor could I teach to the lower end students and lose the interest of the high end ones. I discovered I had to teach to the B students, pulling the poor ones along with the class but still challenging the best students to keep them from getting bored. That plan worked fine for me. Although there were some, even at the junior and senior level, that should have been in different majors. Many were studying engineering for the wrong reasons: either their parents wanted them to, or their guidance counselors steered them in that direction because they did well in math in high school. As a result, some of them weren't very interested in engineering, weren't getting good grades, and needed to find another path. If they were not learning as much as they could, graduating might not be worth it, and some of them would be unemployable when they left AU.

It turned out that my very first astrodynamics class had many high-end senior students. It was one of the best I had at AU because of their ability and enthusiasm. That made it fun, and it was much easier to teach than some of my later classes. My class on structures wasn't as good, and I'm not sure why. Perhaps it was because they were juniors and less mature, or maybe it was because I didn't have as much enthusiasm for teaching structures. I still had excellent students, but more poor ones.

I remember one student in particular who thought he would try to show up the new professor by acting like a know-it-all and showing off his arrogance. Well, he didn't know as much as he thought, and his continued distractions impinged on the learning experience of the rest of the class. I already knew how to deal with disruptive students, and I could handle this one too. Since he thought he knew so much, I raised my expectations for him and he couldn't measure up. He may have wished he hadn't been such a jackass, as his grades didn't turn out to be as high as he expected. He even apologized to me months later for his inappropriate behavior. Over the years, that student type was the rare exception rather than the rule. Most were from the South and taught to respect their teachers. They always addressed me as Doctor or Professor. I had very few problems with students throughout my career. Except for a few outliers, it was a pleasure to have most of them in class.

One way I hoped to help establish a relaxed class atmosphere was to not wear a necktie. I never did at UT or ACC, and I didn't plan to wear one at AU either. I always wore slacks and a shirt, but not a tie. When I arrived in the department, every other professor wore a necktie, and some even dressed in sport coats or suits. I thought that set too formal of an atmosphere for my taste. I was the only teacher who didn't wear neckties to class when I arrived. Sometimes I'd just wear jeans and a polo shirt. Being the only one not to dress up lasted quite a while, but nobody ever said anything to me about how I dressed. Over the years, and as they hired more new faculty, fewer and fewer professors wore ties. By the time I retired, it was unusual to see anyone wearing a tie to teach.

Every faculty member in the College of Engineering had to do research and perform service or outreach, besides teaching classes. The university's mission was defined as teaching, research, and service/outreach. I knew building a research program was important and that it would not be easy or fast. I also knew that getting tenure at a major university depended on it. A typical professor's assignment was 45% teaching, 45% research, and 10% service, which translates to eighteen hours per week of teaching, eighteen hours performing research, and four hours of service. The service portion comprised serving on department, college, and university committees, advising students, or working with student groups, things I thought I'd also enjoy doing.

What I didn't count on, being the first faculty member hired in several years, was that I would inherit a lot of assignments immediately upon my arrival. A few older professors were waiting for the new guy to show-up so they could unload some of their service responsibilities on him. I understood it, but it still surprised me.

A couple of weeks into my first quarter as a professor, I inherited being the Graduate Program Officer, who managed the graduate students and their academic programs, and the advisor to the local student chapter of the American Institute of Aeronautics and Astronautics (AIAA). Plus, I became a member of several departmental and college committees. It seemed like I was spending all my time and energy teaching and preparing to teach, then an avalanche of additional responsibilities hit me. Not to mention planning how to build a research program. It was quite overwhelming and something I didn't count on. It was all part of the job, as I found out. I just didn't expect to get clobbered with so much work so soon.

Most professors only receive a salary during the nine-month academic year, which was my situation. Any summer pay must come from other sources. Sometimes there was teaching available during the summer, but not always. Many faculty members got paid from their research contract, while others went to work off-campus, e.g., in industry or government labs, for the summer months. Very few professors took the summers off altogether. Those with families needed to have a steady income. In that regard, building a research program was a way of helping to ensure you'd have a paycheck year-round. I felt I had little time for doing that. My top priority was teaching and what I loved the most. I wanted to do it well, so I put most of my energy into that and tried to carve out pieces of my time for those other activities. It wasn't easy, at least not in the beginning. I ended up spending about 80% of my effort on my classes and about 20% on research and service. I also worked at home nights and weekends to accomplish what I needed to get done. The time I spent working at home, however, didn't figure into the percentages of my work assignment in the department.

It didn't take long until I found I loved my job and couldn't wait to get to my office each morning. I even hated to leave in the afternoon because I wanted to keep working. If I had my choice, I'd have spent all my time teaching, but I didn't have that option. My days were very busy with many responsibilities besides teaching. It seems there were always committee meetings to attend, students to advise, and research contacts to cultivate.

The best thing about being a professor was the flexibility it offered. I had to meet my classes and satisfy my other obligations, but I was free to manage the rest of my time as I saw fit. Such flexibility allowed me drive the boys to school each morning, then Chris would pick them up in the afternoons. I also played noontime basketball with other faculty members two days per week, which was the same game that Mac Cutchins folded into my job interview. He and I went over to the gym together and often played with or against each other in those games. Although, when we were on the same team, I no longer felt compelled to always pass him the ball for him to shoot. I was still a pretty good shooter myself, and I already had the job. It was fun and great for getting some scheduled exercise.

I spent an enormous amount of time preparing for my lectures because I wanted to be the best teacher I could be. When I wasn't teaching, getting ready to teach, making up assignments and exams, grading, or attending meetings, I worked on establishing research contacts throughout the country within the orbital mechanics community. That meant writing letters or making a lot of cold calls to agencies to make connections and try to get research funding. Those agencies included NASA, the Air Force, the Army, the Navy, the National Science Foundation (NSF), and others. I also made many trips to Huntsville to meet and talk with individuals both inside and outside the government organizations there. There were a plethora of space and defense contractors there that could help me. Most of my trips to Huntsville were with John Cochran, who introduced me to many of his technical contacts in the area. Traveling with John was always fun.

Getting research money was something that didn't come easy. I wasn't good at selling my work, or myself, which is what a professor had to do to achieve success in obtaining funding. Research and writing papers for conferences and journals was enjoyable, but finding money to fund my research was difficult and less fun for me than teaching. I knew that was my weakness as a professor. The most rewarding part to me was standing in front of a room full of students eager to learn.

The first journal article I prepared for publication summarized my dissertation. Dr. Tapley was my co-author, which is the customary way to publish a dissertation, and we submitted it to the journal, *Celestial Mechanics.*

As my first quarter sped by, I learned the ropes of being a professor and my teacher evaluations from the students were outstanding. My performance pleased me very much, and I enjoyed it more than I could say.

Not long after I started at Auburn I got a call from my friend at Sverdrup who tried to hire me when I graduated from UT. He wanted to give me a small consulting contract to help on some of their work, which I gladly accepted. It required me to make a few visits down to Stennis Space Center, which I enjoyed since I always made it a point to visit nearby New Orleans during those trips.

Chris applied for admission to the Auburn pharmacy school in the fall quarter for the incoming class beginning in the spring quarter. She was nervous about being admitted, even though she had outstanding credentials. When they sent out decision letters in early December, we were both anxious to hear about her acceptance. But she didn't receive any notification at all. The days passed, then a week, then a second week, and there was still no word. Since the letters only had to travel across town, she should have heard after a few days. She didn't, so we became very nervous. One evening, Chris needed to call Maryanne Campagna about another matter. Maryanne was the friend from church whose husband, Keith, was a professor at the pharmacy school. When Chris called their house, Keith answered the phone.

She asked to speak to Maryanne, and Keith said, "Okay, I'll go get her. And congratulations on being accepted into pharmacy school!" He could tell hearing that news surprised Chris. When he realized she hadn't received word yet, he laughed and said, "Oh, well, you didn't hear that from me." And that's how Chris found out they had accepted her for the spring quarter class. We were both thrilled at the news! A few days later, she received her official letter, but Keith saved a good bit of anxiety. Keith and Maryanne became wonderful friends to us in the ensuing years.

When the winter quarter was ready to begin, they assigned me two structures classes to teach and no astrodynamics class, which aggravated me. When I received my assignment, I went to speak with Jim Williams to express my displeasure. He understood my unhappiness and explained the reason. Since he needed someone to cover structures again during the winter quarter, and since they scheduled no astrodynamics, he assigned the two structures classes to me. I again clarified with him I came to Auburn to teach orbital mechanics, not structures. Jim assured me that was the case and the reason they hired me. After our discussion we agreed on my teaching one structures class and one in dynamics, a class I'd expected to teach anyhow, which was fine with me. They hired a new structures professor before the next academic year, and I didn't have to teach those courses ever again. Steve Gross joined our faculty in 1988 and became a trusted friend and one of the best colleagues I've ever had.

Since quarters were only ten weeks long, as compared to fifteen for semesters, they always seem to speed by. Before I knew it, the spring quarter had arrived, and I was back teaching astrodynamics, this time the second course required for undergraduates. I also created some graduate classes in orbital mechanics and estimation theory, my specialty. I patterned them after the ones I had at UT because they didn't exist at AU before my arrival. It was very satisfying to get to help design a new graduate curriculum.

It was a tradition in the department that each spring the AIAA student chapter held a banquet for the members, the faculty, and their spouses or significant others. These banquets comprised an enjoyable meal and some entertainment, which often included a roast of each professor. They also gave out awards to students and professors, as voted by their members. It surprised and humbled me when I was selected as the winner of the Outstanding Faculty Member award in my first year. It was a great honor to receive recognition for doing something I loved so much. I felt that all the hard work and the long road I took were worth it. I enjoyed connecting with the students and playing a role in their learning experience at Auburn. It was a wonderful and satisfying night for me.

A new tradition I started that helped the AIAA raise money was a student-faculty basketball game at the recreation center. But since very few of our professors played, we drafted a few from other departments and also used some of our graduate students on our team. The faculty members from my department who played with me were Mac Cutchins, John Cochran, and Butch Foster. It was fun to play against the students because we kept the games competitive. Our record after six years of games was three wins and three losses. The problem was that the students were always 21-22 years old, and the faculty members weren't, so we discontinued the contests when we got too old to compete. Fortunately, nobody ever got injured playing. Those games were fun, and the money we raised helped pay for the student banquet.

I flew back to Austin in May 1988 to attend my graduation. It was a day full of events, which included three separate ceremonies: one each for the college, the Graduate School, and for the university. The university ceremony was outside in the evening beneath the Texas Memorial Tower. The tower was lit in orange lights and we were each hooded on the front steps of the tower at the end of the sprawling tree-lined lawn. It was a beautiful night and a remarkable ceremony, commemorating all our hard work. And I graduated with a few of my friends. One of my more competitive classmates was there who always claimed she'd graduate before me but didn't since I finished the summer before she did in the spring. As we were standing in line getting ready to step onto the stage to be hooded, she jumped in front of me and snickered, "I told you I'd graduate before you!" I believe I may have responded by calling her a 'witch', or something similar, but I can't be sure. It was a fun and memorable experience for all of us.

As I mentioned, teaching wasn't often available in the summer term since they offered so few classes, and I didn't have research funding to provide me with a salary. In my original job offer, Jim Williams guaranteed me my summer salary for the first year, something common to help new faculty establish themselves. It gave me a few months to focus on developing my research program and lining up funding for future summers. That also included financial support for graduate students needed to build a research program. They only promised me one paid summer, so I had to figure out ways to generate income for the summers after my first year. That fact was the most disconcerting part of being as a professor and what I disliked the most.

Chris already started pharmacy school and would attend through the summers in order to graduate in two-and-a-half years. The kids enrolled in some summer activities on campus so I could work in my office while they were busy. I worked at home when they weren't. We spent a lot of time together when Chris had class. Sometimes we played ping pong in the Foy Union basement, and other times it was Sjoelbak (Shulbok), i.e., Dutch shuffleboard, at a little restaurant off-campus. Corey and Darby loved to play that game and drink their Dr. Peppers while I sipped a beer and cooled off from the Alabama heat. It was a wonderful summer of hanging out together and bonding, which was another perk of the flexibility of being a professor.

The next year, the Air Force Office of Scientific Research awarded me a Summer Faculty Fellowship. That grant award required me to spend the summer at Eglin Air Force Base in Fort Walton Beach, Florida, on the coast of the Gulf of Mexico. It was a great opportunity, but I had to be away most of the summer since Eglin was a four-hour drive from Auburn. I didn't enjoy being away from my family for the summer, but they got to spend a few weeks with me at the beach. Working at Eglin was an enjoyable experience, and it helped me make important contacts. Little did I know that spending the summers away would become common practice for me in future years.

14

CHASING TENURE AND PROMOTION

During the next several years, I focused on doing the things necessary to get tenure. Any faculty member will tell you that the most important step in their career as an educator is getting tenure at their school. In higher education that means your position becomes permanent and you can't lose your job unless there's justifiable cause or extreme circumstances, such as financial exigency. It also guarantees a professor academic freedom, or the ability to teach without outside interference.

The problem with earning tenure at most universities is that the requirements are moving targets and institutions are unwilling to quantify those targets. In order to get tenure, one must excel in two of the three areas of teaching, research, and service/outreach. Often they include the notion of collegiality as a fourth area, which refers to cooperation between colleagues who share responsibility in an academic unit. Collegiality is also difficult to measure.

Faculty members seeking tenure are told when hired what they needed to do to earn tenure. They're told they needed to teach, develop a funded research program, publish the results of their research, and perform service or outreach for their department, college, and/or university. However, nobody would quantify those requirements as far as how much funding they had to get or how many articles they needed to publish to be tenure-worthy. At AU, a faculty member could apply for tenure after their fifth year of employment. If declined on the first attempt, they had one more chance after their sixth year. Failing a second time meant the university would end their employment after their seventh year, and there was no way around it. The best information about the requirements to achieve tenure was for a candidate to be aware of the achievements of professors who received tenure in recent years.

Seeking tenure was an arduous process, and should have been, because it guaranteed a professor a job for life. The procedure began with a faculty member creating a dossier of their qualifications, which was a detailed summary of everything they'd done since being hired. Then, the tenured members in the candidate's home department assessed the package of credentials and voted yes or no for tenure. If the vote was positive, they sent one's package to a college committee to compare against other applications within engineering. If the college committee voted yes, they forwarded it on to a university committee for evaluation and comparison with others from across campus. An affirmative vote by that committee would then serve as a recommendation to the president, who would either approve or decline granting tenure. The process would stop if any committee voted no on an applicant, but it was still the candidate's prerogative whether to send their application forward to the next committee with a negative vote. However, in doing so, even though a candidate had nothing to lose, it was uncommon to receive tenure from the president under those circumstances.

Over the next several years, I geared my activities to get through the tenure process; I worked hard to develop a research program through extramural funding; I published in technical journals as much as I could; and I continued to teach the best I could. I also performed a great deal of service in my department, my college, and the university. It took an enormous amount of time to do those things, and I spent many nights and weekends working at home. But in doing that, I could also be at home with my family every evening and continued doing school drop-offs and pickups for both boys. I knew I still had to make up for the sacrifices they made when I was getting my doctorate.

Chris was attending pharmacy school just a few blocks from my office. We'd often have lunch together or, when she was working in the lab through lunch hour, I'd grab a bag of Krystal burgers and we'd eat in the lab. It was fun, and she did great in school, even while taking care of two young children and a busy husband. I did as much as I could to help, but nothing compared to her. She often stayed up late, or woke up very early, sometimes both, in order to get her work done. She succeeded and graduated in 1990 and won several outstanding student awards. I was very proud of her, and I don't know how she did it!

When it came time for Chris to find work, she got lucky. We both did! She could have found a job in Montgomery or Columbus, although that would have meant an hour commute each way. There weren't many local jobs, and she didn't want to commute far. However, after undertaking a student rotation at our local hospital, East Alabama Medical Center (EAMC), they hired her as a temporary replacement for a pharmacist who was a member of the National Guard and was deployed to serve in the Gulf War. However, when his deployment concluded, he'd get his job back, and Chris would have to find a new position elsewhere.

When the EAMC pharmacist returned from active duty, Chris's boss, Buddy Young, liked her work so much that he wanted to keep her on staff. So he went to the hospital administration and fought for more funding so he could create a new position just for her. Her job then became permanent because of his actions. We both appreciated Buddy's effort on her behalf, which made everyone's life in our family a lot easier.

Now the pressure was on me to make my job a permanent one. It was our original intention for me to stay in AU until I got tenured, and then look for a something in a more desirable location. It was easier to find a new faculty position after receiving tenure at one school, because a professor could receive tenure-on-hire at another institution, which was a major advantage. I knew it would be difficult to leave AU. I loved my job, Chris was now becoming established in her career, and Corey and Darby both liked school and were doing well. We all enjoyed living in Auburn, which was a wonderful and safe place for kids, so our plans changed.

I applied for tenure in the fall of 1992 after I completed five years as an Assistant Professor. I had five publications, great teacher evaluations, and I performed a lot of service. Although I was short on obtaining funding, having only received a few small grants and no large ones, although I had a prestigious one from the NASA JPL. Not knowing the target numbers, I wasn't sure if I met them or not. It seemed the least important measures of performance were the quality of your teaching and the amount of your service, which I felt were my strongest areas. They placed more weight upon a candidate's research record than anything else.

AU permitted faculty members to do outside consulting up to one day per week, which also counted towards tenure and promotion. I consulted a little over the years, but it wasn't something I sought or liked to do very much, although I had some listed in my credentials by that time in my career.

I believed I had a strong package in most areas, but I may have been short on the research side, so I thought it was unlikely I'd get tenure on my first try. I was right. I received an affirmative vote in my department and a mixed one in my college. The firm support from my departmental colleagues was very satisfying, and it pleased me to receive their endorsement, which was also a sign that I was collegial. It was my option if I wanted to send my package forward or not. After much deliberation, I sent it on to the university for consideration there, and I was unsuccessful. It wasn't unexpected, but I still felt bad. I received some good feedback regarding my shortcomings, and they encouraged me that the results would be different the next year if I kept doing what I'd been doing. One thing I was told was that candidates are often unsuccessful on their first attempt unless they were research superstars, which I wasn't. Although I believed I was one of the better teachers at Auburn. Then again, being an excellent teacher was not the most important quality of being a professor, at least not according to the administration. So I persevered and went back to work on improving my package.

One interesting event occurred before being turned down, which I feared may have hurt my chances, but ultimately didn't. I failed a student in my astrodynamics class because he didn't do the required work, learned little, and bombed most of the exams. I'd always try to give conscientious students the benefit of the doubt and curve final grades a bit to pick up the borderline cases. However, this guy's performance wasn't worthy of such consideration, so I failed him in the course. He wasn't happy about it and thought he should have passed. I disagreed, so he filed a grievance against me with the Student Academic Grievance Committee. He claimed I didn't treat him fairly by failing him. The committee would review his evidence and determine if the grievance had merit or not.

The grievance process was such that the student had to submit documentation to support his claim. This student wasn't aware that the faculty member named was asked to review and comment on the material the student submitted before the hearing. When I received his documentation to review, I found he falsified the documents by changing grades on his exams after I returned them to him. For example, when I wrote '59 - F' at the top of one exam, where 59 was his score out of 100 potential points, he changed it to read '59/60 - A'. He also altered his grades in several other places to make it appear he deserved to pass the course. I returned his package to the Grievance Committee, informing them of my findings. Then I asked them to please forward the material to the Academic Honesty Committee for review of his falsification of the documents he submitted. They did, and in a subsequent Honesty Committee hearing, found him guilty and suspended him from school for two quarters. He still didn't feel he deserved to fail, nor did he think he deserved a suspension. So he protested both AU and me for being 'unfair'. His protest comprised picketing at Toomer's Corner on the hottest summer day in July, wearing a sandwich board proclaiming his innocence. He also passed out fliers describing his plight. My colleagues thought it was all very amusing and joked with me about it for weeks afterward. I perceived the event may have hurt my chances for tenure, but both Jim Williams and the dean of engineering assured me it didn't. In fact, they commended me for upholding the academic standards of the university. I'm not sure when this student realized that, since I was the only one who taught astrodynamics, he'd have to retake the course from me if he ever hoped to graduate. I wished I could have seen his face when he learned that news. I knew this student worked part-time as a mechanic at a local car dealership, which sold the make of car that we owned. When our car needed servicing, I'd sign it in under a fake name so, if he worked on it, he wouldn't sabotage it somehow because of me.

During my sixth year, I worked even harder because I only had one more chance to get tenure, and I didn't want to fail. I published five more research articles in refereed journals and secured some additional funding. I also kept up my record of quality teaching and a lot of service. When I applied for the second time, I knew my credentials were much stronger than they were the previous year. I was proud of the package I assembled. I felt I had a decent chance of success this time. When my department colleagues reviewed it, they gave unanimous support to my application. Later, both the college and university committees agreed, and they awarded me tenure beginning in the fall of 1993. When they did, they also promoted me to Associate Professor. Both were enormous achievements for me, and a great honor at such a fine institution as AU. It was a major milestone in my career, as it is with anyone in academia.

After becoming a tenured professor, I looked at a few jobs at other institutions, although I didn't think there were any better ones out there for me. Plus, Chris had a great job at EAMC, and the boys enjoyed living in Auburn. That would have been a lot to give up. There wasn't anything I disliked, except maybe living in a small town around so many conservatives and religious people, but I could handle that. One position that came open for which I applied was one in my old department at UT. I think we all would have enjoyed returning to Austin. Although, it was still very difficult to get hired there, having graduated from the same program. I'm a firm believer that universities should hire faculty from different places to create a broader educational experience for their students. Although I applied anyway to satisfy myself, I wasn't successful. Being unsuccessful was best for us all in the long run. There would have been many uncertainties giving up what we had in Alabama to move back to Texas. But we didn't have to make that decision. After that brief flirtation, we stayed in Auburn, and looking back, it was the right thing to do.

The next step in the ladder of higher education to climb was promotion to Professor, i.e., full professor. The general rule was that a faculty member had to work at least ten years before becoming eligible. I intended that my effort would focus on building my credentials for that possibility when the time was appropriate.

As unclear as the requirements were for being awarded tenure and promotion, they were even more vague for promotion to Professor. Targets moved fast and quantifying the standards was something nobody would, or could, do with much certainty. The general guideline was that you had to have established a national reputation through your research program to get promoted. Once again, both teaching and service were of lesser importance than research and publications. The old saying, 'publish or perish' was true at any major research institution, and especially true at the full professor level.

I didn't feel my credentials were strong enough until after my twelfth year at AU. By then I had twenty publications and received a large research grant from the U.S. Air Force. Considering my national and international professional activity and connections, I believed I had established a national reputation, so I felt confident of my success. In addition, I'd won several more teaching awards and checked off many other boxes necessary in the service and collegiality areas.

In the fall of 1999, I submitted my package for consideration of promotion to Professor. I thought my credentials were comparable to other applicants, even though I had less extramural funding than some others. But I was better in teaching and service. Since there weren't any limitations on how many times a person could apply for promotion, I had nothing to lose by trying.

I received positive support from my department colleagues, but the college only gave me mixed support. The process was that the dean would report those votes to the university committee in a letter in which he'd either recommend supporting my application or not. If the dean didn't support the candidate, he must provide reasons for not doing so.

When my package reached the university, even though I had some support there, I got a negative vote and didn't get promoted. The provost informed me of the decision and explained the reasons. The major reason was because of the lack of support from my dean.

I believed we had a dean who was inept and should never have held the position. His actions in my case confirmed my opinion. In the letter he wrote about me, he claimed I wasn't worthy of promotion because I hadn't brought in enough extramural funding to have established a national reputation. However, the AU Faculty Handbook sets the rules for promotion. It stated that a candidate's publication record in refereed journals determined national reputation and not research dollars. Upon learning the details of his letter, I discussed the matter with the AU Provost, who was the Chair of the University Tenure and Promotion Committee, in a private meeting. During our conversation, he told me he thought I had an excellent case to appeal the university's decision based upon the dean's erroneous reasons, and he urged me to do just that.

The Faculty Handbook also defined the appeal process, and I followed it to the tee. I wrote a letter citing my reasons for appealing, which I based upon the fact that the dean was incorrect in his assessment of my national reputation. He didn't understand the rules. I made a powerful case for myself, and the university committee agreed and granted my appeal. The president promoted me to Professor beginning in the fall of 2000. I thought it was another tremendous accomplishment for an overachiever!

After being promoted, I wanted to thank the person I felt was most responsible for leading me to the path I'd chosen, Professor Gencsoy. I'd heard he retired to Florida years before, and I didn't know how to reach him. So I phoned my old department at WVU and they provided me with his address in Ft. Lauderdale. I wrote him a letter to thank him for everything he did for me, and inspiring me to want to teach.

A week after sending that letter, I received a phone call in my office one afternoon.

When I answered I heard a somewhat familiar, "Is this David Chi-chi?" Professor Gencsoy called to thank me for writing such a pleasant letter and that he appreciated me doing so. He told me he framed my letter to hang on the wall in his home so his grandchildren would know he was important once. I enjoyed speaking with him again after so many years. It saddened me to hear of Professor Gencsoy's passing in 2007 at age 82.

Becoming a full professor put me in an excellent place to flirt with changing jobs again. I contemplated moving up to be a department head somewhere, and I looked for such a position. I interviewed and received an offer to become the Head of the Aerospace Engineering Department at Embry-Riddle Aeronautical University (ERAU) in Daytona Beach, Florida. It was a great location and seemed like it would be a good stepping-stone for me to move into higher education administration later. That was until I met with the provost at ERAU during my interview. I asked him about the number of students in their program, and his response shocked me.

The provost described how the enrollment in aerospace engineering was booming and they had too many students to handle. He said their enrollment 'strategy' was to admit an excessive number of students, knowing they couldn't teach them all. Then once they arrived on campus, try to get them to switch into another engineering program where the enrollments were lower. It astounded me that a university administrator would act in such an unprofessional way, which I felt it was deceitful and unethical. His philosophy sickened me, and I lost all interest in working at Embry-Riddle. Of course, I turned down the offer and stayed at AU once again.

In the late 1990s, a couple of years before I came up for promotion to professor, Chris began an online Doctor of Pharmacy degree program through UF. She and a few of her work friends enrolled together, but they only had to travel to Florida once per semester. She worked very hard for three years and in December 2002 graduated with her doctorate. I was very proud of her for such a monumental accomplishment! She amazed me with what she'd done yet again. After that, every time somebody called our house and wanted to speak to Dr. Cicci, we had to ask which one they wanted.

When the kids were growing up, my infatuation with colleges continued. Anytime we took a vacation, we'd have a look at nearby universities whenever we could. I forced my family to visit many schools through the years, although I think our kids eventually learned to enjoy it. Corey was a huge sports fan and wanted to see the football stadiums and basketball arenas on every campus we visited. It was great fun when they were getting ready to go to college. We did family 'college tours' to look at the schools on their lists before they decided where to attend. We visited universities all across the country, from Massachusetts to California and from Florida to Washington, and throughout the South and Midwest. I told them they could go anywhere they wanted, but there were five schools they couldn't attend, based on my biases. That list included Pitt, Penn State, Alabama, Texas A&M, and Miami. But they didn't like any of those schools anyhow.

By the time the boys started high school, they both made lists of potential colleges and put them on the refrigerator door with magnets. It was a long process narrowing down that list. Both chose schools with great academic programs and beautiful campuses. Corey attended the University of North Carolina at Chapel Hill (UNC), and Darby picked Indiana University Bloomington (IU). Chris and I spent a lot of our time at both institutions during their college days, and we developed a special affection for those schools too. Corey and Darby were both double majors that included theater, and were each in two plays every semester. We never missed a show, so we made many trips to Chapel Hill and Bloomington. Those were all such great trips!

15

MAKING IT FUN
WHENEVER I COULD

I tried to make my classes enjoyable, or at least provide some lightheartedness while covering an abundance of tough material. To do so, I had to be friendly, informal, and show my sense of humor as much as possible. It was important for the students to feel at ease, which was the first step in creating an effective learning environment. I thought the key to being an excellent teacher was making everyone feel comfortable enough to promote interaction and participation. That wasn't always easy to do, but it was my goal. Every class had a distinct personality, but sometimes it was difficult to find and connect with. I believed if I did that, everyone could have a successful learning experience. Sometimes I couldn't connect at all, but that was a rarity. Those classes were harder to teach and less fun than the ones where I connected with students from the beginning. Sometimes a single outgoing student could carry everybody through the entire semester. However, the more talkative students there were in class, the more fun we all had.

I started every period by asking how everyone was doing and chatting for a few minutes. We'd discuss what was going on with them, the latest or upcoming football game, or any current and/or important topic that may have been on their minds. Then I'd ask if anybody had questions about anything. Many students were forthcoming and conversational, although not everyone. When I began lecturing, I spoke from my notes and wrote on the chalkboard. I wrote a lot of notes, and talked fast, while stopping to explain or to expand on certain topics or ones about which someone had questions. When I spoke between writing on the board, I often paced back and forth and rolled chalk between my hands. Students teased me a lot about that habit of mine.

Most of the things I put on the chalkboard were drawings, equations, and derivations. I asked for questions throughout my lectures in case anyone didn't understand something or I hadn't explained it clearly. Students understanding the hard material and all the formulas was the key to them doing well. On examinations I tried to emphasize the most important topics and not the minute, unimportant details, much like I did as an undergraduate myself. My drawings were neat and multi-colored, reminiscent of Professor Gencsoy's sketches at WVU. When I ran out of space on the board, I'd sometimes extend my drawing onto the white cement block walls. Those actions always drew laughter from the students and consternation from the janitorial staff.

Some days I felt the class needed a break from the normal fire hose of information. On those days, instead of lecturing I'd chat with them the entire period, talking about anything they wanted to discuss. I think they appreciated the occasional break from being lectured to and enjoyed asking questions that weren't class-related. Most of their inquiries were about finding jobs and having careers as engineers. My having nine years of professional experience was very helpful in answering those questions and giving them advice. Sometimes I'd just tell jokes and stories the whole time to lighten the atmosphere.

I tried to be accessible outside class as well and I spent many hours chatting with students in my office, not just about school, but also about life issues. I wanted them to feel comfortable enough that they could come to me if they had problems, or when they were dealing with some personal matters they needed to discuss with somebody. Not all students would do that, but there were often a few who would. Sometimes our discussions dealt with social matters, and once in a while, even romantic ones, as if I knew anything about that. One student in particular would come by and tell me how she was far from home and lonely and wanted to find someone to date. I told her over and over that she'll meet a great guy soon and to just be patient. She cried a time or two while talking with me, the reason I always kept a box of tissues handy. One day she came in very excited to tell me she met a nice guy, and he asked her to go out the coming weekend. They ended up dating for quite a while, and it pleased me to see her so happy. She continued to let me know how it was going with him. Then one afternoon she showed up with tears in her eyes.

When I asked her what was wrong, she said, "You'll never believe what he did."

I didn't know what she might tell me and all I could say was, "Oh no, what?"

She answered, "Well, the other night we went out, then after, he took me down to the football stadium and nobody else was around. We walked out onto the field and then he asked me to marry him!" Then she cried more. It thrilled me to hear that story and it was great to see her so excited, even through all the tears. They later married and raised a beautiful family together. I always thought I provided sound information to students about engineering, but giving romantic advice was never in my realm of expertise, although it worked out for her.

Except for exam days, most of my other class hours were lectures, and even though I did my best to make them interesting and light, they sometimes became monotonous for all of us. I tried to break that monotony by changing things up a bit. If I had a small class, every once in a while I'd find one of those portable chalkboards and have class outside on the lawn. It wasn't ideal, the chalkboard was too small, and I'd have to erase a lot, but it was a pleasant change from the classroom lectures and everyone enjoyed doing it. On nice days, they often asked if we could have class outside.

I gave three exams and a final exam in my undergraduate courses, although I rarely gave exams in my graduate courses. Most of my exams were problems to solve. Part of each exam also included general information questions, such as completion or matching exercises, or drawing or labeling sketches. I always allowed students to use a formula sheet so they wouldn't have to memorize the multitude of equations they might need. But my final exams in orbital mechanics differed from the regular ones. I'd make up a mission where the students would have to solve a series of related problems in order to complete it successfully. The missions were often about a UFO crash in Roswell, New Mexico, traveling to faraway planets, completing the refueling of spy satellites, or some other science fiction type of problem. Many students found them fun and enjoyed the experience. I learned during my career that a student's performance on the final seldom changed the grade they had before taking it. Once in a while, their grades improved, but they rarely got worse.

The biggest reaction I ever got from students in class was each semester when I returned their first graded exam. Before calling their name for them to walk up and collect their individual papers, I'd always walk to the board and write the average score for the test and how many students earned each letter grade. They never knew what to expect on that first exam, so I'd trick them and write: A: 0 (meaning nobody got an A), B: 0, C: 1. After I wrote each line, I'd hear more and more gasps groans as everybody thought they totally bombed the test.

Then I'd turn around to see their shocked faces before turning back to the board and erasing those numbers and saying, "Just joking…"

The laughs of relief were almost raucous, and it broke their tension and lightened the mood. In actuality, most of the grades on my exams were As and Bs and the averages were usually in the 80s.

There were a few years when I'd assign what I called a 'Scavenger Hunt'. I created a long list of obscure questions, dealing with orbital mechanics, mathematics, physics, or scientific history that were educational but not common knowledge. Some weren't easy to answer (before Google searches) and others were very hard. A few answers could only be found in the library. Then I'd break the class up into teams, each with four-six members, and have a contest pitting the teams against each other. I'd award points for the assignment individually and how they did in the team competition. It was fun, and most of them learned a lot.

I think many students felt I was more of a regular guy than someone in authority. Even though I'd joke with them about how I was holding their futures in my hands. A lot of that came from our class discussions and my hosting those AIAA picnics each year. Sometimes they'd try extra hard to get on my good side. One who knew I liked to drink beer once covertly left a six-pack outside my office door. He confessed later, but didn't receive any special consideration in class. He was an excellent student though, and didn't need help. But I thanked him and drank the beer at home.

Students viewing me as a normal guy lightened up my classes and I believe made me more credible to them. As a result, they sometimes listened to guidance from me rather than from others, even their parents.

One of the funniest things that ever happened in my classroom occurred only a few years into my time at Auburn. I had an outstanding student who was a senior in his last quarter before graduating. But he had a severe case of senior-itis and was failing my class, which he had to pass in order to graduate. Late in the term, he realized his plight and came to my office to discuss his situation. I looked at his grades and told him he had a solid F, and that he needed to get an A on the final exam to pass the course. They scheduled the exam just a couple of days before the end of the semester and graduation day. When he walked in, he took a seat at the last desk in the row in front of where I sat during exams, and I couldn't see him very well. Before anyone else had finished, I heard a rustling noise coming from his direction, but thought nothing about it. I could hear him taking something out of his backpack, but I couldn't tell what he was doing. A few moments later, he stood up and walked up to turn in his completed exam wearing his cap and gown, knowing he did well enough to pass and graduate! The other students must have known of his situation, as they all stopped working and applauded him as he left the classroom. It was hilarious! He aced the final and graduated, which I expected him to do!

Occasionally a student would become too comfortable with my easygoing demeanor. One evening when I was at home the phone rang. It was a student in my class who was working on his homework assignment that was due the next day. The problem he was working required him to use the mass of the moon for the calculations. But rather than look it up in his textbook, he phoned me and asked me to give him the number. That plan didn't work out well for him, and I had to perform an attitude adjustment. I didn't give him the value of the mass of the moon, nor did he ever call my house again to ask silly questions.

I taught some of my graduate courses as a video outreach class. They held those classes in a studio and recorded the lectures onto DVDs, then sent them to the off-campus students to watch at their convenience. The classrooms had whiteboards rather than chalkboards, and we used erasable markers instead of chalk. They also equipped those rooms with overhead projector/camera systems where a professor could also write class notes on sheets of paper using a permanent marker. One fateful day, I walked into the classroom and began lecturing and writing on the whiteboard. However, I inadvertently grabbed a permanent marker rather than an erasable one. I didn't know what I'd done until I filled up the board and went to erase. Once I realized my huge mistake, all I could think was, 'Oh no! What do I do now?' I couldn't hide from either the on-campus students present or the student cameraman who was recording my lecture. Not being able to fix the problem, I stopped lecturing and asked the cameraman to call the office to see if somebody could help. A few minutes later, a very annoyed office assistant came in with a bottle of marker-remover and a rag and slowly cleaned off the whiteboard while I stood nearby in silence. As she did this, she scolded me the entire time in front of the students. I apologized several times and thanked her for helping me through an embarrassing situation, although she became more annoyed with me as the board got cleaner. The worst part was that the cameraman recorded the entire episode. I didn't know he did that until he sent me a copy of the recorded event in the mail a few days later. What a wise guy! I still have that DVD somewhere, but I haven't bothered to watch it to relive the experience. My wife enjoyed seeing it though.

I was teaching in that same classroom on the day of my fortieth birthday. Soon after I began lecturing, the door opened and Chris and a few of her friends walked in and interrupted class singing "Happy Birthday" to me. They even brought a cake to share with everyone. A different cameraman kept the camera rolling that time, and they gave me a copy of that recording too. They had a lot of funny cameramen working in their studio!

Chris's friends who came to my classroom were all wives of faculty members and were always cooking up some scheme, usually to embarrass their husbands somehow. One Valentine's Day, they played a trick on the guys. They sent us each an anonymous valentine in the campus mail so they could see which husbands would tell their spouses about receiving it and which ones wouldn't. Funny, right? It turned out that about half of them told their wives and half didn't mention it, thinking it was just some student prank. I wasn't one who confessed to receiving it because I knew it had to be a joke. I even mentioned the mystery to my class after I received the valentine. What made it funny was that a week before, there was some controversy on-campus regarding incidents involving the gay and lesbian student organization. When we discussed it before a lecture one day, I was clear to express my support for the group when it happened.

So when the valentine mystery arose, I asked the class if anybody wanted to admit sending me the card. I tried to make it into a joke and said, "When I received it, my first thought was that one of you ladies wanted some extra points. Then when I reflected on our discussion about the gay and lesbian group, it hit me that perhaps one of you guys might have misinterpreted my support for the organization." That brought a huge laugh, and that's as far as it went. It wasn't until days later that our wives admitted their practical joke, and, of course, those of us who didn't confess to receiving the card got in trouble. Funny women too!

My stories of classroom recordings bring me to our friend Mike Tuggle. Mike attended the University of Georgia (UGA) with my niece Marnie in the early 1990s and studied broadcast journalism. Marnie always brought Mike and a few of her other friends to Auburn for the Georgia football games during their time in college. They all camped out on our living room floor for those weekends. It was great fun having them there. Mike used to call me 'Uncle Dave' like Marnie did. In fact, when Marnie got married years later, Mike served as her man of honor instead of her having a maid of honor for her wedding. After graduating from UGA, Mike took a job as a reporter for WTVM-TV in Columbus, Georgia, and covered the East Alabama area, which included Auburn. When Mike moved to Auburn for his new job, he lived with us in our spare bedroom for several months until he could find an apartment and get settled. He and his family were always very appreciative of us taking him in for that short time. And Corey and Darby both loved having him stay at our home. He was energetic and fun to have around. It was like Chris and I had a third son.

When there were slow news days, Mike had to generate ideas for stories so that he'd have one for the evening broadcast. When he was desperate, he'd call and say, "Uncle Dave, I need something for tonight's news. Can I come to your classroom and do a story about your class?"

I was always happy to help, and I'd answer, "Sure Mike, come and do any kind of story you want." My class enjoyed having Mike and his camera visit and seeing themselves on the evening news.

One Thanksgiving Mike even did a feature from our kitchen comparing the holiday meal at our house to one people had at local restaurants. It was all fun. Mike later became newscaster in Montgomery and then a national correspondent for ABC News covering the Gulf War. He now lives in Los Angeles with his wife, who's a CNN Senior Correspondent, and their two children. The funny thing is that when Darby moved to LA a few years ago, he ended up living very close to Mike and his family. They helped Darby get settled, still socialize together often, and have served as Darby's California parents in our absence. We meet up with them every trip we take to LA. I still have those videos he made in my class, including the one showing our Thanksgiving dinner.

Although there weren't many summer classes taught in my department, I'd sometimes get to teach one or two if funding was available. When I did, I'd teach them in an even more laid-back style than I did during the academic year. Since I still spent a lot of the summer with the boys after Chris began working full time, they'd sometimes come to campus with me. Occasionally, Corey would even sit in my class while I taught. When he did, I'd often play a trick on my students. In my office beforehand, I'd tell Corey that I was going to ask the class a very hard question, one I knew nobody in class could answer. Then I gave him the answer and told him to raise his hand and answer the question when I asked it.

I'd say to my class, "Okay, who can answer this question?" I asked them the hard question, and nobody replied, as I suspected. Then Corey would put up his hand and give the correct answer. It embarrassed my class that my son answered it and they couldn't. It took them quite a while to realize that I staged those events. Some students in those classes still remind me of how I tricked them when I see them now.

One of my most rewarding experiences at Auburn came when I became the Director of the Minority Introduction to Engineering (MITE) Program. MITE was a summer program that brought rising high school senior minority students to campus to introduce them to careers in engineering and science. The kids were at AU for a week at a time and spent their days taking introductory classes and hearing about different careers, along with other social and athletic activities. They stayed in the dorms and got a brief taste of college life. There were three separate groups of students each year spread out over the summer. As Director, I'd select the students to attend, plan and oversee many of their activities during the week, and teach them some classes in computer programming. It was a wonderful and successful program and a significant benefit to minority high school students. They learned about career opportunities in math, science, and engineering for the first time. Many of the students that attended our MITE program attended Auburn and other universities. I was proud to have served as the MITE Program Director for six years. That ended when the same Dean of Engineering that wrongfully denied my promotion to full professor canceled MITE in 2000.

I sometimes had to be harsh in my advice to students. Most of the time, it was for their own good. I developed an outstanding perception of what they were up to by either their performance or their attitudes. Some tried to get by doing as little as possible, while others worked very hard to succeed. It was easy to teach bright students, but teaching the lazy ones was much more difficult. The most rewarding teaching came from reaching students who weren't the brightest but worked hard and succeeded. The worst experiences were trying to reach kids who were bright enough but just didn't care about learning. Many of those were wasting their time and someone's money. I never thought it was worth it for them to muddle through four years in a rigorous curriculum, only to graduate with a low GPA and be unemployable.

One such student was in ROTC and had a guaranteed job with his future already planned out. He took my class in his last semester before graduation and was not doing well. He didn't care to do the work required, thinking the material was unimportant to him for his job in the military. After he failed my final exam, he knew he was going to get an F in the course. He came to my office groveling for a D so he could graduate, get commissioned into the Air Force, and begin his career a few weeks later. Failing wouldn't allow him to graduate, and could cause him to lose his commission, and he'd then be forced to enter the military as an enlisted airman rather than an officer. As he groveled in tears before me, I told him that perhaps he should have thought about the consequences if he failed. He apologized and asked what he could do to pass my course. I reluctantly agreed to allow him to take a second final exam, and if he passed that one, I'd pass him for the semester. That was something I seldom did, but some other things he had done at Auburn warranted that special consideration.

After taking the second final, he came to find out the results. It turned out that he squeaked by. When I told him he would graduate, he thanked me over and over, knowing that it would have ruined his life if I hadn't given him a second chance. Before he left, I felt compelled to give him some parting advice that may help him in future years.

I said, "When you go into the Air Force, try to keep your head out of your ass, otherwise you could really screw up your life. Everybody won't give you a do-over like I did." I don't know if he took my advice or not.

I'm happy to report is that, to the best of my knowledge, I only ever went to class with my fly down once. The day I did, my very best student noticed it when I entered the room and walked up to me and whispered, "Dr. Cicci, your fly's down."

I replied, "Oh my, thanks for telling me. I'll give you some bonus points on today's quiz as a reward."

He replied, "No, I don't want any extra points." I did anyway, although he didn't need the points. But I very much appreciated his help in saving me from another embarrassing situation.

If I taught class with my zipper down any other days, nobody ever told me.

16

MY RESEARCH LIFE

Many describe the university mission of teaching, research, and service/outreach as the three-legged stool of academia. Some assume that a faculty member must excel at all three activities in order to have a successful career in higher education. To a certain degree, that is correct. But many view research as the most important leg of the stool. The thinking was that if faculty excelled in research, they could transfer that new knowledge to the classroom. That was true if the professor was an excellent teacher; if not, then that premise falls apart. In that regard, I always felt that teaching was the prominent leg, because without the ability to teach well, students wouldn't learn about the state-of-the-art research. Progressive thinkers believed that very few professors can excel in all three areas but should be excellent in one area and be above average in the other two. That viewpoint wasn't prevalent in my college until they named Chris Roberts as the dean of engineering. Dean Roberts understood people are better at different things, and only rare individuals excel at everything. His thinking resulted in stronger programs and more qualified faculty across the college.

It always made more sense to me for universities to establish separate research and teaching tracks for professors. Hiring the best of both would secure a well-rounded faculty. Having brilliant researchers who can't teach doesn't help students learn. And having outstanding teachers who didn't perform quality research wasn't a viable model to introduce new concepts into the classroom. It's my belief the best researchers must be at least acceptable teachers, and that skilled teachers should be decent researchers. Of course, everyone should take part in service or outreach and be collegial. Those activities are necessary in order to complete the university's mission and ensure the university functions effectively.

I considered myself to be an acceptable researcher, not a superstar like some. I believed I was more than adequate in performing research and publishing my work. My weakness was being able to get funding for my research. I was not as adept at doing that as many others. But there wasn't much money available for orbital mechanics research. My problem, to which I've already admitted, was not being a good enough of a salesperson to squeeze funding out of agencies. I got a little money at first, but doing so wasn't my strength or my ambition. It satisfied me to be an excellent teacher and an adequate researcher and perform great service. That was my idea for myself, and it was the assignment I preferred. I strived to make that formula work, which I did, but I was one of the lucky ones. Faculty members who'd like to build a similar career nowadays would fail because the 'publish or perish' world has become more of a 'get funding or perish' world. These days it would be better for someone who wanted to focus on teaching to work at a community or junior college. That, and online education, might be the only places to get to spend an entire career primarily teaching. If I were graduating with a Ph.D. now, I don't think I'd be interested in finding a tenure track faculty position. The expectations are too high and I wouldn't be able to concentrate on teaching like I did at AU.

When Dr. Nacozy at UT advised me to pick a subject that I loved for a dissertation topic, his reasoning was that by the time I finished, I'd hate it. That wasn't the case with me. I never moved from loving my topic to hating it. So after I became a professor, I sought to develop a research program in that same general area, known as estimation theory or orbit determination. It involved using observational data to improve the accuracy in determining the orbits of objects in space. Related areas were space vehicle guidance and control, spacecraft navigation, and satellite geodesy. All those subjects used the same tools: dynamical and mathematical modeling, numerical analysis, and statistics. I enjoyed the topic because while it encompassed the theoretical development of dynamical and mathematical models, the solutions were numerical. The work used the tools I learned from Dr. Greenspan at UTA and Dr. Tapley at UT, and I did it well. I found that it's a lot easier to be good at something you like than at something you don't!

With this in mind, I continued working on projects related to my dissertation subject, and I published five or six more journal articles on extensions of that work. I generated so much data during my time at UT that I didn't include as part of my project there, it was easy to extend that research to produce more important results. I enjoyed the topic, even after several more years of working on it.

I spent as much time as I could trying to establish connections within the orbital mechanics community to get extramural funding and build a research program. In my first few years, the Air Force Office of Scientific Research (AFOSR) and NASA JPL awarded me small grants to do so. The AFOSR grant was a follow-up to the work I did in the summer of 1989 at Eglin AFB. It was a project that required me to make occasional trips back to Fort Walton Beach, Florida over the following two years. Those trips were fun since it was near the beach and only about a four-hour drive from Auburn. I welcomed the NASA grant since I'd never been to JPL and visiting there was fascinating. It appeared to be a very laid-back place, as I judged from seeing many employees coming to work in shorts and t-shirts. Both those projects were similar in that they dealt with how to track space-based interceptors to improve lethality. I learned a lot during both projects, and they generated several more conference papers and journal articles.

During the next few years, and with the help of some outstanding graduate students, we perfected some of the numerical techniques I developed at UT. Then we used them to improve the accuracy of the gravity fields of both Mars and Venus. We did so using satellite observational data provided to us by some of my former UT classmates who were working at JPL. Those studies extended the state-of-the-art of gravity field determination for those planets, but have likely been far surpassed by now. More publications came from that work, along with at least two theses for hard-working students.

I didn't receive any large research grants until 1998 when John Cochran and I teamed up to win another AFOSR grant, this one for $400,000 over a three-year period. That was a sizable amount in those days and would cover our summer salaries and support graduate students over the life of the grant. It was a project that dealt with the tracking and identification of satellites in low-Earth orbits that were connected by a cord or tether to a second satellite. The Air Force was very interested in being able to determine quickly if the two satellites were connected. It was an important problem. If they tracked one of the connected satellites (not knowing there were two), its motion would appear to be that of an incoming missile instead of a satellite. If they mistakenly identified it as an incoming threat, they may take countermeasures to neutralize that threat. But if they identified it to be part of a tethered satellite system, no such actions would be necessary and they'd avoid a major conflict.

We worked on the tethered satellite program with the U.S. Air Force Space Command in Colorado Springs, Colorado. In doing so, we made several trips to Colorado to discuss the project and coordinate our efforts. On one trip, they invited us to visit the Cheyenne Mountain Air Force Station (AFS), which was on the Front Range of the Rocky Mountains. The Cheyenne Mountain Complex was an underground facility, built for the North American Aerospace Defense Command (NORAD) Combat Operations Center. NORAD moved its daily operations to its headquarters on Peterson AFB in 2006; however, the day-to-day operations returned in 2011 after a major overhaul and renovation. The location now supports U.S. Strategic Command's Missile Warning Center, along with other strategic warning and survivable capabilities. It provides a ready alternative operating location for NORAD's command center. They built the complex beneath 2,000 feet of granite within five acres of excavated tunnels to protect it from a potential nuclear attack from adversaries. For protection against earthquakes, they mounted the buildings in the complex on systems of huge springs. It was an extraordinary facility to visit and a very memorable trip.

As a team, we made some enormous advances regarding the quick identification of tethered satellites. We developed computer algorithms that identified orbiting bodies within five minutes of tracking. Our work generated fifteen research articles about our work, and John Cochran and I became experts on the dynamics of tethered satellites. It was an exceptional project to take part in and a career-builder, for me at least. Some of our algorithms were based on concepts from my research back at UT, so my dissertation topic was a very good one.

I was very fortunate to have many exceptional graduate students over the years. Most of them earned master's degrees, and only a few earned doctorates. All of them were outstanding scholars and hard workers. Quality graduate students always made my job easier. I benefitted from each of them. Looking back, I don't recall ever having a poor one, a claim I'm sure few professors can make.

One of my graduate student helped me write seven journal articles and six conference papers dealing with tethered satellites and missiles. That amount of productivity from a graduate student is extremely rare in academia.

It used to be impossible to track the number of reads and citations one's publications received. That all changed in 2008 when they launched the website ResearchGate.com. ResearchGate is a commercial European social networking site for scientists and engineers to share their research, ask and answer questions, and find collaborators. According to recent studies, it's the largest academic social network in terms of active users. Researchers can upload copies of their work and allow open access to their journal articles, conference papers, books, and technical reports. Other researchers can then read, cite, and use it in their own work. ResearchGate also publishes statistics summarizing how your publications are being used, and how others perceive your research. A service of this type was a long overdue addition to the scientific community. Since its inception, I've uploaded all the research publications and reports I generated during my academic career.

One activity that connected research, service, and teaching was serving on graduate student committees, both at the master's and doctoral degree levels. I viewed it as research and teaching when it was my student, but more of service and teaching when it was another professor's student. Being on a committee was a lot of work, much more so for my own students, although still time-consuming when the student was someone else's.

Since I worked with my graduate students on their research, I was very aware of what they were doing and how they were doing it. When it came time for them to write their thesis or dissertation, there weren't any surprises for me. We'd discuss everything they did and always let me proofread the first draft before putting it all together in one document. Then I'd pore through it in great detail, often many times, until they got everything right and in an acceptable form before they could schedule their defense. I wouldn't allow anybody to rush the process and attempt to defend their work before they were ready. Once they felt prepared, they'd practice their presentation a time or two for me before I permitted them to proceed. So I never had much apprehension about how they'd do defending their research. As a result, none of my students ever had trouble during their final examination and they all passed on their first attempt. There was never anything more than just making small editorial changes or clarifications before everyone on the committee signed-off on their document.

It was much different when I was a member of the committee for another professor's student. Even though I was familiar with their research, I didn't know all the details of their work. The students would keep me updated on their overall project, but until they handed me the draft of their complete document, I was unsure of what they were planning to defend. Once they did I'd study it and use my red pen to mark-it-up, sometimes a devastating amount, with suggested corrections and changes. I tried not to be too particular since it was someone else's student and rather tried to look at an overview of their projects instead of the smallest details. I felt that should be the role of the student's major professor, not each committee member. If I had a lot of suggestions, I'd return it to the student before their defense. I wouldn't return it to them until after their examination if I only had a few minor suggestions.

During student thesis or dissertation defenses, I attempted to pose big picture types of questions. I wanted to make sure they understood the very fundamentals of the problem they were addressing. Students often become so buried in the details of their work they lose sight of the overall focus. For example, I always asked students a question like, "What's unique about how you solved this problem?" Or, one on the order of, "What contribution will your work make to advance the state-of-the-art in your field?" I thought those were important questions because the point of doing independent research was to do something nobody had done before, or doing something differently than everyone else. I never wanted students to overlook the big picture. To emphasize that idea, I'd also ask them to use one sentence to describe why their work was relevant, something all students should have been able to do. Most of them, however, had trouble keeping it to only a single sentence.

I never attempted to play the role of blocking a student's graduation. That was the job of their major professor if they felt it was necessary. I viewed my participation as someone to make sure they met high standards and students satisfied the overall qualifications to earn their degrees. I know I didn't keep anyone from graduating, even though I'm sure I sometimes suggested they change many things in their documents.

When students from the mechanical or electrical engineering departments took my graduate classes, they often asked me if I'd be on their committees, and I always agreed. Serving on those committees was very interesting because their projects differed from the kind with which I was most familiar. They seldom involved orbital mechanics or space vehicles, but still used the same mathematical fundamentals and analysis techniques.

I also served on many dissertation committees in the History Department as an outside reader who the Graduate School appointed to offer a unique perspective on the research. Auburn had a remarkable program in aviation history, led by two friends of mine, Jim Hanson, and Bill Trimble. They often recommended me to be the outside reader because of my experience in the aerospace industry. Jim is the famous author who Neil Armstrong selected to write his biography in 2005, entitled, First Man: The Life of Neil A. Armstrong. His book was the basis for the 2018 movie, First Man, and he also served as a co-producer for the film. Jim honored Chris and me by inviting us to the local premier when it opened in theaters. Prior to the guests viewing the movie, he told many funny and interesting stories about its production.

Serving on committees in the History Department was very different and very interesting to me. The dissertations were all quite long and didn't have any equations, charts or tables. The academic perspective of a historian differed from that of an engineer or scientist by a sizeable amount. I always enjoyed my experiences working with Jim and Bill's graduate students, and I'd offer the viewpoint of a non-historian. After each involvement I had in that department, I came away happy that I studied engineering and not history.

As I state earlier, research wasn't the primary reason I wanted to become a professor. While research my production wasn't as great as many other faculty members, I finished my career having sixty-seven journal articles, conference papers, and research reports.

17

MY SERVICE LIFE

Service to one's department, college, and university is essential to ensure the efficient and fair operation of all units. They required all faculty members to take part in these activities on some level. While many professors welcomed such participation, some found it distasteful and would rather spend time on something 'more productive'. I discovered the more I undertook, the more I enjoyed it.

The service component of my assignment entailed serving in a variety of ways. I was the Graduate Program Officer (GPO) for thirteen years and the AIAA advisor for five more. My departmental service also involved taking part in academic, curriculum, search, planning, and tenure and promotion committees. Those assignments were mundane, but they gave me an opportunity to play a role in my department's operation. There was always something that needed done, studied, or decided for our future well-being. I also served on many theses and dissertation committees, which was crucial in helping our students navigate their graduate programs. My service just to the department took over 10% of my time, besides my other types of participation.

My additional service to the college involved taking part in planning, quality improvement, curriculum, and tenure and promotion committees, which were long-term activities and less interesting to me. Other than my involvement in the MITE Program I described earlier, I didn't find college service to be very satisfying.

I enjoyed performing university service the most. I believed it helped ensure academic integrity and assisted students in achieving success at AU. Unlike department and college service, faculty members weren't just assigned duties. Professors could volunteer for committees they found interesting. Many professors didn't wish to do much university service because it often took significant time. However, they could seek acceptable opportunities and decline others.

A position I volunteered for soon after my arrival on-campus was to join the Alumni Board of Sigma Phi Epsilon, my fraternity at WVU. I took part in that capacity for five years, one of which I spent serving as Faculty Advisor to the chapter. It was fun for a while. But a few incidents of reckless behavior by undergraduates convinced me to resign from both positions. I didn't want to be held responsible for the activities of immature fraternity boys.

Later I served as a member of the Traffic Appeals Board, which heard appeals from anyone who received traffic or parking tickets on-campus and didn't want to pay their fines. Every college has parking issues, and AU was no exception. Students often parked illegally to avoid driving around to look for a space or walking far to class. Many times they'd come up with transparent excuses, which weren't very believable. They seldom won their appeals, unless they were women who claimed they felt unsafe walking far in the dark. They always prevailed in those cases, and rightfully so. Sometimes students got tickets because they thought they were entitled to park wherever they wished. One student parked in the same faculty lot three days each week all semester and got ticketed each time. He received forty-five tickets, each carrying a fifty-dollar fine. Because his bill was so large, it automatically came before our committee. The student didn't even bother showing up for his hearing, and I doubt he paid the $2,250 himself.

I also volunteered for the Student Academic Grievance and Academic Honesty Committees, thinking I could help students get through the obstacles of academia. I intended to be an advocate for them, but I found it more compelling to help enforce more appropriate student behavior. Many of the issues that came before the grievance committee were ones where students received a poor grade in a course and claimed they weren't treated fairly by a professor. Those were usually cases where they didn't want to do the work needed to succeed in class. Many times, they had breezed through high school, never learned how to study, and got good grades without working very hard, which was much more difficult to do in college.

Students often claimed their issue was the professor's fault. Most of the time students didn't have a case and realized it after appearing before the committee. The formal hearing required them to provide evidence against a faculty member, which they couldn't usually do. During three years of service on that committee, I don't believe we ever determined that a professor was intentionally unfair to a student. There were a few times when students disagreed with assigned grades. In those situations, we'd request an outside grader to become involved and re-grade the student's work for comparison. When we did, we seldom found a grading discrepancy, which resulted in an unfair outcome for the student. I came away from my service on that committee, being more of an advocate for the faculty than for the students. It also gave me even more insight into the minds of undergraduates, which was itself amusing.

While my experiences on the Grievance Committee were enlightening, the ones on the Honesty Committee were eye-opening. And they were much more entertaining. Cheating is very popular in college, even though most universities have an honor code that students agree to abide by when they enroll. AU was no exception.

I served on the Honesty Committee for three years and was chair for two of them. A wide range of penalties existed for violations of the honor code. They included receiving a failing grade on an assignment or exam, an F in the course, suspension, and even expulsion from the university. And I witnessed the entire scope of sanctions.

There were many cases of plagiarism that came before the committee, most of which involved freshmen students. It appeared young students weren't aware of what plagiarism even was, or that it was inappropriate to use someone else's work as their own. They didn't understand the seriousness of doing so. I'm sure much of that

was because of the weak school systems in Alabama, but that wasn't an
excuse. Students wouldn't hesitate to borrow material from others for
their assignments, including work they downloaded from the Internet.
It was quite easy for professors to know when a student didn't write
something but claimed they had. They could also find where students
got it. Most plagiarists tried to hide their deed, but some were too
lazy to even do that and turned in work which included the website
address where they copied it. The most blatant case of plagiarism I saw
was from a student whose assignment in a communications course
was to write a report on a current event. Rather than do it himself,
he reproduced the headline story, word for word, from the front page
of the most recent edition of the campus newspaper, the Auburn
Plainsman. I should note that the faculty member who taught the class
was part of the journalism department, which published the weekly
paper. The notion that the student thought his professor wouldn't
recognize the week's lead story was astounding.

There were many cases of students cheating on exams, not only
by looking at another student's paper, but by bringing contraband
materials to the exam that would help them do better. Cheating
occurred more in classes where Teaching Assistants (TAs) proctored
exams rather than professors. But they were trained to look for those
offenses like a faculty member would, so they caught cheating too.
Being a teacher, I never had much cheating in my classes. I walked
around the classroom during every exam and quiz, looking for
problems. My exams were hard enough that students had to work
the entire time just to finish and couldn't waste time trying to look at
someone else's paper.

One fall afternoon, we had two football players appear before our
committee in the same case. They were part of a situation involving
students sharing material during an exam, but adequate proof wasn't
available and we dismissed the matter. Both players were polite and
showed respect for the process and the committee throughout. As one
player got up to leave when the hearing ended, the other remained
seated and asked if he could stay because he was also part of the next
case. The second charge against him also involved cheating, but this
time we found him guilty of the offense. The sanctions were that

he received a grade of F in the course, along with a notation on his official transcript that the failure resulted from academic dishonesty. It was a university rule that the notation must remain on his record for an entire year before he could petition to have it removed.

A few months later, during the spring semester, I received a phone call from the NFL agent for the player. Since I was the chair of the committee, he asked me if I could have the notation removed from the player's transcript early. The player was going to attend the NFL Draft Combine and thought his academic record might hurt him in the upcoming draft. I explained that wasn't possible until the one-year period had elapsed. Then he'd have to petition the university to have the notation removed, but there was no way to do that before a year had passed. The agent was very pleasant and accepted what I told him, but just wanted to ask about the possibility. It didn't appear to harm the player as he ended up being a top draft pick and having a long professional football career.

Of the many cases that came before the Honesty Committee, the most egregious case involved a work-study student who worked part-time in the Registrar's Office. He somehow gained access to a regular employee's computer login credentials that allowed him to change grades on student's official transcripts. So he did! He changed a lot of his own grades and those of some of his friends. However, this student didn't know about the security measures that were in place. Whenever a grade was changed in the system, both the department head and the instructor received notification to verify that they had requested the change. Since that was not the case, the student got busted. All the grades he changed were reversed, and they suspended him for a year.

My service wasn't only for the university. I always had an interest in national politics, and in the late 1990s I also became interested in local politics. The reason was that I didn't like how the city was changing. Developers were driving it in directions to make a profit without regard to the esthetics of our town. Growth was inevitable, but smart growth wasn't on their agenda. The City of Auburn had a mayor-council form of government, which included an elected mayor and eight council members. They elected our family friend, Cheryl Gladden, to the council in 1994 because she didn't like the ongoing development either. We had much the same viewpoint about city politics and, being the only non-businessperson on the council, she was always fighting a futile battle. Cheryl somehow talked me into running for the city council in 1998 to help her fight for smart development. I did, and they elected me to a four-year term. The best part of running for office was that Darby served as my campaign manager and we got to work together planning our strategy. It was a fun thing to do with him. We knocked on every door in my ward and handed out fliers describing my platform. I was proud because I funded it myself and didn't accept money from anyone, so I wouldn't feel like I owed donors something if I became a council member.

Being on the council was a lot of work, but I got paid… one hundred dollars per month. That worked out to be about two dollars an hour for the time I spent. This was in addition to the demands of my regular job. It was very frustrating trying to accomplish anything against the 'good old boy' network, which ran things in town. The mayor was even a developer, so Cheryl and I weren't successful in changing much at all. Wins for us were rare, and we had little impact on the city's direction. They made most all decisions in favor of developers and protecting their profits. Just about the only thing I could do for anybody was being able to get their trash picked up when the truck missed it. When that happened in my Ward I'd get a phone call from them complaining. We had a great City Manager in those days and all I had to do was let him know of the problem and he took care of it. I enjoyed helping people, just as I did with students as a professor.

My career as a 'politician' was short-lived. Although I reluctantly ran for re-election in 2002, I lost at the hands of the same network I worked against. Big surprise! I think that the City of Auburn is worse off than it could be, because the individuals who controlled the city in those days still influence the decision-making today. Although I still enjoyed my involvement, and it opened my mind to opportunities I'd have later, so it was worth the frustration and fighting the constant battles.

Because of my experience on the Auburn City Council, I also volunteered to represent my department in the University Senate. It was much more enjoyable than being a council member. The primary responsibility of a senator was to take part in the legislative process for the university and keep your colleagues informed of important issues and policy changes. It was an interesting position, and I enjoyed learning about how they governed AU.

As a senator, I got to know many individuals in charge of deciding issues within the governance structure. Those decisions included choosing faculty volunteers to assign to individual committees each year. The best committee assignment, and the one in the highest demand, was membership on the Committee on Intercollegiate Athletics, which served as advisors to the Auburn Athletics Department. I volunteered for the athletics committee several times earlier, but never got chosen. However, after becoming friends with many faculty members involved in university governance, they selected me to serve on the committee in 2004 for a three-year term.

Besides learning about the inter-workings of AU athletics, there were several perks that went along with the position, which was the reason the committee was in such high demand. They gave the members tickets to all AU sporting events, including seats near the fifty-yard line for the home football games. The tickets even included parking passes close to the stadium. I attended all the home football and basketball games during those years, and many of the baseball games. Although I didn't make it to a lot of away contests, I went to the Southeastern Conference (SEC) Football Championship against Tennessee in Atlanta in 2004. And Darby and I went to the 2005 Sugar Bowl game in New Orleans against Virginia Tech. What a fun trip that was! He and I saw the last game played in the Superdome before Hurricane Katrina devastated the city.

I also became friends with some coaches and assistant athletics directors during my involvement on that committee. Each year they invited me to attend the on-campus NFL Pro Day for football prospects. When I did, I got to meet several top players and their agents, a few of which were first-round draft picks and had long NFL careers. Although I must admit, attending a Pro Day was one of the most boring things I'd ever done. Watching college kids run, jump, lift weights, and do drills for hours was as dull as it sounds.

The most interesting and biggest honor I had occurred one day when the AU men's basketball coach, Jeff Lebo, held a special clinic for kids attending his summer camp. Since Coach Lebo was a former player at UNC, his special guests one evening were the current and former head basketball coaches at UNC, Roy Williams, and Dean Smith. An assistant athletic director friend invited me as a visitor because he knew I was a UNC fan, and I met and chatted with both of the legendary coaches. Even better, the three men each autographed a personalized copy of Dean Smith's latest book for me, A Coach's Life, which I brought along. It was an honor of a lifetime meeting those men. Coach Smith became ill soon afterward, and he didn't make many more public appearances.

There were also plenty of professional service activities in which I took part. During most years I attended two conferences per year, to present technical papers about my research or just to learn what others in my field were doing. I served as a Session Chair at many of those meetings and as an AIAA Technical Chair for one conference. They also selected me to be on the AIAA Education Committee and the Board of Directors for the American Astronautical Society (AAS) for a four-year term. In addition, I reviewed articles for a few journals and was a textbook reviewer for several book publishers.

The best part of professional service was attending the conferences and getting to visit many places I hadn't been to before. One of our yearly meetings was always at a warm location in the winter, while they held the second in the summer. My family often came to those with me, so they also visited a lot of interesting U.S. cities.

One activity that was more of a combination between service and teaching was when Auburn switched from quarters to semesters in 2002. As part of the academic calendar conversion, each curriculum in the university had to reduce the number of credit hours in their degree programs by one-third. All engineering programs had requirements for their students to take nine quarter hours of engineering mechanics courses: three hours each covering the subjects of statics, dynamics, and mechanics of materials. Many programs, other than aerospace, mechanical, and civil, proposed combining those three courses into one three-hour semester course, which included the mountain of material covered by each of them. It was a terrible idea, and I expressed my opinion, which didn't matter to the decision makers. They made the change, anyway.

Besides it being too much material to cover in fifteen weeks, another big problem was that no single book existed that covered all three subjects. Students would have to purchase two separate books costing over one hundred fifty dollars each. To avoid the high cost to students, they asked me if I'd be willing to write a textbook for the course. I reluctantly agreed. Even though I knew the material well enough to create such a book, I hesitated because I only had the summer to complete it since it had to be available for the upcoming fall semester.

The most difficult part of writing the textbook for me was going to be generating the graphics. Darby possessed better computer skills than I, and I knew he'd be able to do it much faster than I could. So I offered him some of any profits to do the artwork, and he agreed. Darby just finished his first year in college and didn't have a summer job, so he had plenty of time. I planned to take the summer off to work on the book at home the entire time. Darby was more of a night person while I was a day person, and we weren't awake at the same time much. So we devised a process to accomplish our task. I worked in the daytime typing the text and the equations, etc., and making hand sketches of the drawings I wanted in the book. Then before I went to bed, I'd leave my sketches on the table for Darby to turn into computer drawings overnight while I slept.

When I awoke in the morning, he had stacked his finished drawings on the table and was asleep. We operated that way the entire summer, and by fall we had a textbook ready for the class. Corey later went through and checked the math to verify the calculations were correct. It was an amazing undertaking for us. I had it printed at a local copy shop and they sold them in the bookstores for students to purchase at a cost of forty-five dollars. They've continued to use our book every semester since 2002. Over the years, I made revisions and modifications and have now published a version of the textbook through Kindle Direct Publishing, which is available for sale online. We worked hard that summer, but the results were worth our effort.

Our book ended up being 244 pages long and contained 500 of Darby's computer-generated drawings.

In 2013, I undertook another interesting summer service activity. I volunteered to perform a study for my college to determine how other engineering schools were planning to use online engineering mechanics courses in their course offerings. Our new dean, Chris Roberts, funded me to visit six universities and meet with faculty and departments to discuss their programs and plans. He wanted the information to help define AU's future direction in online education. I spent the entire month of July driving between schools to talk with professors and collect data. I'd spend an entire day in meetings, then have a couple of days to enjoy the towns and campuses before going to the next institution. It was a perfect project for me! The schools I visited were Maryland, Virginia Tech, Illinois, Purdue, West Virginia, and Tennessee. It was a very interesting experience, and I learned a lot, met many educators, and wrote a final report for the dean presenting my findings. It was a fun project to work on and I enjoyed spending time on those campuses, some of which I hadn't been to before. I pleased Dean Roberts with the recommendations I made when the study ended.

I had a unique experience during my trip from Virginia Tech to Purdue. I drove out of my way to Milan, Indiana, so I could visit the Milan '54 Hoosiers Basketball Museum. It was a museum dedicated to the 1986 film, *Hoosiers*, which told the story of tiny Milan High School unexpectedly winning the Indiana state championship in 1954. I arrived in Milan on a Monday afternoon, only to find that the museum was closed on Mondays. As I peered through the glass front door to see whatever I could, the very kind museum director opened the door and invited me in to look around even though they were closed to the public. It felt as though destiny guided me to visit that piece of basketball history on that day, and I thoroughly enjoyed spending time alone in such an interesting and reverent place.

Darby and Corey at home in Auburn, 1987

Our visit to Dodgertown, Vero Beach, FL, 1988

Jim Williams, Auburn, AL, 1988

Grandma Cicci, Auburn, AL, 1989

Aerospace Engineering Building groundbreaking, 1990

Easter in Auburn, 1993

My first office in the AE Building, 1993

Accepting the Birdsong Teaching Award, Auburn, AL, 1999

At the Astrodynamics Specialist Conference with John Cochran, Girdwood, AK, 1999

18

SHORT COURSES AND SUMMERS AWAY

A couple of years after I began teaching at AU, I received a call from a former student. He worked in the Propulsion Directorate at the NASA MSFC in Huntsville. They needed someone to teach a short course about ascent trajectories for the space shuttle. Since the subject related to orbital mechanics, he thought of me and asked if I'd be interested in teaching such a course.

A short course is intensive instruction on a specific subject offered over a brief period. They teach short courses in the professional engineering world from a few hours to twenty hours of instruction over a time of between one day and a week. At this point in my career, I didn't have any experience with short courses. I suppose the Professional Engineer's Exam review I taught in Pittsburgh might qualify as a short course. However, that review course differed in the sense that it was one night a week rather than intense instruction over a few days.

I pondered teaching the short course at MSFC and discussed it with some of my colleagues before I accepted the challenge. They wanted a course with twenty hours of instruction in one week, or four hours per day of teaching, which is very hard to do alone. Plus, not being very familiar with space shuttle ascent trajectories required me to do a lot of preparation. I needed to cover advanced topics and not introductory or simple material. So I had to learn a good bit before I could teach NASA professionals. We scheduled the course for mid-December 1989, which was only a few months away. I got busy researching the material they requested I cover and producing several hundred overhead slides from which I could lecture. Doing that took a great deal of time. A big advantage was that I could work as a contractor and not through AU, which they allowed us to do under the university's official consulting policy. That meant I'd get paid directly by NASA, separate from my university salary. I could charge NASA by the number of hours taught and students enrolled. I had to research the pricing structure of other professional short courses to determine what cost would be appropriate.

It turned out I had about fifteen enrollees for the twenty-hour course. Several of those who enrolled were former students of mine at AU now working at NASA Marshall Space Flight Center (MSFC). I priced it to compete with similar short courses that were being taught around the country, and the extra money was a substantial amount for our young family. Chris and the kids came up for part of the week after school was out for the holidays. It turned out that week was one of the coldest in Huntsville history. It snowed and temperatures were below freezing for the entire time we were there, which was quite unusual for north Alabama, even in December.

A short course was far different from a college course for several reasons. Teaching four hours per day by myself was intense. I spoke from the overhead slides I made, but it was exhausting, and I tired of hearing myself talk. They wanted me to start at 8:00 a.m. and teach all morning so the employees could return to work in the afternoon. Only having a ten-minute break every hour was brutal. It drained me by the end of the week.

Another reason it was so difficult was because of the high level of the students enrolled. They were all sharp and interested professionals, unlike my normal classes at AU. Their questions weren't easy to answer. They questioned me on a lot about what I told them, which was both invigorating and challenging. But I thought the course went well, and I enjoyed the experience. By the time I finished, I wasn't sure if I ever wanted to do another one because it was so tiring. However, it was nice having extra money for the holidays, and we had a delightful (and warmer) Christmas back in Auburn.

I was right when I thought the short course went well. They hired me to do two more, in December 1990 and in March 1992, although those courses covered different subjects. The 1990 course was about orbital maneuvering, and the subject of the 1992 course was estimation theory and filtering. I was also hired to teach one at Eglin AFB in 1991, dealing with the same subjects. Being more familiar with those topics required less preparation than the first course, since my learning curve wasn't as steep. Both courses were fun but also tiring, and once again I enjoyed the experiences. In addition, I made more money, which came in handy with two growing sons and the expenses of raising a family. However, I didn't agree to teach any more short courses until after I worked my way through the tenure and promotion process. I needed to devote all of my time and effort in that direction to achieve success in academia. So that's what I did. Once I became a full professor, I returned to teaching short courses. From 2001 to 2006, I taught seven more for a variety of organizations. Those included: the Army Aviation Missile Research, Development, and Engineering Center (AMRDEC) at Redstone Arsenal; the Naval Surface Warfare Center (NSWC) in Dahlgren, Virginia; the Naval Research Center (NRC) in Washington, DC; NASA MSFC again; the DIA, MSIC, and Dynetics in Huntsville; and the Central Intelligence Agency (CIA) in Langley, Virginia. The subjects of each of those short courses dealt with state estimation and Kalman filtering, the subjects I knew best. By then I had my short courses perfected and streamlined. I didn't need to prepare an extensive amount, and they weren't as hard to put together as my first ones. The subjects were also ones that I taught yearly in an on-campus graduate course, so covering much of the same material in a short course wasn't difficult. It was still very tiring though, as most of them averaged four hours per day and extended over a few days to a week. In later years I taught more courses at the CIA, which I'll discuss in an upcoming chapter. They invited me back to teach at the NSWC again in 2018, after I retired. The offer came as a complete surprise from a member of NSWC management staff, John Lundberg, who was a friend from UT and a former colleague at AU.

A lot of the graduates from our department went to work in Huntsville, either for a government agency or one of the aerospace or defense contractors located there. As a result, I had a built-in network of contacts in many of those organizations, which opened doors to many opportunities for research, short courses, and consulting. Our graduates were always willing to help when I needed funding. Likewise, we always helped their organizations in hiring quality graduates. I'd refer our best students anytime they'd call, and our department provided a constant supply of summer interns to their companies. The relationship benefitted all of us, which only strengthened over the years as our graduates moved into management positions and became responsible for funding and hiring decisions. I always viewed one of my primary responsibilities as a professor was helping students find jobs. I took great pride when I could assist them, which I did many times throughout the years.

Our friends in Huntsville also hired many of our faculty for summer positions if we didn't have research or teaching opportunities. And I was one of them.

I mentioned that in 1989, I worked on an Air Force grant at Eglin AFB in Fort Walton Beach, Florida. Most of the other summers I taught classes, had research grants, or directed the MITE Program, which covered all or a part of my summer salary. I appreciated the opportunity to stay in Auburn and spend relaxed summers with my family. In 2001, I didn't have any source of income, so I looked to my connections in Huntsville. It only took a couple of phone calls to the U.S. Army to find a summer job at Redstone Arsenal. George Landingham was a technical manager in the lab who graduated from AU before I arrived. He hired me to work in his group on a very interesting project, analyzing the separation dynamics of a two-body missile. It was a complicated problem in which an inner body separated from the outer body boost vehicle after launch. Understanding the motion of each body besides their interactions required me to develop detailed computer simulations and significant dynamical analyzes for many launch parameters and scenarios. I worked the three summer months on the problem, and George provided me with additional funding to continue studying it after I returned to campus in the fall. We co-authored a paper about that research a few years later, and the work is still pertinent today.

Huntsville was about a four-hour drive from Auburn, so I couldn't commute to work and had to find an apartment and live there. Corey was already in college and Darby just finished his junior year in high school, and they both had summer jobs. Of course, Chris was working, too. So it wasn't a bad time for me to work in Huntsville. Plus, we needed the extra money for tuition for Corey. I rented an apartment for three months at a complex off Water Hill Road in Madison, Alabama, only a short drive from Redstone Arsenal. I rented furniture, and I enjoyed living there for the summer. Living alone was quieter than I was used to, but Chris visited a few weekends when she could get away. Huntsville's a great city and I found a lot to do besides work. One of my favorite things was to see the Huntsville Stars minor league baseball games. They were a Double-A farm team of the Milwaukee Brewers but are no longer in existence. I went to one game advertised as 'bring your dog to the game' day, and many people did. They even had a dog trained to serve as the bat 'boy' and ones that carried water out to the umpires between innings.

It was an interesting summer for me at AMRDEC. I worked with an outstanding group of engineers, some of whom were former students of mine, and I could work at my pace on the project. There was a very relaxed atmosphere in the lab, and that made for a pleasant experience. I enjoyed another taste of the engineering world, but looked forward to getting back to campus when the summer was over. The best part about working time in Huntsville was strengthening my connections there, both inside and outside the government. I also drank some beer with a few former students who had become responsible adults and outstanding professionals. It made me proud to see them succeeding in their careers.

Late that summer Corey was moving into an off-campus apartment at UNC in Chapel Hill, and I promised to help move some furniture from Auburn. I rented a small Penske truck in Huntsville on a Friday and drove to Auburn that night. On Saturday we loaded the truck, and I drove eight hours to Chapel Hill, while Chris followed in her car. We spent the rest of Saturday helping him move into his new apartment. Then on Sunday, I drove the truck all the way back to Huntsville through the Great Smoky Mountains of East Tennessee. The entire trip was a nineteen-hour drive and a brutal one overall. But Corey got moved into his first apartment. Even better, I felt like I outsmarted the truck rental companies. For a local rental, there was a basic fee for the truck plus a fixed price per mile driven when it was returned to the same location. But Penske's pricing structure for a one-way rental had a major flaw. If you rented at one location and returned it to a different one, you'd only have to pay mileage between those two rental points. I rented a truck in Huntsville and dropped it off at a different location across town. So I only had to pay for ten miles instead of the 1,200 miles I traveled. Otherwise, the cost would have been very high.

In the spring of 2005, I received a call from another former student, who was a technical manager at Dynetics Corporation, also in Huntsville. Dynetics was a large defense contractor, and he needed someone to perform filtering studies on a project and asked if I'd be interested. That meant me spending another summer in Huntsville. Since I needed summer funding yet again, I agreed. It was a simple decision since I enjoyed being there a few summers before, and I knew it would be fun again. This time I rented an apartment off Zerdt Road in south Madison and rented furniture once more. I lived on the first floor and there was a small lake a few steps from my back patio, which had a walking path around it I used a lot. It was a peaceful and serene setting. This time I worked at the Dynetics building in the Cummings Research Park and not at Redstone Arsenal. It was an easier drive in the morning with less traffic, and much more convenient for going out for lunch and happy hours. It was another fun summer living in Huntsville. I thought I did some excellent work and learned a lot. I also got to ride one of the original Segways at Dynetics. It was quite an interesting thing to do and a very creative application of feedback control systems, which was something I studied for many years in school and taught a few times at AU.

The following spring, I met the father of one of our undergraduate students who was a co-owner of Dynamic Concepts, Incorporate (DCI), and another NASA contractor in Huntsville. Her father was an aerospace engineering graduate from UT before me, so and we hit it off well. He called one day to tell me that his company had a need for someone to work on a project at MSFC over the summer and wondered if I'd be interested. I couldn't say yes fast enough, and it was back to Huntsville for me in the summer of 2006. DCI hired me to be a Faculty Associate, and I was going to be working on site at NASA, which was also on Redstone Arsenal. I found an apartment in a brand new complex off University Drive in northwest Huntsville, but a furnished one this time, which made the move much easier. I just showed up with my suitcase the day before I was to begin work and the apartment was set-up for me when I arrived.

The project I worked on at NASA was developing mathematical modeling techniques for inertial measuring units, which are instruments used in controlling spacecraft and missiles. I hadn't done that type of work before, but it involved basic mathematics and feedback control concepts I was familiar with. It wasn't orbital mechanics or filtering, but it was interesting and fun. And a very ironic circumstance occurred that summer. When I arrived at work my first day, I found that my immediate supervisor was one of my classmates at UT, which made it even more fun working at NASA.

Both Corey and Darby had graduated from college by then: Corey in May 2002, and Darby in December 2004. Corey just moved from New York to LA, but Darby was still in New York. He developed a strong interest in music and wanted to attend the Bonnaroo Music and Arts Festival. Bonnaroo, which was a four-day music festival held each summer in Manchester, Tennessee, about a ninety-minute drive from Huntsville. So he flew to Auburn and drove up to go to the festival. He arrived a couple days early so we could hang out a little before he headed to Tennessee. Darby enjoyed the experience. He saw some fantastic bands and slept in a tent as thousands of others did, but wasn't able to bathe for four days. When he got back to Huntsville, he direly needed a long, hot shower and a lot of food. But he had a very memorable time and talked about how great it was for months afterward!

It was ironic that a few of years later in 2012, Darby was a member of the indie rock band, The Antlers, and got to perform at Bonnaroo in 2012. They bussed the band in to play their show, then left by van immediately afterward. He found that playing at the festival wasn't as much fun as attending as a spectator.

One funny thing about his trip to Huntsville was that he had flown to Atlanta, where Chris picked him and drove him to Auburn. His car was at home since he didn't need one in New York, so he drove it to Huntsville to take to Bonnaroo. After the festival, he flew back to New York from Huntsville and left his car with me. So I found myself alone with two cars. I ended up driving one car home to Auburn, having Chris drive me to the Atlanta airport, then flying back to Huntsville and taking a taxi to my apartment. It would have been cheaper and easier if I rented Darby a car in Huntsville to drive to Tennessee, except he wasn't old enough to get a rental car.

The people at DCI liked the work I did at NASA, so they hired me again to work as a Faculty Associate the following summer. This time, however, it was a project I could do in Auburn and I didn't need to go back to Huntsville for a third year in a row. This project was also interesting and one I was more familiar with, performing a survey of ascent trajectory reconstruction methods for use by NASA's future launch vehicles. After two straight summers away, I was happy to have a summer at home, although it would not be a relaxing one.

When I was working at NASA in the summer of 2006, I had just become Chair-Elect of the Auburn University Senate. Soon thereafter, there was a controversial issue that occurred regarding courses that athletes took that might not have been up to the standards of other classes across campus. Since I was the Chair-Elect, a journalist from the New York Times called me to discuss the matter. They wanted to hear a professor's viewpoint about the situation. I gave him some thoughtful quotes, and they appeared in the Times later that week. Ironically, Darby worked at an art gallery in New York and made some photographs of his art installation, which were published in the Times that same week.

The sad part about the summer of 2006 was that my mother passed away at age 84 back in Pennsylvania. She fell ill and was hospitalized and I flew up to see her, but she died a few days later. I stayed for a week until the funeral was over. My family few to Pittsburgh to be there too, and Chris took care of their travel arrangements. She booked all the flights and did a remarkable job. She flew from Atlanta, Corey from LA, and Darby from New York, and everybody arrived in the Pittsburgh International Airport within thirty minutes of one other. It was an amazing feat, and I only needed to make one trip to the airport to retrieve everyone. After the funeral, I flew back to Huntsville and finished out the summer working at MSFC. It was an eventful time for sure.

19

MY EXCESSIVE SERVICE LIFE

My time serving in the University Senate along with the experiences I had as a council member in the City of Auburn inspired me to consider running for Chair of the AU Senate. I thought it would be much more interesting, and I expected I could be a lot more productive than I was on the City Council. Running for Senate Chair was a very easy process. It required me to submit a resume and outline my platform, and a university-wide election took place online. There was no campaigning, no debates, no forums, and no cost to run. Many people remembered me being a council member, so they may have assumed the experience was a good preparation for leading the Senate. I'm not sure if that was true, but I won anyhow.

Winning the election for Chair of the Senate meant making a three-year service commitment. The first year, as Chair-Elect, was an intense period of learning about the university and its governance, attending a plethora of meetings, and being involved in many decisions affecting the university's operation. However, the intensity level increased even more in the second year as Chair. There were many leadership responsibilities and even a larger number of meetings to attend, which entailed working closely with the university administration. The third year, as Immediate Past Chair, comprised serving as the faculty representative on the Auburn University Board of Trustees (BOT), and assisting the Chair and Chair-Elect in their duties. The last year was much less intense than the previous two.

The three years of service required a major professional and personal commitment, which took most of my time. Since the position was so demanding and didn't attract a sizeable amount of interest, they wanted to encourage people to run for Senate Chair. To do so, they provided several incentives. Those included a reduction in teaching load to a single class and a bonus of one-third of your salary during your year as Chair.

However, the biggest perk was a paid sabbatical leave after finishing one's term as Immediate Past Chair. It meant taking a yearlong leave from AU and getting your full salary for doing whatever you wanted. Since it wasn't a normal academic sabbatical, there was no requirement to do something educational or related to your field. I suppose you could take off from doing anything productive and play golf every day, if you desired. But the former chairs I knew all partook in some professional activity while refreshing themselves to return to academia after an exhausting three years. They often worked on their research full-time, wrote a book, traveled, taught at another institution, or pursued other professional activities. Marketable faculty, like I was, could even find a job in industry or with the government for the year. Any pay received from other sources would be in addition to your full salary from the university during that year. So, you could 'double dip' and receive two salaries during your sabbatical. University policy permitted doing that because it differed from regular academic sabbaticals. In those cases, they deducted any money you received during your sabbatical from your university salary. That wasn't the case in the one I'd receive from my Senate Chair service.

I began my three-year term in the summer of 2006, which meant serving as Chair-Elect in 2006-2007, Chair in 2007-2008, and Immediate Past Chair in 2008-2009. Then I had an additional three years in which to take my sabbatical. All I had to do was tell the university my plan and when I'd be gone. There wasn't even a requirement to write a report describing my activities when it ended.

Chris was very familiar with the commitment I made when I ran for Senate Chair because we had several friends who served in that capacity before me. She supported my decision to run and knew about the sabbatical I'd receive when I finished.

When I gave her the news that I won the election, her first response was, "Congratulations! So what are you going to do on your sabbatical?" Being at least three years away, I hadn't thought about it or made any plans yet. It was a long way off, although sabbaticals took time to arrange.

I responded, "I don't know!" All I knew was that I wanted to do something different and interesting, and that I hoped to get paid for doing it.

When I became Chair-Elect, I found it overwhelming. There were so many meetings I couldn't do much of anything else. And that included teaching and research. My Senate duties took over 60% of my time, and I spent the rest of it on my classes. There was no time to do any research at all. But it was fun, if not all-consuming. There was an immense amount to learn about how the university ran and who made the important decisions. I also had to figure out the best way to be an advocate for the faculty, which was the reason I wanted to serve.

The Chair-Elect at that time, Rich Penaskovic, a good friend of mine, was a renowned professor in the Religion Department and someone I played softball with for years. Rich did an excellent job, and we worked well together. He had great insight and fought hard for the faculty.

I enjoyed getting to know the people in the upper administration very much. Although after a few years of internal turmoil, Auburn had an Interim President who I thought was hurting the university. He tried to play a dictatorial role, but alienated the faculty and the staff, and never connected with the students. I believe his presidency represented a low point in AU history and we needed a change. Some members of the BOT, who were clueless and complicit in the inept running of the university, also needed replaced. But during my first year of service, they were undertaking a national search for a new president to replace the interim disaster.

One very interesting experience I had as Chair-Elect was to represent AU at a conference sponsored by the Knight Commission on NCAA rules reform. They held it at Stanford University in Palo

Alto, California, in 2007, and my entire family went along and we
made it a vacation after the conference. A highlight of the meeting
was getting to meet Dr. Myles Brand, who was the Executive Director
of the NCAA and former President of Indiana University. He was the
person who fired the famed basketball coach Bobby Knight in 2002.
We had a friendly chat about his time at IU during a social hour. It
pleased him to hear that Darby had a wonderful experience as an IU
student. After the conference, we stayed in downtown San Francisco
for a few days. We even drove over to Berkeley to see Cal, where we'd
never been.

We stayed in a big hotel near Fisherman's Wharf in San Francisco,
which was wonderful. The funny thing was the hotel only had valet
parking, and it was very expensive. Corey and I noticed that there
were several places near the hotel where we could park on the street
for free. He devised a brilliant plan where we could park during our
entire stay for free instead of paying to park at the hotel. All we had to
do was move the car a few times because of street cleaning.

When I became Chair, it meant taking part in even more high-
level university committees, such as the President's Cabinet, and the
Budget, Curriculum, Executive, Rules, and Steering Committees.
There were additional study groups that arose that required significant
amounts of time and work, not to mention energy. It continued to be
overwhelming, and I devoted many of my evenings and weekends to
Senate business. In addition, they required me to set the agendas and
conduct the monthly University Senate meetings, which took many
more hours of preparation. And it was always a battle trying to work
with the Interim President who showed little respect for the faculty
and had no interest in shared governance. I was fortunate to serve
with an outstanding Senate Secretary who made our work possible.
I couldn't have survived that year without the many talents and hard
work of Ann Beth Presley.

Halfway through my term as Chair, things at AU changed in a
major way. The presidential search concluded, and we hired a fantastic
new president to lead us: Dr. Jay Gogue, an Auburn graduate and
former basketball player and the sitting president at the University of
Houston returned to AU as president. Upon his arrival, Dr. Gogue

endeared himself to the faculty, staff, students, and the BOT. He soon became a trusted and respected leader and made my job much, much easier. It was a pleasure to have Dr. Gogue back on campus and for us to get to work with him.

One major initiative I headed as Chair was rewriting the Faculty Dismissal Policy. This project came about because a single member of the BOT didn't think that the Auburn faculty members were doing their jobs. He had the impression that professors were spending most of their time at home or on the golf course. His claims were absurd, and he had no evidence to support his accusations. This BOT member wanted to have the power to walk into a professor's office and fire them on the spot without due process. In modern day academia at institutions with faculty tenure, there was never a chance of that occurring. Still, this individual persisted in his efforts that the university have a policy where they could dismiss professors for both misconduct and poor performance. Even though AU had such a policy in place, he didn't like it for a variety of reasons, mostly because it didn't allow him to fire faculty at will. I accepted the responsibility of writing a new policy and having it approved by the Senate, the administration, and the BOT. It was an enormous task.

I worked several months studying dismissal policies at other universities and talking with the various constituency groups across campus. Those groups included the leaders of the local chapter of the American Association of University Professors (AAUP), senators, administrators, BOT members, and many past Senate chairs. It was an experience that taught me a lot about all the groups involved. Based on what I learned during the process, I came away with a much higher level of respect for our faculty and a much lower level of respect for some board members.

My work culminated in me rewriting Section 3.9.2 of the AU Faculty Handbook, entitled Dismissal of Tenured Faculty, which is still in existence today. The three major parts of the new policy it addressed were clarifying just cause resulting from misconduct, defining just cause resulting from performance, and describing the guidelines for the dismissal process, including the hearing, the final determination, and the sanctions. The policy specified the misconduct for which they could consider a professor as unfit to continue on the faculty. These included convictions or admissions of guilt of various crimes, misdemeanors, or felony drug offenses, and repeated violations of substantive university policy, rules, or regulations. Most all constituency groups believed these types of violations should bring about sanctions for a faculty member found guilty of those offenses, up to and including dismissal. They also believed the well-defined process for hearing such a case would determine a reasonable decision while protecting the rights of the individual being charged.

There was, however, a great deal of contention about the guidelines for dismissing a faculty member based on performance. This conflict resulted for many reasons. Assessing someone's performance was subjective, poorly defined, and standards differed. Many questions arose, such as, 'What comprised inadequate performance?' Also, a professor's duties are wide and varied, so, was it fair to single out someone for not being as skilled in one area of teaching, research, or service as opposed to the other areas? This goes back to the three-legged stool analogy, although everyone may not subscribe to that concept. I found that many BOT members felt faculty members should be excellent in all areas, and if they weren't, they should be fired. Most people on the BOT were from the business world and knew little about running a university, and they didn't understand or appreciate the notions of tenure and academic freedom. Faculty members and others across campus did not share their viewpoints. In addition, the BOT wouldn't support the idea that if someone had already earned tenure, it was a clear sign the individual was competent to hold a professorial position. Not to say a person's performance couldn't deteriorate over the years, only that it would be difficult to prove it justified dismissal. Although I believe much of it came down to the sanctity of tenure. If they could dismiss a tenured professor based on subjective evaluation, it would damage the institution's reputation, and it would hinder hiring quality faculty members in the future. Tenure not only protected professors, it also protected the university. Constructing an acceptable Faculty Dismissal Policy became a significant challenge. The BOT demanded absolute power over the faculty, along with the ability to fire individuals without adequate justification. "That wasn't doing to happen!"

As Senate Chair, I couldn't and wouldn't let that occur, and neither would the rest of the faculty. Therefore, I constructed the 'performance' portion of the dismissal policy with great care. I had a strong desire to protect our faculty from unfair or retaliatory actions by certain members of the BOT. I believe I accomplished my goal.

The BOT wanted to dismiss a faculty member for poor performance in any part of their assignment, e.g., teaching, research, or outreach/service. However, when I wrote the new policy, I included the following three conditions for dismissal based on performance:

1. Serious or substantial violation of professional ethics in administrative, teaching, research, or outreach activities.
2. Demonstrated incompetence in teaching, research, and outreach activities.
3. Serious or substantial neglect of professional or academic responsibilities.

The first condition cites violations in professional ethics, while the third condition cites a neglect of responsibilities. Those were actions deserving of faculty dismissal, if proven to have occurred, and weren't points of contention.

However, I had to be clever when I wrote the clause regarding faculty incompetence to provide the utmost protection to my colleagues. I put a great deal of thought into addressing that point in writing the second condition. I cited 'incompetence in teaching, research, and outreach activities', rather than 'or outreach activities', which makes an enormous difference. It means that a faculty member must be incompetent in all areas of his assignment, and not just one area. I intentionally included the word 'and' instead of 'or' to prohibit any unreasonable attempt to dismiss a professor. I believe it would be difficult to prove that anybody is incompetent in every phase of his or her assignment. As a result, I doubt they could ever dismiss someone because of incompetence under the second condition. I view that as my eternal gift to the AU faculty, and after seeing the disdain

204   My Teaching Life

the BOT had for professors, I was proud to do it. I'm not sure many people know what that provision entails, but perhaps someday it will be useful in protecting a faculty member against an unfair charge.

After spending many hours educating our faculty, administration, and the BOT on the new policy, it received unanimous approval when I presented it to each body. I felt my work provided an added layer of protection for both tenure and academic freedom at Auburn. I think it passed the BOT because they didn't take time to read it and may not have even understood it. Or perhaps they were just as incompetent in doing their job as they accused our faculty of being so many times in doing ours.

I enjoyed working with Dr. Gogue. I appreciated his efforts to bring the university together after a decade of turmoil and tension between the faculty and BOT. Not long after his arrival, they replaced several BOT members with individuals who were more interested in the university's betterment rather than wanting to control it as a part of their own fiefdom. As a result, we undertook many new initiatives and made substantial progress in positioning AU to be an academic leader in the twenty-first century.

I was proud of everything Senate leadership accomplished during my year as Chair. I am thankful for the experience and for the trust the AU faculty placed in me to lead them. By the end of the year I was exhausted, so becoming Immediate Past Chair in the summer of 2008 was a welcome change. I passed the gavel to another good friend of mine, Bob Locy, who took over and did a fine job during his term. And I was happy to get back to teaching my normal class load again.

My primary duty as the Immediate Past Chair was to serve as the faculty representative on the BOT. That meant attending board meetings and providing input on behalf of the faculty on important issues. I was still a member of many committees, but as more of a consultant than an active member. It was much more relaxed with reduced responsibility for me. I still felt involved, but with a lot less pressure. Under Dr. Gogue's leadership, the turmoil at the university had subsided, and everything seemed to go much smoother. We all appreciated the new culture he established and the direction he was taking the institution. My year as Immediate Past Chair was uneventful, but I was still looking forward to finishing my three years of service in Senate leadership. I needed a break from being involved to such a large degree.

Each spring semester, at the General Faculty Meeting of the university, the local chapter of the AAUP gave its Academic Freedom Award. They humbled and honored me by naming me the winner in 2010. But I was on my sabbatical when they announced the award winner and couldn't attend the presentation. Chris took off from work early that day to accept it on my behalf.

I've won many awards over the years, but this is the one I'm most proud of since the AU faculty presented it to me for my service to them, and I will be forever grateful.

20

MY SABBATICAL LIFE

The sabbatical leave I was due to receive was one where I'd get my full salary no matter what I did during that year. Even though there was no requirement to do so something educational, I always thought I would because I couldn't sit idle for an entire year. When I first won the election, I didn't have any plan for what I'd do during my leave since it was a long way off. Although I began thinking about it soon after I became Chair-Elect.

I knew that being an engineer, I'd have opportunities to do a variety of things and make money. I was going to get my Auburn pay regardless, and I thought that if I could get a second salary, it would be a big financial boost. My friends who received the same sabbatical worked on research, traveled, or wrote books, but most didn't receive any extra money during their leave. I was lucky. I was very marketable, and I knew I could always find work with a company in Huntsville. But I couldn't begin exploring opportunities until about a year before I'd be available, which was the summer of 2009 after finishing my year as Immediate Past Chair.

When that time came, I began looking for possibilities across the country by submitting resumes online in response to advertised positions and talking to some of my contacts in Huntsville. I received calls for several phone interviews and flew to Tucson, Arizona, to interview with Raytheon. It pleased me that a few companies were interested in hiring me for only one year. But it didn't excite me to do a job similar to my past jobs. I wanted to do something different and interesting. Then something happened that I didn't expect.

In the spring of 2008, I received a phone call from a former student who worked at the Central Intelligence Agency (CIA) Headquarters in Langley, Virginia. This student's been a CIA employee for many years and began as an intern when he was an undergraduate. He was also the individual who arranged for me to teach a short course at the CIA a few years earlier. He sometimes called to ask if we had any outstanding students who might be interested in careers in the intelligence community or to just reach out and chat. As we talked, I mentioned I had a sabbatical coming up for serving as Senate Chair, and he surprised me with a question he asked.

"Would you be interested in coming up to Langley for your sabbatical?"

I answered, "Sure, I'd consider doing that. Why do you ask?"

Then he responded, "Well, because of 9-11, the CIA developed an initiative to strengthen our connections to academia. In that regard, I think I could make a proposal to the administration to arrange for you to spend your sabbatical working up here."

I thought it would be a terrific experience for me since I never worked in the intelligence community and always heard great things about working at the CIA.

So I said, "Well, if you could do that, I'd definitely be interested."

"Terrific! I'll talk to the people up here and get back to you," he replied.

I didn't hear anything from him for a few months, so I expected nothing would develop from our conversion. Then one day he called and told me some folks wanted to come down to Auburn to talk with me about it and asked if that would be alright. I told him that would be fine, and I looked forward to talking with them. But he didn't tell me when they planned to visit.

A couple of weeks later, I answered a knock at my office door to find three CIA officers from Langley who came to talk with me. It was late in the afternoon, so we went to dinner at Mellow Mushroom on College Street to get acquainted. One officer was from Pennsylvania and also a Steelers fan, so he and I hit it off great. They wanted to continue our discussions that evening. I had planned to attend the Auburn basketball game, and I asked them if they'd like to go along and chat there, and they did. We walked over to the Beard-Eaves Memorial Coliseum, got three more tickets, and we all attended the AU game.

When we were finding seats, they wanted to sit high in the upper mezzanine away from everybody so we could talk openly about the possibility of me coming to Langley. So that's where I had my 'interview'. I sat a few rows from the top of the coliseum with three CIA officers, watched an AU basketball game, and chatted about how I might help with the CIA's mission.

When they left afterward, all they said was, "We'll be in touch." I felt good that they would try to work something out, and that possibility became an exciting one for me.

Several months passed before I heard anything else. That's when my former student called to tell me that the approval process was underway. He said it was going to take longer than he thought, although he was still felt confident they would approve it. Getting the required sign-offs was just very slow. I also had to have my current security clearance updated. The CIA needed to upgrade my Top Secret (TS) clearance, which I held for many years, to a Top Secret–Sensitive Compartmented Information (TS-SCI) clearance. That took more time and slowed the process even further because they had to investigate my background deeper than in the past.

I understood how the government works, and I also knew how things could get screwed up and the whole thing could fall apart. So I continued to look at other options for my sabbatical and had a few offers. One option was a chance to go back to WVU and teach there, which would have been great fun. However, the department chair didn't have enough funding available to even cover my living expenses in Morgantown. Besides, I felt I needed a break from academia, so I rejected that opportunity.

Then early in the spring of 2009, I got a call from a contracts officer at the CIA. He told me they've received the approvals for me to come to Langley, but we had to work out financial arrangements before they could complete the paperwork. He asked me to submit a funding proposal for me to spend a year there, which, of course, I agreed to do. I also knew how government contracts worked for engineering services, so I did a lot of research to find the price contractors were charging in the Washington, DC area. I came up with an hourly rate based on my credentials and the going rates in the region for professional engineering services for the government. Then I determined the cost for working two thousand hours for the year. I didn't include any money for living expenses in the DC area, as I figured I'd cover those costs out of my salary, even though they would be substantial. The total cost I calculated was a large number, but I submitted it anyhow, along with the hourly rate upon which I based my proposal. I was certain they wouldn't pay as much as I asked for, but I thought all they could say was no.

A few weeks later, I received a call from the same contracts officer to discuss my proposal. I could tell he was a junior employee and had little negotiating experience since I'd dealt with contracts personnel many times before. Our conversation was surprising and went something like this.

He said, "Dr. Cicci, we received your proposal. Can you tell me how you came up with that figure?"

I answered, "Sure, I based it on the current hourly rates in the DC area that contractors charge the government for engineering services for someone with my experience."

He responded, "Oh, so it's based on the going rates paid by the government around DC?"

"Yes it is," I replied.

Then he said, "Well, we don't have that much money to spend." Not thinking he would answer my next question, I asked it anyhow, "Okay then, how much do you have?" In an obvious rookie mistake, he told me the amount they had available to spend, which was exactly 80% of the amount I requested.

Then he replied, "Could you change your proposal to reflect that figure?"

I replied, "I'll be happy to." Then he offered a suggestion I really didn't see coming. He said, "To reach our number, you can either reduce your hourly rate for the 2,000 hours, or you could keep your original rate and only work 1,600 hours for the same amount of money." I couldn't believe what I just heard!

He continued, "You can think it over and get back to us if you'd like."

Before he had time to realize what he'd told me, I said, "I don't need to think it over. I'll re-submit my proposal using the hourly rate I quoted but only working for 1,600 hours over the year instead of 2,000 hours."

He replied, "Great, send us your modification and we'll approve it for that amount." Our conversation left me speechless. They just gave me the choice to work fewer hours for the same amount of money. The government works in strange ways.

However, there was yet another delay in the final approval process. It was already May 2009, and they expected me to start that summer. The semester had just ended and time was short for me to make living arrangements in DC and move up there. I began getting nervous because I'd rejected the other offers and didn't want to restart the process. Besides, I already notified the university that I'd be taking my leave during the 2009-2010 academic year and I couldn't change my plan at that point.

The afternoon after our department's graduation reception I received the call. I was told that they approved all the paperwork on their end, but now AU also had to approve it, which was something I didn't know had to happen. After they did, I could start whenever I wanted. I wasn't sure if AU approving my contract would be a problem or not. It would have highlighted the fact that I was getting a double salary during my sabbatical year. But my friend, President Gogue, supported my working there and happily signed-off on my contract. He told me he had friends at the CIA and had visited just a few weeks before, and my name came up as perhaps going there for my sabbatical, which he encouraged. Once I received AU's approval, I picked a date in mid-July and made plans to head to DC.

I knew Chris couldn't go with me for the entire year because of her job. But she planned to visit whenever she could. A couple of weeks later, I drove to Washington to look for housing. I found a magnificent apartment in Pentagon City, next to Pentagon Row and the Fashion Centre Mall, close to the Metro and the Pentagon itself. In fact, the Pentagon City Metro Station was only a five-minute walk from my apartment and just two stops from Reagan National Airport, which was very convenient when Chris flew up for weekends. I'd be able to drive to work up the George Washington (GW) Parkway, traveling against rush hour traffic both ways, and it would only take about fifteen minutes. It was a perfect place for me to live. My new apartment was on the tenth floor of a high-rise, and I could lie on my sofa and look at the Washington Monument. It was a beautiful sight, and a spectacular one at night!

In a strange coincidence, during those few days I was in town looking for an apartment, Darby's band was playing at a small venue in DC. I got to see him and the show, which made my trip even better.

I drove back to Auburn to pack for a year. My lease began on July 1st, so I returned then to move in and get settled. When I visited a furniture rental store, I ended up purchasing an entire apartment of used furniture for $1,100 and sold it all when I left for $700. It wasa great deal.

Chris flew up a few days later to spend Independence Day in our nation's capital, which neither of us had done before. We had fun learning about the city and enjoyed the holiday celebration. We could watch the fireworks on the DC Mall from the rooftop of my new building, which was an amazing place to see them. The apartment management even provided food and drinks for the event.

One very unusual thing happened that weekend. There was an Irish Pub called Siné in Pentagon Row only a couple hundred yards from my building. It was a great bar and restaurant where I'd end up spending many future hours. Chris and I went out for drinks there on Friday night, July 3rd. Siné was crowded and as we were standing at the bar having drinks; we began chatting with a young couple next to us. We learned that they both worked at the Justice Department, but they didn't appear to be together as a couple. They even commented they were working that night, although they didn't say what they were doing. The couple bought us a round of drinks, and when we tried to return the favor later, they wouldn't hear of it. They ended up purchasing our drinks all evening and refused to let us buy any. Chris and I were both a little unsure of why, but we were enjoying our night out, the conversation, and the drinks. We thought it was very odd that two complete strangers would buy drinks the entire night without letting us buy them any in return. We continued to talk with them, and while we did, it appeared they were constantly looking around, observing others in the bar. That was strange too.

After we left, we discussed what just happened to us at Siné. I think we decided the couple was working counterintelligence for the Justice Department. It appeared they were attempting to observe or identify spies or other individuals who might talk too much about work or were perhaps revealing classified information. It was a well-known fact that the DC area had more spies per capita than any other city in the world. In fact, during my time there, they arrested a spy who lived in the apartment building across the street from mine.

I saw the same couple a few more times at Siné and other bars in the area over the next year, but had no further discussions with them. And they never bought me any more drinks. Regardless, it looked like they had interesting jobs.

I can't say too much about the work I did at the CIA. They assigned me to the Missile and Space Group of the Weapons, Intelligence, Nonproliferation, and Arms Control Center (WINPAC/MSG), which was part of the Directorate of Intelligence. The primary mission of WINPAC/MSG was to identify, assess, and counter foreign missile, unmanned aerial vehicles, and space threats to U.S. interests. They hired me as a Resident Expert to support the WINPAC/MSG mission. I acted as a consultant on a variety of issues and provided technical instruction in areas of need. The CIA was an enthralling place to work, and I learned a lot about the intelligence community. The layers of security I had to pass through each day were sometimes cumbersome, and I often arrived at the main gate in the morning to see armed soldiers guarding the entrance.

There were many fascinating things about the HQ building where I worked. The CIA Museum housed artifacts associated with the CIA's predecessor, the Office of Strategic Services, foreign intelligence organizations, and the CIA itself. The collection includes clothing, equipment, weapons, insignia, and other memorabilia that serve as tangible testimony to the Agency's history. They designed, manufactured, and used many of the objects in the Museum for intelligence operations, many of which were '007-like' gadgets for espionage activities during the Cold War.

As you walk through the hallways and offices of the various buildings on campus, you see many framed movie posters from all the films that included CIA references. They also had a wonderful gift shop that sold a multitude of books written about espionage and the Agency. One thing I liked to do was visit the Map Room, which had maps showing the very latest and ever-changing borders of all the countries around the world.

I found the people who worked at the CIA to be very intelligent, extremely competent, and exceedingly loyal. They were some of the best and brightest I've encountered during my career. After getting to know my co-workers I came away confident that our country's intelligence mission was in expert hands. The group I worked in comprised scientists, engineers, and mathematicians, but also included political scientists, economists, and sociologists, all of who played a specific role in the assessment of foreign threats.

Besides providing technical support on specific issues connected to missiles and space, I created and offered a series of short courses dealing with a variety of subjects. They covered topics related to orbital mechanics, inertial navigation, and guidance, orbital station keeping, orbit determination, and spacecraft perturbations. I taught several short courses that similar to the ones I did in the past. Those courses sharpened my teaching skills to an even higher level because of the quality of the seasoned professionals enrolled. My skill set was an excellent match to the needs of WINPAC/MSG, and I believe my being there was a benefit to the Agency.

Many of the people I met in DC outside of work also had government connections, and they were intelligent and well educated. Everybody had a story to tell, and they were often very captivating stories. I became friends with a guy who grew up in Pittsburgh and spent many years working as a Secret Service agent assigned to protect President Clinton. He told me he was with Bill Clinton the night

Hillary found out about the Monica Lewinsky scandal, and that they had to take the President to hide out in a hotel because Hillary was ready to kill him.

Living in DC, while lonely, was educational, inspiring, and exciting. Since my contract only called for me to work 80% of full time, I had a day off each week to explore DC. And I did. I visited most all the museums, monuments, and government buildings I found interesting. My favorites were the Newseum (which has since closed), Ford's Theatre, the Supreme Court Building, the Library of Congress, and Arlington National Cemetery. Chris came up a lot of weekends and we explored much of it together. There was so much to see and do in DC and there wasn't enough time to do everything, even living there for over a year. But I tried.

Visiting the Smithsonian Air and Space Museums was imperative for me. Both the National Air and Space Museum on the Mall, and the Steven F. Udvar-Hazy Center in Chantilly, Virginia, were splendid! Although, I felt old when I saw the actual XV-15 tilt-rotor plane in the Udvar-Hazy Center I worked on at Bell many years before.

When I attended the Memorial Day services at Arlington National Cemetery, I saw Vice-President Joe Biden speak. I also went there on the day of Ted Kennedy's funeral and saw his motorcade, but they closed the burial to the public.

I signed up for tours of both the U.S. Capitol Building and the White House, but had to arrange them through my congressional representative, Mike Rogers. For my Capitol tour, I reported to his office in the Rayburn House Office Building (HOB) and met one of his staffers. She was to be my guide for a personalized tour of the Capitol and spent two hours showing me every corner of the building and telling many stories of its history. Although I'd been there before, I learned much more this time thanks to such a knowledgeable staffer. We walked from the HOB to the Capitol and back through the underground tunnel that the members of Congress used each day. I never cared much for Mike Rogers as a congressional representative, and I found during my tour with his staffer that she felt much the same way.

My visit to the White House was even more memorable. They scheduled it for a Friday afternoon at 4:00 pm, and I was to be part of a small group touring together. I arrived at the White House thirty minutes early and was the first member of my group to appear. When I went into the security tent to present my identification, a friendly young man in his twenties, who worked for the U.S. Secret Service, checked my ID. When he read my driver's license and saw I was from Auburn, he said, "Hey, I'm from Birmingham and I graduated from Auburn University a couple years ago." We chatted for a few minutes. When I told him I was a professor there, it turned out that I knew some of his former teachers, one of whom was my close friend, Rich Penaskovic.

Then he said, "I'll tell you what, since you're the first one here, you can do a self-guided-tour, if you'd like. Take as long as you want, but just stay behind the velvet ropes wherever you go." I liked that idea, so I thanked him and went in and walked through the White House alone. It was an amazing way to see such a beautiful and historic building.

Another thing I did that I found very fascinating, although it may not be to others, was to visit the famous Deep Throat Garage in the Rosslyn section of Arlington. That was the parking garage where Washington Post reporter Bob Woodward met Mark Felt of the Federal Bureau of Investigation (FBI), also known as 'Deep Throat', during Woodward's Watergate investigation. The information that Felt discretely provided Woodward in this underground garage helped to bring down the Nixon administration and resulted in President Nixon's resignation in 1974. The particular parking stall where the two men met, D-32, was located two levels below the garage's North Nash Street entrance. When I visited in 2012, it was a very dark and deserted, and an overall creepy place. I can see why they chose that location to exchange information and hide the identity of the secret informer. Since I lived through Watergate, I found my visit to the garage to be captivating, and a little scary.

I also visited a lot of great restaurants, bars and music venues. My favorite eateries were the Old Ebbitt Grill near the White House, Theismann's in Old Town Alexandria, and Cantler's Riverside Inn in

Annapolis, Maryland. The best music venues I liked best were the 9:30 Club in DC and the Birchmere in Alexandria. I also spent a lot of time watching sports at the Crystal City Sports Pub, a three-level sports paradise for watching all types of sporting events. There were several days I was there for such a long time watching back-to-back-to-back college football games, I had more than one meal while hardly moving from my bar stool.

During the year I was there, Darby's band played a few more shows at various venues around town, and I attended each one. They were all marvelous and fun nights. On a couple of occasions, they even stayed at my apartment to save money on hotels, which made it even more enjoyable! Corey even flew to DC from Spokane, WA to ride with me back to Alabama for the Christmas holidays. Unfortunately, there was a huge snowstorm just before he arrived and much of the city was closed, so I couldn't show him around the city.

My year of working at the CIA went by fast. I don't think I could have gone to a better place for a sabbatical. And living in DC was far greater than I could have imagined. They must have thought my being there was beneficial to the Agency as well. Before I finished in July 2010, they extended my contract for me to return in the summers of 2011, 2012, and 2013 to continue my contribution to their mission.

When I returned to DC the following summer, I rented another apartment in the same building in Pentagon City. This time it was on the sixth floor and didn't have a view of the Washington Monument. Although it was still close to Siné, which had become my favorite bar since the first night Chris and I went there and got free drinks, courtesy of the Justice Department.

In the summer of 2012, I sublet an artist's condominium in Old Town Alexandria, a marvelous area filled with shops, restaurants, bars, and art galleries. It was a little farther out than Pentagon City, but it was fun exploring another part of town.

Bad news came the following spring, however, as budget cuts hit the Agency. Those cuts resulted in my contract for the summer of 2013 being canceled, and my abbreviated career at the CIA ended. Overall, my time at the Agency was an amazing experience and I wouldn't trade it for anything. I was very lucky to have worked there.

If I had known what a great place it was to work, I might have applied there after graduating from WVU, or CMU, or maybe even UT.

One thing I did with the extra money I made during my sabbatical was to buy a regulation NBA glass backboard and basketball goal. I had it mounted next to my driveway, and I started shooting again. I found that I can still shoot pretty well, but I still can't dunk.

My leave from AU was a sabbatical like no other, and I'm very proud to have done it!

21

BACK TO CAMPUS AND WINDING DOWN

My experience working at Langley was an exceptional one, and I feel very lucky to have had such a great opportunity. I came away with even more respect and admiration for the people who devote their lives to keeping our country safe. But after thirteen straight months of being away, I was ready to return to Auburn and get back to my academic life.

During my years at AU, every student who graduated in aerospace engineering had to have me for orbital mechanics, because I was the only professor who taught it. Spring semester of 2010 was the exception. My colleague Andy Sinclair took over the class in my absence and did a great job. The students who had him for orbital mechanics were the only ones who went through our department that didn't have to take me for a course, which may have been lucky for them. I enjoyed knowing that I had almost everyone in class who graduated from our program from 1987 until 2018.

On my return from DC, I began thinking about how I would finish out my career. I was 59, and I thought I'd work another seven or eight years until I was 66 or 67. Knowing that I had my summer salary covered for a few more summers working back at the CIA, I didn't feel pressure to find funding. As a result, I wanted to focus more on teaching and even less on research during the rest of my career. I was very fortunate to have a department head in John Cochran who agreed to allow me to do that. So instead of teaching the customary two classes per semester, John allowed me to teach a third class in place of research. Of course, I still had the obligatory service assignment, but knowing I could focus on teaching pleased me very much. I think it worked out well for the department too. I dabbled in research and publishing some of my past work, but doing that only involved writing up results I already had and not doing much new research.

I enjoyed being back in the classroom for fall 2010, returning to the flexible schedule of a professor, and not having to commute through traffic each day. Although I missed DC and everything it offered, I didn't miss the intense job and lifestyle I had there. When I returned to AU, I brought back plenty of delightful stories about my CIA experience, and the students had a million questions about my time there. I couldn't answer many of them because so much of the information was classified or at least highly sensitive.

For the ones I couldn't answer, I'd often respond with my version of the old joke, "I could answer that question, but then I'd have to shoot you. Would that be alright?" I got no takers with that response, only laughs.

Student questions often dealt with what the CIA knew about flying saucers and space aliens. One story I'd tell them was how my desk at the Agency was in a large office and there was a filing cabinet against the wall behind my chair. It had three drawers, always locked, and a label on each drawer described its contents. The three labels read: 'Area 51', 'Moon Landing', and 'Kennedy Assassination'. I didn't mention that those labels were just a joke placed there by a clever CIA officer in our group. The students enjoyed the story and may have half-believed the Agency humor.

I received a lot of questions about what exactly I did at the CIA. The only thing I'd tell them was that I came away amazed at what other countries were doing and even more amazed at how much we knew about it all. They'd also ask, knowing what I know now, how did I feel about our country's security? I always answered by telling them I felt safer than I did before, because of what our country knows about what's going on in the world. Our intelligence community does incredible work, and it astonished me daily!

I also told them about the Oktoberfest party we had in WINPAC/ MSG. On a Friday afternoon the WINPAC director brought in a buffet of hors d'oeuvres and snacks, along with several coolers filled with German beer. He invited everybody to enjoy the social atmosphere and take part in a beer-tasting contest. I'd never been in a work environment where they held a drinking party in the office during the day before. Everyone enjoyed the festivities, and it was a nice reward for the employees who labored so hard to support our nation's intelligence mission.

Besides teaching, I also did some consulting for Broadcom Corporation in Irvine, California, during my year back. That project involved developing filtering software for Global Positioning System (GPS) applications on certain brands of cellular phones. I didn't enjoy consulting because I always spent too many hours working on it and it ate up most of my free time. But the money was nice, and if I get offered another interesting project, I'd consider doing more of it.

After my three-year stint in senate leadership positions before my sabbatical, I didn't want to do more university service. As a result, after I returned I focused my service effort more at the department and college levels. It wasn't as interesting, but it was still worthwhile. Much of it involved serving on faculty search committees. When they hired Chris Roberts as dean, he set in motion a conscientious effort to provide aerospace engineering with resources by adding new faculty positions and enhancing our facilities. Our previous dean-yes, the inept one-hurt our department through budget cuts and intentional neglect. His actions damaged our programs and our professors. But with Dean Roberts we were back on-track to become competitive again, not only within the university but also in our region and also across the country.

I always had a few graduate students, but I never had a lot at any one time, like some other professors, and not anywhere near the number Dr. Tapley had at UT. Before I went to DC, I tried to get most of them graduated, but then I attracted a few more when I returned. Thinking I'd be retiring soon, I didn't want very many more. And I wanted no more doctoral students because of the length of their program, but I took a few more master's degree students with the idea that they could all finish by the time I retired. That plan worked out well as I wound down my research activities. I was lucky to always have excellent graduate students, and those experiences were important for me and for them. They did many great things that made me very proud of them after they graduated.

Before my sabbatical, I won six teaching awards in the department and one in the College of Engineering. After I returned, I was lucky enough to win six more, three departmental and three college awards. They included the prestigious William F. Walker Teaching Award for Excellence, the Fred H. Pumphrey Award, and the AU Student Government Association Award. A few of those even included monetary gifts in addition to nice plaques. I believe I became a better teacher after my sabbatical, from my experience teaching high-level CIA employees, and because I could focus more on it than before. I enjoyed being back in academia and able to help students succeed. I still couldn't wait to get to work each morning and didn't want to leave when the day ended.

As I mentioned, I felt an important part of my job was helping students to find jobs when they graduated. Many would ask if they could use me as a reference, and I always agreed. I'd often receive phone calls from perspective employers inquiring about a student's work ethic, character, honesty, and how they'd fit into working on a team of engineers. When asked, I tried to emphasize their strong points and speak as highly of them as I could. I was proud that I helped so many of them find employment to kick off their careers.

Students who didn't do well in my classes seldom asked to use me as a reference. I suppose they might not like what I'd say about them. But I often suggested names and companies for them to contact if they were having difficulty finding jobs, and even for internships while they were undergraduates.

I was always honest in my recommendations. Anytime I recommended that a company hire a student, it was a reflection on both our program and me. If I believed someone wasn't capable of doing the job well, I wouldn't recommend them for it. Sometimes I'd suggest a company consider them for alternative type of work based upon their skill set, and they appreciated my honesty.

There was only one time I may have hurt a student's chances of getting hired. I had a foreign graduate student that took my graduate course who missed a lot of class and didn't complete all the assignments. He got a C in the course, which is a terrible grade for a graduate student. (I know, I got one once.) Most of the students who took my graduate courses get As, and only a few got Bs. I seldom gave anybody a C.

After I posted the grades, this student came to my office to 'discuss' his poor grade. Our conversation went something like this:

Student: Dr. Cicci, I got a C in your class.

Me: I know you did.

Student: Well, I don't want a C. It looks bad on my transcript.

Me: Yes, getting a C is terrible for a graduate student.

Student: Can you change my grade to a B?

Me: Well, do you think you did enough work in class to deserve a B?

Student: No, but I want a B, anyway.

Me: Then you should have worked harder.

Student: But can't you just change it from a C to a B so it won't look bad on my transcript?

Me: No, that wouldn't be fair to the other students. But I can change it from a C to a D. Would you like me to do that?

Student: No, I'll keep the C.

This student got a poor grade because he was not focused, didn't do the work, and didn't learn the material. Although, he graduated with his master's degree that semester. He was one of those who didn't ask me to be a job reference.

But ... a few months later I received a call from my friend, Jimmy, at DCI in Huntsville, who I worked with at NASA during the summer I spent there. This student had applied for a job at DCI and Jimmy saw on his transcript that he got a C in my class. So he called to ask me about the applicant, knowing that I'd give him my honest opinion. And I did. I described how the student didn't do the work, earned his C, and wanted me to change it to a B because he didn't want a C on his transcript. Jimmy knew this wasn't someone he wanted to hire and thanked me for my comments. I would not be untruthful about a prospective employee as that would be a terrible reflection on me as a professor. I'm not sure where this student ever found a job but I don't think he got hired at DCI.

When I arrived at AU in 1987, they housed our department in Wilmore Laboratories. By 1993, we moved into a brand new building just across the parking lot. They called it, cleverly, the Aerospace Engineering Building. At the groundbreaking ceremony, all faculty members were given shovels to pose for a photo, and we pretended to be digging a hole to start the construction.

When one of my students saw the photo he said, "How appropriate Dr. Cicci has a shovel, he's already buried me a few times on his orbital exams." I thought his comment was funny and very accurate.

Our new building wasn't a well-built one, likely because it went to the low bidder under a state contract. When construction first began, the outer wall was built so crooked it needed to be taken down and redone. A little later, a large crane fell backwards into the faculty parking lot and flattened someone's car a few spaces from mine. They were lucky that nobody got injured or killed. When the building opened and the first heavy rain came, we could see water gushing out of electrical receptacles on the bottom floor. That was quite a frightening sight! Several times over the years, they installed scaffolding around the building's perimeter to protect passersby from being struck by pieces of blocks falling from the top edge of the exterior. Even worse, they built the roof to be flat, and it held water like a swimming pool. As a result, the ceilings in many of the offices on the top floor leaked whenever it rained. I know each office I had in that building had leaks. When they became bad enough, a maintenance crew would try to find and patch them. But even if they succeeded, the repair never lasted long. I spent many mornings cleaning up from overnight rains that flooded my office.

Several years later they changed the building's name to Charles E. Davis Aerospace Engineering Hall after they received a large donation from 'Buddy' Davis. He was a former engineering student at AU who'd done well in the business world. I'm not sure I'd want my name on that poorly constructed building.

Over the years, I occupied four different offices, all on the top floor, where I have one now that still leaks. The first two were just standard rectangular-shaped rooms, as most of the offices in the building were. But my last one before I retired was a large L-shaped corner office that had tall windows on two sides. I spent about fifteen years in that office and I loved it there, even with the leaky roof. It was quiet, roomy, comfortable, and it had a splendid view of Samford Park and it's beautiful lawns shrubs, and blossoming azaleas in the spring. After I retired I had to surrender that wonderful office, and I returned to one of the standard rectangular ones with a much worse view. But I always loved being on-campus regardless of what office I had. I suppose a campus was my happy place where I felt comfortable and content.

When I returned to AU in 2010, I spent the next two summers working back at the CIA. Those experiences were also good, but I was tired of being away from home and having to find places to live. And DC was getting harder to navigate alone. So I wasn't too sad when budget cuts canceled my contract for the summer of 2013. I was glad to not have to go back, and by then, I didn't feel like I needed to work in the summers any longer. Chris had been working full time for many years now. The kids were both out of college, grown and gone, and we were enjoying our lives. We weren't very materialistic and spent little money. So I took the next few summers off. I played golf; we traveled whenever we could; and I drank more beer. We went to New York many times over the years because Corey lived there from 2002 to 2006, as did Darby from 2005 to 2016. Although we loved the city, we did everything we wanted to do there during those fourteen years and have only been back once since Darby left.

I published a couple more journal articles after I finished at the CIA, but they didn't relate to any of the work I did there. I lost interest in technical writing and became more interested in creative writing. I even took a class to learn more about it, which I enjoyed. I began planning a story for a novel and worked on an outline. I always wanted to create some kind of art, and I thought writing might be something I could do. It was hard though-much more difficult than technical articles for conferences or journals, although it was a fun learning experience.

But nothing was as good for me as teaching. The longer I taught, the better teacher I became. I felt comfortable in the classroom, and I found better and better ways to connect with students. And the longer I taught, the more stories I could tell, which was always an important part of my classes.

As a joke, I'd sometimes begin my class by asking how many of them would like it if I canceled class that day, even though I had no intention of doing so. Of course, nearly everybody's hand went up. Then I explained to them how education was the only commodity where people would happily pay more money for less product. I'd ask how they'd like it if they went to the gas station and paid to fill up their tank, but only got half the gas they paid for. They didn't appreciate that idea much, but they'd be okay if I canceled class and not refund that day's tuition. I told them they were probably paying the university twenty dollars for each scheduled class, and that money was being wasted if I didn't teach. I just wanted them to realize that not having class wasn't in their best interest. Of course, many of the students' parents were paying their tuition, so it was sometimes a hard point to drive home. But the ones who were putting themselves through school understood what I meant.

I never had very many students who were athletes in my classes. When I did, they were usually swimmers, soccer players, and baseball players. Only rarely did I have a football player, and I only had one basketball player. I offered to give him bonus points if he could out-shoot me on the court. He turned down my offer. I don't think he wanted to embarrass an old man, since he was 6 feet, 9 inches tall and I wasn't. He was also twenty-one, and I wasn't that either, but we both laughed about it. He was an excellent student, as were most of the athletes I had in class, because they were hard-working and dedicated individuals and that carried over to all aspects of their lives. They had to be in order to manage both going to school and playing their sport.

It's too bad that more student-athletes don't select demanding majors. The reason for this isn't because they aren't capable of doing the work, it's because a National Collegiate Athletic Association (NCAA) rule discourages students from taking difficult majors. If athletes want to study engineering, for example, and find it too difficult or time-consuming, they'll lose athletic eligibility for a time if they change their major. That's because their current coursework wouldn't count in their new degree plan, which violates NCAA eligibility rules. So a student will major in something less demanding and not risk losing their eligibility by changing majors. It's a ridiculous rule and one that they should change. I have many gripes about NCAA rules that I'd like to see changed. When I had athletes in class, I could relate to them and what they were going through to get an education and play their sport. And I know it's much more demanding nowadays than it was when I was a student-athlete.

I also update our engineering mechanics textbook each semester as they continue to use it for that same class Darby and I wrote it for years before. After I make changes, I deliver it to a local copy shop where they duplicate it and sell. That process works well, and it's nice to know that our book is being used to help students succeed in their academic careers.

I could always deal with just about anything that happened in my classrooms. The students were usually respectful, and I never had many problems. One thing that bothered me, however, was the use of cell phones in my classes. I found it to be very distracting, not only to me, but also to the others in class. As the years went by, the problem became worse and eventually unbearable to me as a professor. I knew I had to devise a policy so students wouldn't want to risk playing with their phones during my lecture. I tried several measures before I came up with a solution that worked.

My first attempt was telling students they had to keep their phones in their backpacks and if I saw them at all, I'd confiscate their phone for the rest of class. That wasn't very successful, even though I collected a few phones. Next, I tried a policy where if I saw their phones out, I'd dismiss them and count them absent for the day. That didn't work great either. Then I adjusted it to an even stricter policy: I'd dismiss them and they'd lose half a letter grade in their final average for the semester each time it happened. Now that plan got their attention!

But even though it solved the problem, I felt it might have been a little harsh. By my last year of teaching, my policy became having the students turn off their phones and place them on a table in front as they entered the classroom, then they could retrieve them when they left. That was the best policy. A student even came up to me after class one day and thanked me for having a strict rule on the use of phones. He said that he never used his, and it was very distracting when other students used theirs during lectures. I appreciated him telling me so.

Cell phone usage is a big problem in class, but even a bigger one in our daily lives. Some people, and not only students, become addicted to their phones and focus on them at the expense of everything else. And I'll admit I fall into that category myself sometimes. The problem arises when people's phones interfere with the rest of their lives, including their jobs and their relationships.

I met one of our alumni several years ago that often came to Auburn to hire recent graduates for his engineering company. During our talk, I asked him about how a graduate he hired the year before was doing. The student was talented student, and I thought he'd make an excellent engineer. Well, this alum told me he had to let our graduate go because he couldn't stay off his phone long enough to focus on his job. He said the employee spent most of the day texting and playing on his phone and was unproductive. Companies pay engineers to produce, so I understood his position. Then he asked me if I'd please try to break students of their cell phone addiction, at least when they were in class. So I tried my best to do that. I'm not sure if it helped in the long term, but I hope so. I know it benefitted me in the short term.

The CIA had a simple phone policy for the employees that worked great. They prohibited cell phones on site altogether. Part of the reasoning for that policy was because there was so much classified information around; they didn't want to risk any of it being leaked through cell phone use. But a big part of it was also to keep employees focused on their jobs so they could be productive. I thought their plan was a good one, although I know there wasn't any way students could come to class without their phones.

22

AN UNEXPECTED TURN OF
EVENTS

As I moved toward my mid-sixties, I thought more seriously about retirement. I still loved teaching, but I wanted to have time to do other things before I was too old. So like anyone contemplating retiring, I calculated how much money I'd have to live on after I stopped working. Since my father died at a young age, I knew I could, too. I had already outlived him by fifteen years, so I didn't want to wait too long to retire and die at my desk, or worse, in my classroom.

Alabama may not have been the best place to live for most of my life, but it had an outstanding retirement program for state employees, and I was one since I worked at a public university. I often said that the Retirement System of Alabama (RSA) made up for many of the negatives of living in the state, and I was right.

The RSA retirement program for teachers was a fixed-benefit plan. Private investments fund the program, part of which included the Robert Trent Jones Golf Trail, a group of twenty-six championship golf courses at eleven sites across the state. The RSA program provided a retirement pay equal to two percent of the average of your three highest years of salary over the last ten. So if you worked for thirty years, your pay would be about 60% of your highest three-year average salary. As a result, when employees get close to retirement, they try to maximize their salaries in order to get a higher pension.

That's accomplished by working through the summers, either by teaching or doing research, to drive up the income upon which they based our retirement salary. Faculty could also roll their unused sick leave into their total service time, which generated higher pay. I never used my sick leave during my career and that counted for a couple of extra years of service, which would provide an additional 2% pay for each of those years. Therefore, when employees think about retiring, a significant amount of planning and calculating occurs, and it was no exception for me.

My concern was to have an adequate retirement income, but not work too long and miss out on getting to do the other things I hoped to do after retiring. I never cared to work into my seventies or beyond, like some people, even if I could still teach. That just wasn't me. Besides, Chris was only a year younger than me and she didn't want to work too long, either. I knew she was tiring of her job, and I wouldn't keep working after she retired. So there was a lot to consider. I often thought back to my first job out of college and remember thinking that I'd reach my expected retirement age of 65 in the year 2016, which seemed like a lifetime away. But that time had now passed, and I still hadn't retired.

I first began calculating what my retirement pay would be once I reached age sixty. When I finished at the CIA in 2012, I was sixty-one. It was my intention to work a few summers to raise my salary. I still enjoyed teaching enough that I wasn't ready to give it up just yet, but I thought I might be when I hit sixty-six in 2017, which also coincided with my full retirement age for Social Security. So, 2017 became my target date for me to quit working.

Besides the study about online education I did for the dean in the summer of 2013, I planned to teach in the summers of 2016 and 2017 after taking the summers of 2014 and 2015 off. I ended up teaching one summer class in 2016 and two in 2017. My thoughts were that, depending on how the academic year of 2016-2017 went, I'd be in an excellent position to retire in the summer of 2017. If I wanted to. Chris was planning on retiring in 2018 when she turned sixty-six, so if I left in 2017, she'd still be working, which I'm sure would have resulted in me getting into some kind of trouble with my friends.

Before the start of classes in Spring 2017, they invited Chris and me to attend a WVU basketball reunion for former players back in Morgantown. We attended the game against Texas Christian University, which WVU won. They introduced former players to a filled coliseum at halftime, where we got to walk to center court as they announced our names. We also took part in the new Mountaineer tradition of singing 'Country Roads' after the game ended. Later, Coach Bob Huggins hosted dinner at a local restaurant. It was a great weekend seeing old friends and making new ones, and I appreciated being invited to attend the reunion. Basketball was still affecting my life, and that wasn't about to change yet.

The next day, we drove to Pittsburgh and attended the Steelers playoff game against the Miami Dolphins, which the Steelers won in a lop-sided victory. They played the game in bitter cold weather, and I believe the temperature was barely above zero at kickoff. On the walk from our car to the stadium, Chris and I had to stop in two bars just to get warm. It was the first time in my life that I sat at a bar and ordered hot chocolate. The weekend was a fun one all around, despite the freezing temperatures. It's always nice to go back home to Morgantown and Pittsburgh.

I still taught three courses in the spring semester, and I continued to love it. Even after all those years, I got butterflies from excitement before class each day, and I didn't feel like that would end in only a few more months. Then Sunday, March 26, 2017 happened and things changed, with basketball playing yet another role in my life.

Chris was in Florida visiting her mother and I was at home, upstairs in my man cave getting ready to watch the NCAA Men's Basketball Tournament Elite 8 game between UNC and Kentucky (UK). They set the tipoff for 4:05 pm CDT. At about 3:30 I started having terrible chest pains that I'd never experienced before. Of course, I thought it was indigestion from all the crap I'd been eating while my wife was out of town. But it wasn't. I knew that when my arms got numb and I broke out in a cold sweat indigestion wasn't the problem. I called 911, then I phoned Chris, who was sitting in the Melbourne,

Florida airport waiting to board her flight home. We only talked for a minute, and she told me to take four low-dose aspirins, which we had stockpiled in the medicine cabinet, and lie down, which I did. Then I texted my brother in Atlanta and told him what was happening. He and Jean dropped what they were doing and headed for Auburn at once.

The paramedics, along with a city police unit and a fire truck, arrived in what seemed like only a few minutes. I'd unlocked the side door to the house so they could come right in. When they did and performed a quick electrocardiogram on me, they determined I needed to get to the hospital. As I was lying in the ambulance, I remember thinking that if this was going to be the end for me, I did the best I could and had a pretty good life. Not that I was ready to go, but if I must, I wouldn't go out having any regrets. Those thoughts gave me some peace and relaxed me. But hell no, I wasn't going anywhere yet! I was in the middle of the semester and had class the next day. After all, I couldn't miss my classes!

We only lived five minutes from EAMC. Everything was happening so fast I didn't even get to call Chris back and tell her what was going on. After not being able to reach me, she called one of her coworkers at the hospital that she knew was working that day, Danna, and asked her to be on the lookout for my arrival. Since the paramedics alerted EAMC about my condition ahead of time, they wheeled me straight into the catheterization (cath) lab to diagnose my condition when I arrived, where Danna soon found me to see how I was doing. It was great to see a friendly, smiling face! Danna called Chris to update her before she boarded her flight to Atlanta.

I didn't worry once I arrived at the hospital because I knew I'd be in expert hands. As the nurses prepared me to get a catheterization, I asked if anybody knew the score of the UNC-Kentucky basketball game. When nobody did, I commented they needed to have a TV in the cath lab since it was March Madness and patients like me wanted scores!

Then they told me that Dr. Rhodes, the heart surgeon, was on his way in and would be there in a few minutes. I immediately thought to myself, "Oh no, not Dr. Rhodes!"

Now, I didn't know Dr. Rhodes at all. I'd heard that he was one of the best cardiologists at EAMC. But Chris and I both watched the TV series, Chicago Med, because one of Darby's college buddies was an actor on the show and played a heart surgeon named Dr. Rhodes. My first thought was, "Wait, he's not a doctor, he's an actor. I don't want Colin working on me!" But this Dr. Rhodes wasn't the actor; he was an outstanding cardiologist. Dr. Rhodes, the actor, agreed with my sentiment when I described my experience to him a couple of months later.

I had to have one heart stent implanted to open a blocked artery. It wasn't a big deal at all, and I was awake the entire time. I felt lucky that a single stent was all I needed.

In fact, when I told a good friend about my procedure later, he responded, "Just one stent? That's hardly worth mentioning!" He was almost right.

As they wheeled me out of the lab, I asked once more if anybody knew the score of the UNC game. One guy in the room said UNC was up by five points at halftime. I thanked him and reminded them again that they needed a TV in their lab for when they brought in sports fans.

Danna wasn't the only person Chris called. On my way out of the cath lab, six or eight of our closest Auburn friends had rushed to EAMC to find me. I saw them in the hallway as I rolled past when my catheterization was over. It made me feel great seeing them all there, and it touched me they would come to the hospital so fast. Those are the best friends anybody can have!

They took me to a private room in the Intensive Care Unit (ICU). It may have been because Chris was a friend to everybody there and they wanted to take good care of me. At one point I even heard Dr. Rhodes say to a nurse, "This is Chris's husband, we're not letting him go," for which I was very thankful!

After I got settled in my room, the first thing I did was turn on the TV to find the basketball game. I saw the last five minutes and watched the incredible ending where UNC won 75-73 on a shot by Luke Maye with 0.3 seconds left. That ending may have sent me to the hospital if I hadn't already been there. I found out later that one of our friends, who was also a UNC fan, texted Chris and, not knowing what happened to me, jokingly said that the exciting finish to the Tar Heels game probably gave Dave a heart attack.

It wasn't long until Ed and Jean arrived. It sure was great to see them both. Then a short while later Chris made it from the Atlanta Airport, a little frazzled and flustered, although she calmed down when she saw I was still alive. But she'd been talking with Danna all along and knew everything that was taking place. They kept me in the ICU for a couple of days before moving me to a regular room for two more. Then I went home on Thursday.

I always felt lucky being married to a healthcare professional, except when Chris was standing next to my hospital bed staring at my patient monitor and making comments like, "Well, that doesn't look good." Then she wouldn't tell me why it didn't look good. That was my only complaint. She took great care of me in every aspect of my recovery and life since that day. But sometimes she gives me 'too much information' or, in this case, 'not enough information'.

I called my department chair, Brian Thurow, early Monday morning, and he canceled my classes for the entire week. I wanted to get back to work on the following Monday. My doctor, however, disagreed and said I had to take another week off. So, I taught all my classes during the following week online from home. It wasn't very easy or much fun, but it was better than canceling more classes. I never liked to cancel any of my classes, even when I had to be out of town for meetings or a conference. My classes were thrown off-schedule, and I wasn't giving the students what they paid a lot of money for, which just wasn't something I preferred to do.

I'm not sure if my students ever heard the reason for my absence. I don't think they did. However, when I returned the following week and walked into class for the first time, one student was suspiciously standing near my podium as I arrived.

Before I could say anything, he handed me an envelope and said, "Dr. Cicci, everybody chipped in and we bought you this to welcome you back." They gave me a gift card to a local restaurant. It shocked and touched me they would do such a considerate thing.

I said to the class, "Oh my, thank you so much, I'm very touched that you would all do this for me! I appreciate your thoughtfulness more than I can say. Now it's time to get to work, you've been off too long already!" At the end of the hour, I thanked them all again. I can't express how much their gesture meant to me. And it felt wonderful to be back where I belonged. At the student AIAA banquet a few weeks later, I received the 'Most Likely to Teach Class From a Hospital Bed,' award.

By that time, it was late April, and the semester was winding down. The epiphany I had during my health scare caused me to rethink my retirement plan. It made me realize that I just wasn't ready to say goodbye to the students I spent so many years educating. I still loved my job and looked forward to going to work every morning. So I pushed my retirement plans back for another year and signed-up to teach two more classes that summer. But as I taught them, I had second thoughts about working another year. I didn't want to work away my last few years. Having reached full retirement age, I filed to receive my Social Security benefits. I thought that if I wasn't going to live much longer, I at least wanted to get back some money that I've been paying the government since my very first job. When I did that, I think I mentally retired.

In the big scheme of things, having that blockage may have been a good thing for me. It was minor but could've been much worse. It opened my eyes and caused me to change my lifestyle. I ate better, got a lot more exercise, lost weight, and took better care of myself. As a result, my health improved, and I felt great. I never missed taking my meds, and overall, my life improved. Of course, Chris kept me on track and wouldn't let me slip back into my old bad eating habits and not exercising.

When classes began in the fall of 2017, I returned to teaching my full course load. But what people say is true. Once you think about retiring, you're already retired in your mind. And that was the case for me. Beginning that fall and for the first time, I no longer looked forward to going to class. In fact, I dreaded it. That's the point when I realized I stayed too long and should have retired in 2017. I knew I hit my wall and this would be my last year. Once I made that decision,

I was sure it was the right one for me. Besides, I was now having students whose parents I also taught, which was a clear sign to me it was time to retire.

By that time, I was in my thirty-first year of teaching at Auburn, besides those few years at UT and ACC. Facing retirement, I couldn't believe the time went by so fast, or that I had a career I enjoyed so much.

Somehow, I bumbled through the fall and spring semesters. Brian agreed to allow me to teach a class in the first half of the summer term of 2018 to increase retirement pay. My official retirement date was June 1, but I taught my class until it ended later that month.

A few weeks before I finished, my department held a retirement party for me at the home of my colleague, Roy Hartfield. It was a fun night and great to see everybody together, including some colleagues who retired years before. One of my master's graduates even drove three hours to attend. During the party they presented me with some gifts, one of which was a binder containing letters, photos, and congratulations from many of my former students and former and current colleagues. It was a lovely gift loaded with beautiful sentiments. One entry touched me deeply: it was a photo taken that very morning at Dynetics in Huntsville. Twenty of my former students who were employees there all left work to take a group photo to send to me for my retirement party that night. I will keep that binder forever, and it was the best gift I could have received.

Chris retired at the same time. I don't think she wanted me to have any fun without her. We planned to play golf and travel as much as we could in the years ahead. We had a joint retirement party at our home and invited our Auburn friends to celebrate with us. It was a perfect culmination to two long and wonderful careers. It thrilled me that one of them was mine!

23

MY RETIREMENT LIFE

Retirement suits me, although I wasn't sure if I was going to miss teaching or not. I suspected that I'd miss the students and my connection with them, but not making up exams, grading, attending faculty and committee meetings, or cell phones in my classroom. I may also have missed getting to stand in front of thirty or forty hungry minds that wanted to learn everything I can teach them about space. I'd definitely miss being around young adults who always made me feel younger. And I'd miss answering the tough questions they used to ask. That might be the best part about teaching-getting a question you don't expect, having to think fast on your feet, and draw from your base of knowledge or even on courses you took yourself many years before. Then talking yourself through it and explaining it well enough for the students to understand, convincing them you know what you're talking about. Yes, that was satisfying, and it kept me mentally sharp. Faking it was never an option, since they always knew when I tried doing that. They made sure I was on my game, and I liked that.

Chris and I had a simple retirement plan; we wanted to travel and play golf as much as possible and see our children more. Combining those two activities, we're trying to play at all eleven of the sites on the Robert Trent Jones Golf Trail throughout Alabama. We've spent more time with our kids, even though they don't live near us. I also planned to read more and write or do something else artistic. We continued exercising regularly and focusing on being healthy because we wanted to be around for as long as possible. Life was too good to have it cut short. We got off to a splendid start doing all the things we wanted.

When Chris retired, they asked her to keep working a couple of days each month on special projects. She agreed to do that as long as she could do it online so it wouldn't affect our travel plans. EAMC was fine with her request, so she continued to work when she could. She likes to be up-to-date on the pharmacy world and stay current, not only for her own benefit but because Corey is now an Emergency Department Pharmacist in Tyler, Texas. After being an actor and a nurse, and following stops at Eastern Washington University (EWU) and the University of Nevada, Reno (UNR), he went back to UNC to attend Pharmacy School in 2014. He graduated in 2018 and did two years of residency, one year in Chapel Hill and a second year in suburban Milwaukee, Wisconsin. Now we have three doctors in the family, which makes it even more confusing, and an extremely talented musician and artist. We have thirteen degrees among the four of us, and I may be the least intelligent of everyone in a great multitude of subjects. I lose every time we play intellectual board games, and I always get clobbered in Jeopardy. We have a lot of high-level conversations, and Corey and Darby express too many clever quips and jokes to count whenever we're together. It's always a tremendous amount of fun!

Darby quit touring the world with his band and is now writing music for commercials and movies, in addition to his own records. In 2019 he finished the musical score for a full-length film and he also wrote the soundtrack to a film he put together entitled, *I Have Seen The Future*, about the 1939 New York World's Fair. We went to New York to see him present the film's debut in 2019.

In the spring before I retired, McGraw-Hill Education hired me to assist them with their online tutorial systems for their engineering mechanics textbooks. It was part-time work and a splendid match for my background and interests, so, like Chris, I agreed to dabble a bit doing that. I've worked with McGraw-Hill on seven different textbooks so far, and I'll continue to work with them as long as they keep asking me, and it doesn't consume too much time. It's a perfect fit for me since the books I help with cover the same topics covered in the textbook Darby and I created. Working with McGraw-Hill has been fun, easy, not intense, and something I had the qualifications to do.

In the fall of 2018, they offered me a chance to teach another short course at the NSWC in Dahlgren, Virginia. It was a twenty-hour course over five days. It had been several years since I did any kind of short course and it felt good to get back in that saddle, but it was very demanding as always. My friend and former colleague John Lundberg set it up for me again, like he did the last time years earlier. I'm not sure if I'll do any more short courses. I don't seek those opportunities or advertise, but if somebody contacts me and asks, I'd consider doing a few more.

Not long after I retired, I received a letter from AU's president, Dr. Steven Leath. They awarded me the title of Professor Emeritus, which is an honorary title granted to retirees who have a record of meritorious service to their university. It humbled me to receive such a great honor. The letter and certificate are very special to me and always will be.

In Dr. Leath's letter he stated, "I am naming you Professor Emeritus as an expression of our deep appreciation to you for the years of valuable service which you have rendered to Auburn University."

Professor Emeritus is not a paid position, only an honorary one. However, there are benefits that come with the title. I get to have an office on campus, keep a university ID, use the school facilities, keep my email address, have access to the university's licensed software packages, get a campus parking pass, and even purchase athletic tickets at a discounted rate. I'm also permitted to serve on university committees and teach classes if there's a need for me to do so. It's almost as though I continue to have a job, except I don't get paid or have to do anything. But it's very nice to remain a part of the Auburn University community. I feel like I still have a place in my department and a home away from my house I can visit whenever I want. It's great they appreciated my contributions.

Although I lost my big corner office overlooking Samford Park and had to move to a smaller rectangular one similar to those I had when I was a young professor. I don't use it much, but sometimes I'll stop by to see my former colleagues or talk with students, or to just say hello and have lunch nearby. On rare occasions, I'll sit at my desk and work on something productive since they also allowed me to keep my computer and printer. I have a couple of shelves of books there, but little else. It was an enormous job cleaning out my large office, most of which went directly into the dumpster. Decades of work right into the trash, which helped convince me my career was over.

Chris and I began our travels immediately after retiring. During our first year, we took eighteen separate trips. We traveled about half our time and included three trips to California: One to visit Darby, one to meet up with Corey at a Pharmacy conference, and one for the memorial service for Chris's brother-in-law.

One of the most enjoyable things we did since we retired was rent an apartment in the Uptown section of New Orleans (NOLA) for two months. I'd been to NOLA many times, but always as a tourist, and I could never stay long. I've always wanted to spend an extended amount of time there to feel more like a local. We found the great neighborhood restaurants and legendary old bars tourists don't know about. We rented a furnished two-bedroom apartment on State Street, close to Audubon Park, Magazine Street, Saint Charles Avenue, and the universities. We also found magnificent blues and jazz clubs in the Marigny neighborhood and on Frenchmen Street. Plus, we worked out three days each week at the Tulane University Recreation Center, and sought the best happy hours most every afternoon.

We stayed in NOLA for the months of March and April 2019. During those two months, we experienced Mardi Gras, the Jazz and Heritage Festival, the French Quarter Festival, Saint Patrick's Day, and Easter. The city stole our hearts and we plan to spend much more time there. Corey and his fiancé, Christine, and Darby all joined us for Easter in the Big Easy. Our friends from Orlando, Joe and Susan Thomas, visited us for the French Quarter Festival, and our Auburn friends, Larry and Margie Teeter, came down for Jazz Fest. Living there was an amazing experience. By the time we left, I realized that if I could spend my last dollar and take my last breath in a Blues club in the Marigny, I'd leave the world smiling. New Orleans is a truly city like no other!

Besides going to the gym, we walked a lot. In fact, during our time in NOLA, Chris and I walked 168 miles! We could also ride the city busses and trolleys for forty cents since we were over the age of sixty-five.

One hobby I've had for ten years now and continue to indulge in is online betting on sporting events, mostly pro football and college football and basketball games. I find sports betting fascinating, challenging, and entertaining. Gambling on games isn't about what teams are playing each other, not for me at least. I may bet on some of my favorite teams, although I don't feel compelled to do so. It's all about the numbers to me. To be more specific, it's about point spreads, odds, and probability. In fact, it doesn't matter much who's playing in the game at all. I enjoy studying how the point spreads change, and the most important thing-where the money is going as other gamblers place their bets. I'll bet on games such as Ohio University versus Bowling Green if the numbers are attractive. There are many betting philosophies that people use with varying degrees of success. I've even developed a few myself. I started by placing my first bet on Auburn in the 2010 Iron Bowl, the game where Cam Newton brought AU back from a twenty-four-point deficit to win. That's the year AU won the national championship. Now, after ten years of practicing, I'm getting to be competent at it. I don't bet to win a lot of money, only for the entertainment. And even if I lose, I've had fun. Although, even in my worst years I lost little money. It's fun and a challenge, and it keeps me involved with math and statistics. Besides, I love it when I can beat the numbers and feel like I outsmarted the odds makers.

Brian asked if I wanted to teach another four and a half weeklong summer course in 2019. It was engineering mechanics again, which I'd taught many times before. I was still unsure if I missed teaching because we were busy traveling, so I agreed to teach the course and see if I did. They scheduled the class every day for seventy-five minutes; it didn't take me long to realize that I didn't miss it at all. I was a little rusty in the classroom, but my skills returned quickly. After they did, and I was back into the rhythm, I still didn't miss teaching. I doubt

I'll teach again if I'm offered the chance, but I appreciate Brian asking me.

In our second year of retirement, we took thirteen more trips, including a week in Las Vegas and helping Corey and Christine move from North Carolina to Wisconsin. The highlight of our year, however, was a trip to Detroit for Corey's marriage to the incredible Christine Metry. She's a marvelous addition to our family, and we love her to death! We had an outstanding time in Detroit and with all her wonderful family members. Besides the wedding, one highlight of that trip was to visit the Motown Museum, which houses Hitsville U.S.A., the original Motown recording studio and administrative offices. It was a fantastic trip, and that we now have two people named Christine Cicci in our family, which only adds to the fun.

Our travel pace slowed in our third year because of the COVID-19 pandemic. We made a few trips safely, including two weeks in Austin, Texas, over the Christmas holidays of 2020. We hadn't been back to Austin in almost twenty years, and it was fun spending some time there again. Chris and I rented a house on Lake Travis, and our family joined us, with Darby driving all the way from LA. We barely recognized the city since it's changed and grown so much since we lived there.

I've spent a good bit of time publishing our engineering book, which includes the three topics (statics, mechanics of materials, and dynamics) that I've already described. It's published through Kindle Direct Publishing (KDP) and it's available online. KDP offers it through a print-on-demand service, and I've sold a fair number so far. AU used it again, through the summer of 2021, and will continue to use it, for a while, at least. We've also sold a few copies in foreign countries and have been in touch with some other academic institutions to market it at those schools. I've taken the single, three-topic textbook and broken it up into separate and combined subject versions, all published through KDP. For example, there are now versions of statics, mechanics of materials, and dynamics separately; combined versions of statics and mechanics of materials, and statics and dynamics, along with the original three-subject version. So we now have six different textbooks available online. Creating all those versions was fun, but very time-consuming to publish the entire series. I found I like online publishing. I've also published some material I created for short courses, since I had four great ones with thousands of slides. They might be useful to practicing engineers. Although it was a large task to convert them into publication worthy documents, which kept me very busy.

My retirement has been splendid, so far, and I hope it continues for a long time. We plan to keep traveling, and at some point travel internationally, but only after the COVID-19 pandemic allows us to do so safely. Then we'll see.

In the spring of 2021, Chris and I returned to New Orleans. We just couldn't stay away from that incredible city! This time we rented a beautiful apartment on St. Charles Avenue in the Garden District. We leased it for a year and plan to make it our second home. It was fun furnishing a new place and learning all about a different part of NOLA. After a few more months we began to feel like native New Orleanians.

I had a new retirement adventure recently. I always thought it would be fun to be in a movie. It turns out that the film industry is huge in New Orleans, so I thought I'd give it a try. I answered an ad and got cast as an extra in the movie, "Where the Crawdads Sing." I was actually picked to portray a professor, ironically from UNC.

But I was wrong! Being an extra in a movie was one of the most boring things I've ever experienced!! There was a lot of sitting around and a lot of standing around, and after nine hours, I only saw about 20 seconds of the movie being filmed. I didn't have any lines and I don't know if my scene will make it into the movie or not, but there really wasn't anything fun about it, to my disappointment. The movie is an adaptation of the best-selling book by Delia Owens, and will probably be a very good movie. If you squint really hard, you might be able to see me somewhere, or not.

As boring as my experience on 'Crawdads' was, I got called for a couple more opportunities to be an extra in shows, which I accepted. I portrayed a restaurant patron in the limited TV series, "Hans Bubby," which was an overnight shoot at a fancy New Orleans restaurant. I may actually be visible in that scene, or at least my arm will be. Then ironically, I was asked to play a Catholic priest in the NBC series, "The Thing About Pam," staring Renee Zellweger. I'm not sure they could have picked a more unpriestly-like person for that role. Those last two experiences were more fun than my first one, and if asked, I'll likely accept more opportunities in the future if they sound interesting.

I also want to continue to write. As I mentioned earlier in this memoir, I attempted to write a novel, something I always wanted to do. I'd been working on it since I finished at the CIA in 2012. It was much more difficult than I thought it was going to be. But I persevered and, after many iterations, I completed it this past spring. When I retired, I told some friends I wanted to try writing a romance novel. Of course, my wife laughed at me. It turned out a lot different from I expected when I first started. I don't plan on letting anybody I know read it, nor will I even reveal the title, so nobody should ask. It was more of a gift to myself to prove I could create a piece of art. It was fun, but an enormous challenge. I might like to try a mystery next time, perhaps something involving space travel.

Chris suggested I write this memoir so our kids would understand more about my professional life and the long road it took for me to become a professor. Darby, who's also an amazing artist, has agreed to help with the cover design, so it's another project we'll get to work on together.

Some of my former students might be interested in a few of my stories, but they may have had enough of me by the time they finished taking orbital mechanics. I know they've heard most of my old stories already, anyway. It doesn't matter if many people read this as I didn't write it for others or for money, the same way I didn't become a teacher to get rich. I could've made more working in industry, but having a great deal of money isn't the most important thing in life. Loving what you do is, and that's why I feel as though I had a successful career, a lot more successful than it could have been. I suppose that's what makes me an overachiever.

24

REFLECTIONS AND BEYOND RETIREMENT

I was very lucky. I didn't want to be a teacher in the beginning, but I believe something destined me to become one. An unknown force I couldn't control drove me, and I had to follow its path. Ultimately I feel that I didn't choose teaching, but teaching chose me. When it did, I found a long career that I loved. I was fortunate to know what my calling was early in life, even though it took me a while to get there. Along the way I received inspiration from many and help from even more. Although, I worked hard, too. Everything aligned perfectly for me to succeed like I have. In my case it was a perfect storm.

I don't think many people have careers where they looked forward to going to work each morning and didn't want to leave at quitting time. Those who do are lucky as well. But those years in a job I loved flew past me in a blink of an eye. It continues to astound me I could somehow carve out the career I had from such unlikely beginnings, but it happened.

When Chris first read this manuscript, she commented that our lives could have gone sideways many times during our time at UT and throughout our careers. She was absolutely right, but I'm thankful our plans didn't fall apart like they could have.

I'm also thankful for every person who inspired and helped me along the way. I was happy to accept help from others because I know

I couldn't have gotten where I wanted to go without it. Few people can do everything alone. I was just very fortunate to have the people in my life that I did. They all played a meaningful role, and I never would have ended up where I am without them. I'm sad to say that one person who did so much for me, Dr. John J. McKetta, Jr., passed away in 2019 at the age of 103. He was a truly a magnificent individual.

I'm not sure why destiny drove me to be a teacher. Perhaps it was the influence of my father, or maybe it was from being exposed to great teachers early in my academic career. But I believe it was more than that. I feel like I had a unique skill set that translated well to higher education and that with my experiences I could give a lot to college students as an educator. Somehow doors opened to give me an opportunity to do just that.

During my thirty-five-plus years of teaching, I taught over 4,000 students. I think I've affected many of them and had a big impact on some of them, although I'll never know to what extent. I hope I've inspired a few along the way. In the notebook I received at my retirement party, one former student wrote that he stayed at Auburn for graduate school because of the classes he took from me. Then he met and began dating his future wife, so my impact extended well beyond just teaching him in class. There are other similar stories I'm aware of and others that I don't know about.

I'm very proud of all the wonderful things my former students have accomplished. Most of them became outstanding engineers serving the aerospace industry, many had distinguished military careers, and a significant number have reached high-level positions at places like the CIA, NASA, JPL, and Space-X. A few even became professors themselves, who I claim will somehow carry on my legacy, whether that's true or not. Several changed career paths altogether. They became doctors and lawyers, and I know of one who's now a dietician. Another even became a meteorologist and can be seen forecasting the weather on a Birmingham TV station. I'm honored if I played even a small role in any of their many successes.

When I grew up in that small Pennsylvania town, I always knew I needed to do something meaningful and in a different place. That drove me too. I supposed I dared to dream, even though I was unaware of what I was dreaming about when I began. It's strange to me that, looking back, things I did so many years ago when I was just a boy played a part in my adult life and career. Those common threads were music, basketball, math, an inexplicable draw to colleges (most of my casual wardrobe still consists of college t-shirts and sweatshirts), hard work, and a desire to succeed. It also helped to have a fear of not succeeding. Perhaps I was an overachiever because I was afraid of being an underachiever.

I am still very lucky. Besides having the career I always dreamed about, I have an amazing wife, and two incredible sons, and now an exceptional daughter-in-law! We're thrilled to have her in our family. The things I accomplished never would have occurred without my family's love, encouragement, and sacrifice. Corey and Darby astonish me daily with their talents, their accomplishments, and the outstanding men they've become. Chris had more to do with that than me, so she deserves most of the credit for how they turned out. I'm just glad I didn't screw it up.

Everyone else who inspired me and helped me through my journey is entitled to my thanks as well. I'm especially thankful to Auburn University for allowing me to have a career I never could've imagined. I was very fortunate to get to work at such a beautiful and welcoming place as Auburn. It, along with EAMC, gave our family a chance to have wonderful lives.

I was lucky to work for three outstanding department heads/chairs in my time at AU: Jim Williams, John Cochran, and Brian Thurow each gave me freedom to mold my career the way I wanted. I also got to work with one visionary dean in Chris Roberts and an exceptional president in Jay Gogue. They all cared about the department, the college, and Auburn University. AU is truly a special institution, as anybody with any Auburn connection already knows. Even better, my departmental colleagues were professional, supportive, friendly, and more like a family than just people I worked with. They were always focused on what was best for our department and never wavered in their commitment to make it the best it could be.

I truly appreciate the students I taught at UT, ACC, and AU. Each day was fun, challenging, adventuresome, and my career was wonderful because of all of you. I hope I gave you something good that will stay with you throughout your lives. To those of you who I've had some type of special connection with, you made it even better!

The phrase 'beyond retirement' that I used in the title of this chapter is unusual because I never plan to unretire, even though I still read ads for faculty jobs and still love to visit college campuses. I used that phrase only in the sense that I want to show my lifelong love for colleges and universities after I'm gone. My desire is to be on a college campus forever. To do that, I've left instructions for when I leave this world, to have some of my ashes spread at each of my favorite places on this Earth. Doing so is probably illegal, but I'm sure my brilliant sons can figure out a way to pull it off. They will, if they think of it as a puzzle to solve, like the time in San Francisco when Corey and I figured out how to avoid paying the high parking fees at that downtown hotel. Working together, I know they can. They already know I'd like a small portion of my ashes dispersed in a lovely green area on each of the following campuses: West Virginia University, Carnegie-Mellon University, The University of Texas at Austin, The University of North Carolina at Chapel Hill, Indiana University Bloomington, and of course, Auburn University. Then, if there are any left, I'd like to have those spread beneath the 'Tree of Life' in Audubon Park in my beloved New Orleans, near the banks of the Mississippi River, where we visited as a family during Easter of 2019. Those are the places I'd like to rest forever. That would be the crowning accomplishment for this overachiever. With that thought in mind, I'll finish by saying:

Let's Go Mountaineers!
Go Tartans!
Hook 'em Horns!
Go Heels!
Go Hoosiers!
War Eagle!

And finally to all the wonderful people of New Orleans:

Laissez les bon temps rouler!

Darby on tour with The Antlers, Istanbul, Turkey, 2011

Jean and Ed, Peachtree City, GA, circa 2013

At PNC Park with Mike Cochenour, Pittsburgh, PA, 2013

At one of Darby's shows, Raleigh, NC, 2014

A return to Washington, DC, 2016

Another cutthroat family board game in Auburn, circa 2016

Celebrating the 2017 Iron Bowl victory, Jordan-Hare Stadium, Auburn, AL

My retirement party, with Elizabeth Hayes, Rhon Jenkins, and Steve Gross, Auburn, AL, 2018

WVU Homecoming, with Jay Gordan, Linda Arnold, Al Verstein, and my college roommate John Catselis, Morgantown, WV, 2018

Happy hour with Aubie, Auburn, AL, 2019

Darby, Corey, and Christine, Orlando, FL, 2019

John McKetta celebrating his 103rd birthday, Austin, TX, 2019

A lasting tribute to an incredible educator and friend, Austin, TX, 2020

Made in the USA
Columbia, SC
12 August 2024

b8e095b3-7575-416a-bdf5-82c4e01edd87R01